KU-161-209

Feminism and the Women's Movement in Malaysia

This study provides an account of the multiple struggles of the Malaysian women's movement – from securing gender equality in a patriarchal society to achieving unity among members of a multiethnic society that are further divided along class and religious lines. While most historical versions of national struggles have created icons out of male figures – usually prominent politicians – this study provides a corrective. It details the important role of the women's movement, led by numerous unsung personalities, in promoting social change in Malaysia. A crucial argument is made: that in the context of an ethnically fragmented post-colonial, authoritarian society, an autonomous women's movement which began in the early 1980s had actually achieved significant political successes, introducing new issues into public debate and confronting the dictates of the state. But the study observes that, by the late 1990s, feminist issues were also readily appropriated and instrumentalized by the state and the market. It argues that the emergence of 'market feminism' poses specific challenges for the future of the Malaysian women's movement. Overall, this book combines both personal and academic insights into the construction of an in-depth account of the Malaysian women's movement and the various feminisms behind it.

Cecilia Ng is an independent researcher and women's rights advocate. She was previously an Associate Professor at Universiti Putra Malaysia and Visiting Associate Professor at the Asian Institute of Technology, Thailand. She has conducted research and published widely on gender, development and work, and is active in women's groups in Malaysia where she is involved in research, training and advocacy on advancing the women's movement in Malaysia.

Maznah Mohamad is an Associate Professor of Development Studies and was formerly the Director of the Women's Development Research Centre at the Science University of Malaysia, Penang. She is a committee member of the Penang-based Women's Centre for Change and sits on the Board of Directors of the International Women's Rights Action Watch Asia Pacific (IWRAW Asia Pacific). She is also author of the book *The Malay Handloom Weavers: A Study of the Rise and Decline of Traditional Manufacture*.

tan beng hui is trained in political economy and economic history. She has been involved in the Malaysian women's movement since 1990, during which time she has also tried to put sexuality rights on the agenda of local women's groups. She most recently worked as a Programme Officer with the International Women's Rights Action Watch Asia Pacific (IWRAW Asia Pacific).

Routledge Malaysian Studies Series

Published in association with Malaysian Social Science Association (MSSA)

Series Editors:

Mohammed Hazim Shah, University of Malaya
Shamsul A.B., University Kebangsaan Malaysia
Terence Gomez, University of Malaya

The Routledge Malaysian Studies Series publishes high quality scholarship that provides important new contributions to knowledge on Malaysia. It also signals research that spans comparative studies, involving the Malaysian experience with that of other nations.

This series, initiated by the Malaysian Social Science Association (MSSA) to promote study of contemporary and historical issues in Malaysia, and designed to respond to the growing need to publish important research, also serves as a forum for debate on key issues in Malaysian society. As an academic series, it will be used to generate new theoretical debates in the social sciences and on processes of change in this society.

The Routledge Malaysian Studies Series will cover a broad range of subjects including history, politics, economics, sociology, international relations, geography, business, education, religion, literature, culture and ethnicity. The series will encourage work adopting an interdisciplinary approach.

The State of Malaysia
Ethnicity, equity and reform
Edited by Edmund Terence Gomez

Feminism and the Women's Movement in Malaysia
An unsung (r)evolution
Cecilia Ng, Maznah Mohamad and tan beng hui

WITHDRAWN

LIVERPOOL JOHN MOORES UNIVERSITY
Aldham Robarts L.R.C.
TEL. 0151 231 3701/3634

LIVERPOOL JMU LIBRARY

3 1111 01157 3241

Feminism and the Women's Movement in Malaysia

An Unsung (R)evolution

Cecilia Ng, Maznah Mohamad and tan beng hui

Routledge
Taylor & Francis Group
LONDON AND NEW YORK

First published 2006
by Routledge
2 Park Square, Milton Park, Abingdon, Oxon OX14 4RN

Simultaneously published in the USA and Canada
by Routledge
270 Madison Ave, New York, NY10016

Routledge is an imprint of the Taylor & Francis Group, an informa business

© 2006 Cecilia Ng, Maznah Mohamad and tan beng hui

Typeset in Times New Roman
by Taylor & Francis Books

Printed and bound in Great Britain by
Biddles Ltd, King's Lynn

All rights reserved. No part of this book may be reprinted or repro-
duced or utilised in any form or by any electronic, mechanical, or
other means, now known or hereafter invented, including photo-
copying and recording, or in any information storage or retrieval
system, without permission in writing from the publishers.

British Library Cataloguing in Publication Data
A catalogue record for this book is available from the British Library

Library of Congress Cataloging in Publication Data
Ng, Cecilia, 1950-
  Feminism and the women's movement in Malaysia : an unsung
(r)evolution / Cecilia Ng, Maznah Mohamad, and Tan Beng Hui.
    p. cm. -- (Routledge Malaysian studies series ; 2)
  "Published in association with Malaysian Social Science Association
(MSSA)."
  Includes bibliographical references and index.
  ISBN 0-415-37479-0 (hardback : alk. paper) 1. Feminism--Malaysia.
2. Women's rights--Malaysia. 3. Women--Malaysia--Social condi-
tions. I. Maznah Mohamad. II. Tan, Beng Hui, 1967- III. Persatuan
Sains Sosial Malaysia. IV. Title. V. Series.
  HQ1750.6N4 2006
  305.4209595--dc22
                                    2005026289

ISBN10 0–415–37479–0
ISBN13 9–780–415–37479–8

Contents

About the authors

Cecilia Ng

Cecilia Ng is an independent researcher and women's rights advocate. She was previously an Associate Professor at Universiti Putra Malaysia and Visiting Associate Professor at the Asian Institute of Technology, Thailand, where she was also an editor of the AIT-based *Journal of Gender, Technology and Development*. Cecilia has conducted research and published widely on gender, development and work, with a focus on globalization, technological change and women's employment. She has also written on the women's movement in Malaysia. She is active in women's groups in Malaysia and is a founder member of the Women's Development Collective (WDC) and the All Women's Action Society (AWAM), where she is involved in research, training and advocacy on advancing the women's movement in Malaysia.

Maznah Mohamad

Maznah Mohamad is currently an Associate Professor of Development Studies at the School of Social Sciences, University of Science Malaysia (USM), Penang. She was formerly the School's Deputy Dean for Research and Graduate Studies and Director of the Women's Development Research Centre. She has done research on development policies in Malaysia especially in relation to women's organizations and the impact of Muslim Family Laws on women's status. Her publications include, *Feminism: Malaysian Critique and Experience* (co-edited, 1994), *The Malay Handloom Weavers: A Study of the Rise and Decline of Traditional Manufacture* (1996), *Muslim Women and Access to Justice: Historical, Legal and Social Experiences in Malaysia* (edited, 2000) and *Risking Malaysia: Culture, Politics and Identity* (co-edited, 2001). She has been a Visiting Fellow at York University, Yokohama National University and held the Visiting Chair in ASEAN Studies at the University of Toronto in 2001. She was awarded the Asian Leaders Fellowship in 2002 by the International House of Japan and the

Japan Foundation. She has been active with the Women's Centre for Change (formerly known as the Women's Crisis Centre) since 1991, holding various positions in the committee at different times, from secretary to president. She also sits on the Board of Directors of International Women's Rights Action Watch Asia Pacific (IWRAW Asia Pacific).

tan beng hui

beng hui is trained in political economy and economic history. She also holds an MA in Women and Development from the Institute of Social Studies, Den Haag, the Netherlands. She has been involved in the women's movement in Malaysia in various capacities over the last 15 years, and is a member of the Women's Development Collective (WDC) and the All Women's Action Society (AWAM). beng hui is a firm believer of sexuality rights and promotes this through her writings, talks and workshops. She has spent the last four years at an international women's human rights NGO based in Kuala Lumpur, the International Women's Rights Action Watch Asia Pacific (IWRAW Asia Pacific).

Foreword

Humanity's ongoing struggle for new visions, principles and possibilities demands that our experiences of struggle are kept in the people's living memories. This is especially critical for women's movements whose stories of courage, pains and victories are often marginalized and invisible. Keeping our political values and projects recognizable is important because our feminist struggles for radical transformations require both collective and inter-generational reflections and actions. Despite being socially conditioned by dominant ideology-forming forces, a majority of people are still in search of alternatives – feminist ideas and ideals certainly offer a refreshing and provocative viewpoint.

For such reasons, we welcome this historical and critical account of the Malaysian women's movement that has been written by three activists whose lives have been intimately shaped by the women's movement. Written from the vantage-point of engaged social actors, the book provides a compelling narrative of the twists and turns, the victories and pitfalls, the convergences and cracks, and the tensions and contradictions of a social movement. It was a movement which negotiated its way through the complexities and sensitivities of a post-colonial society where tensions of ethnicity, class and religion were felt alongside the democratic deficit of a managerialist state. More than just a record of events and happenings, this book interrogates the politics of the Malaysian women's movement, throwing hard questions on how it has engaged with the state, as only insiders can.

For those interested in women's studies, the book fills a void in the literature on Malaysian and South East Asian histories of social movements. For feminist activists, it is a rich resource of strategies and tactics on various forms of women's organizing and mobilization. For those who have had the privilege of sharing political moments with the writers, it is a testament of courage. This book is certainly an academic and political must-read.

Josefa 'Gigi' Francisco
Executive Director, Miriam College – Women and Gender Institute (WAGI)
South East Asia Coordinator, Development Alternatives with Women for a
New Era (DAWN)

Preface

For many years, despite the acknowledged need among women activists to document the experiences of the contemporary women's movement in Malaysia, this intention had failed to materialize. The task at hand was simply not regarded as a priority among those in the movement. While it may have been deemed necessary for the purposes of chronicling its history, in the larger scheme of things – when the everyday battle of fighting for greater democracy together with other civil society groups took precedence – a book project was considered a luxury in the agenda of activism.

Another reason for the delay was simply an absence of a tradition of sharing our stories in a systematic and documented manner. Women activists are more into the habit of meeting, brainstorming, planning and taking on immediate practical actions. It is only occasionally that we step back, reflect and analyse our strategies and their larger purpose. In the main, however, putting our ideas into print to build a knowledge base has not been a popular choice among activists.

It was only in early 2000 that the Women's Development Collective (WDC) earnestly started the process for a publication of this nature. Although the original idea was to document the history of the WDC itself, this was quickly superseded by the realization that there was more to gain by expanding the scope of the project to include a study of the Malaysian women's movement.

When the three of us were commissioned for this task, we were enthusiastic and excited about the possibilities that lay before us. It was indeed a pioneering effort. We agreed to work together because we believed in the value of this initiative. Yet, while we each identify ourselves as feminists and are part of the Malaysian women's movement, we are still different in many ways. And it is our very differences in intellectual approach, career background and social involvement that have contributed to the diversity of insights and analyses in the book's pages.

It didn't take long to discover that we had quite a challenge ahead of us in assigning priorities. If we were to document each and every concern that different women's groups in Malaysia have taken up over the years, it would have meant prolonging completion of this project.

Furthermore, as writers we are informed by our own personal experiences and ideological perspectives. It is inevitable that a partial outlook influences our treatment of many issues raised in the book. Thus we do not purport that it contains an impeccably objective and comprehensive account or analysis of the contemporary women's movement. Rather, this publication should be viewed as one of many accounts that may be written on this subject. We are hopeful that the experiences, roles and importance of women's groups in this country will continue to be reflected, elucidated and debated by many parties.

A major part of our attention is devoted to deconstructing the political feminism of the late 1980s and its subsequent manifestations until today. As scholars we are committed to the integrity of scholarship and impartial assessment by which this book is largely guided. However, we are not simply detached scholars. We have been participants, if not 'participatory researchers', in the women's movement. We have also been part of the activism which shaped the movement's course.

The book is as much a self-critique as it is a celebration. It is as much a denunciation of the past as it is an annunciation for the future. We hope that these critical reflections will provide the women's movement with its continuing momentum to move forward. And we hope, too, that those outside the movement may come to appreciate the complexities of the contributions of the women's movement to the transformation and evolution of ideas and institutions in society.

The title *Feminism and the Women's Movement in Malaysia: An Unsung (R)evolution* was chosen after much thought. It was meant to reflect the understated complexities that women's groups encounter in their struggle to promote women's rights. In conventional understanding, 'revolutions' are associated with sudden cathartic changes. The changes brought about by Malaysian women activists in the last 20 years or so can hardly qualify as revolutionary in this manner. In fact, it may be more apt to regard our achievements as an evolution of conflating factors.

The politics, economics and culture of national and global developments have provided the context for an evolving rather than a revolutionizing women's movement in Malaysia. Yet if we were to understand the context in which such changes are being achieved – essentially one in which the state is repressive and democratic spaces are curtailed – this could give new meaning to the term 'revolution'. Indeed, despite the obstacles posed by the authoritarian state, Malaysian women's groups have done relatively well in going against the grain of patriarchy by breaking the boundaries of women's circumscribed rights and in helping to push the limits of democracy beyond what is safely dictated by the state.

Our limitations

In this book the focus of discussion and analysis is on the experiences in Peninsular Malaysia. This is immediately open to critique. It reflects the subjective inclinations and structural limitations of the authors whose experiences are mainly within this geographical context. The role of the state has constituted the main thread running through the arguments of this book. We felt that women's groups in the East Malaysian states of Sabah and Sarawak have had a different relationship with the state, given the geographical distance and federal-state structure which maintain an almost explicit social, political and cultural gap between West (peninsular) and East Malaysians. As such, the East Malaysian experience can only be discussed through limited treatment. Any attempt to cover the ground fully would not do justice in capturing the distinctive historical and cultural characteristics of the women's movement there.

Also not discussed are the struggles faced by peasant, plantation and indigenous women, mainly because the women's movement has not taken up these concerns in any systematic manner – which also reflects its rather narrow base for mobilization. This is its source of weakness as much as it is the basis of its gains among specific constituencies, particularly the urban middle-class.

Attribution of authorship

This book is the product of a joint-authorship among the three of us. We have contributed collectively to the formulation of ideas within each chapter and we have had an equal hand in editing, paraphrasing and re-writing all of the chapters. Nonetheless, it is only fair to attribute both praises and criticisms to those who are the principal writers of each chapter: Cecilia for the Introduction, and Chapters 4 and 6; Maznah for Chapters 2 and 5; and beng hui for the Preface, and Chapters 3 and 7. We each had a hand in putting together Chapter 8, but Cecilia saw to its completion. It remains to be stressed that the final product is truly a reflection of our collective responsibility and undertaking.

Acknowledgements

This project could not have been realized without the collective experiences and knowledge of many people behind the contemporary women's movement. The foundation of our insights has been built on these efforts and we thank all concerned.

We thank members of the WDC, especially Maria Chin Abdullah, for their enduring patience and trust in us as writers. Alina Rastam, Fathilah Kamaluddin, Meera Samanther, Manohary Subramaniam, Lee Shook Foong, Wathshlah Naidu, Judith Loh, Jac Kee, Zarizana Abdul Aziz, Julaila Mokhtar, M. Puravalen, Bruno Pereira, Chan Lean Heng, Johan Saravanamuttu, Hew Cheng Sim, as well as friends in the Women's Centre for Change, Sabah Women Action Resource Group and Sarawak Women for Women Society – all contributed to the substance of the text, which we deeply appreciate. Thanks also go to Terence Gomez who, on behalf of the Malaysian Social Science Association, encouraged us to see this book to print, and to Gigi Francisco, who despite her busy schedule, consented to writing the foreword. For the book cover, we had the good fortune of locating a charcoal drawing by Wong Hoy Cheong, a Malaysian artist celebrated for his socially engaging art. We found *Girl with Mirror* (1985) an apt reflection of the book and we thank him most warmly for allowing us to use this work.

Two people who played an especially important role in this project are Chee Heng Leng and Padmaja Padman. As our contemporary and peer, and as an uncompromising critic of our drafts, Heng Leng's insights and feedback on our work have been invaluable and we wish to express our deep gratitude to her. As our language and style editor, Padma has been quite remarkable in her tenacity to pursue the completion of the book to its end – we thank her too for helping us see the forest for the trees.

We started this project as friends and are pleased, perhaps even secretly relieved, that we have ended it on the same, if not on a higher, note. It would be an understatement to say that the process of making this book a reality has been a struggle. Its completion speaks volumes for the friendship and solidarity that have been reinforced among us and we end by thanking each other and our loved ones for this invaluable experience.

Cecilia, Maznah and beng hui

Abbreviations

ABIM	Angkatan Belia Islam Malaysia (Islamic Youth Movement of Malaysia)
AWAM	All Women's Action Society
AWAS	Angkatan Wanita Sedar (Force of Awakened Women)
BA	Barisan Alternatif (Alternative Front)
BN	Barisan Nasional (National Front)
CAR	Citizens Against Rape
CEDAW	Convention on the Elimination of All Forms of Discrimination Against Women
CPM	Communist Party of Malaya
DAP	Democratic Action Party
Darul Arqam	House of Arqam
DVA	Domestic Violence Act
HAWA	Secretariat for Women's Affairs
ISA	Internal Security Act
JAG-VAW	Joint Action Group against Violence Against Women
JIM	Jemaah Islah Malaysia (Islamic Reform Congregation of Malaysia); Wanita JIM (JIM women's wing)
Keadilan	Parti Keadilan Nasional (National Justice Party)
MEF	Malaysian Employers' Federation
MNP	Malay Nationalist Party
MTUC	Malaysian Trades Union Congress
NACIWID	National Advisory Council for the Integration of Women in Development
NEP	New Economic Policy
NGO	Non-Governmental Organization
NWC	National Women's Coalition
NCWO	National Council of Women's Organisations
PKI	Pergerakan Kaum Ibu (Mothers' Movement)
PAS	Parti Islam Se Malaysia (Islamic Party of Malaysia)
UMNO	United Malays National Organisation
VAW	Violence Against Women
VSS	Voluntary Separation Scheme

WAC	Women's Agenda for Change
WAO	Women's Aid Organisation
WCC	Women's Crisis Centre; later Women's Centre for Change
WCI	Women's Candidacy Initiative
WDC	Women's Development Collective
WID	Women in Development
WLUML	Women Living under Muslim Laws
WTU	Women Teachers' Union
YWCA	Young Women's Christian Association

1   Introduction

Like any other social movement, women's organized struggle in Malaysia has had to weave in and out through the peculiarities and complexities of the nation's cultural, political and economic circumstances and history. Malaysia's mosaic of state-driven democracy, identity politics and multiculturalism provides the terrain for allowing or frustrating the growth of the women's movement into what it is today – unique in itself but with its feminism existing within the interstices of a state which is authoritarian and nested within a capitalist system.

This book may be one of several accounts of the origin, evolution and establishment of feminism in Malaysian history and cultural consciousness. Yet it deals with a significant and fundamental question: how has feminism, as a cultural influence or a driving social and political force, left its mark on Malaysian society? Does it form the core or merely the fragments of Malaysia's transformation from a colony to an independent nation state? Does it appear as grand politics or micro-narratives in the lives of Malaysians?

To place the contents of the book within a historical framework we first summarize several of the early theoretical perspectives and debates circulated in the West that were applied for an understanding of feminism. Some of the concepts may seem detached from our specific Malaysian experience but we cannot deny the influence of Western-inspired ideas on the course of the women's movement in this country. It is pointless to seek an essential Malaysian feminism unique in its own identity or origins, given that territorial markers cannot curb cultural and ideological exchanges. This said, all of these external influences have had to articulate with realities on the ground. As such, we also cannot negate the fact that national influences and indigenous norms have given Malaysian feminism its distinct character.

Even so, we contend that there have been many variants of feminism in Malaysia. However, this variation is not merely a manifestation of changing history. Feminism as understood and embraced by society can differ even within the same historical moment. Although feminism is not always successful at uniting all women towards a common cause, it is at minimum an ideology that contests power, ranging from colonial systems to patriarchal cultural orders and state regulation. Indeed, Malaysian women are still divided by their ethnic and cultural roots, not to mention differences based on class. However, the construction of a gendered perspective has gained ground because social movements as a whole have depended on women as symbols as well as the backbone of their transformative ideals. Precisely because gender symbolism is a terrain that is easily manipulated by the wielders of cultural and political power, an authentic feminist project of attaining gender and social justice is, at the same time, difficult to realize. The Malaysian feminist project, being a product of historical circumstances and of the way the state has evolved, is an apt manifestation of this condition.

By nature, the state must accommodate many expressions of interests for its own legitimacy – including that of patriarchy as well as that of religious and ethnic communalism. The success of the Malaysian authoritarian state may thus hinge on its construction and subsequently the containment of distinct ethnic communities. Together with this, the phenomenon of Islamic resurgence among Malay-Muslims and religious revivalism in the direction of conservatism among non-Muslims have also provided much leeway for the strengthening of patriarchal authority in society.

Feminists can thus only hope to function within the gaps of this political system which accommodates ethnic-based rather than gender- or class-based demands. This model of governance is often referred to as the consociational model, where the ruling structure is represented by an elite group who purportedly speak for and make claims on behalf of their ethnic communities.[1] However, the state's position on gender equality is inconsistent. On the one hand its authoritarian facet is strengthened by ethnic politicization. On the other it cannot afford to ignore the growth of new, non-ethnicized politics led by civil society groups. These include the women's movement.

This book intends to look at this multilayered and often confounding process. It seeks to explain why the women's movement is not able to fully play a key role in reforming society even though it may have contributed to mitigating the slide of authoritarianism into an even more despotic plane. It is in this context that we review some of the more important early perspectives on feminism elsewhere before drawing in the Malaysian experience as a basis for rethinking the issue. The later section of this chapter sets out the purpose and main arguments of each chapter within the book.

Understanding feminism and its discontents

The term 'feminism', which refers to the struggles of the women's movement, became widely used in Europe, the United States and the colonized countries in the nineteenth and early twentieth centuries. According to well-known Sri Lankan historian Kumari Jayawardeena, the concept of feminism is neither a recent phenomenon originating from the West, nor was it imported or imposed from the West into Third World countries. In her classic book

Feminism and Nationalism in the Third World (1986), she argues that debates on women's rights and education were held as early as the eighteenth century in China. Furthermore, feminist struggles were already evident in India, Iran, Turkey, Egypt and Japan in the nineteenth and early twentieth centuries.

In Malaysia, Muslim intellectuals in the 1930s, educated and influenced by the reform movements in the Middle East, demanded Muslim women's right to education. The Malay Women Teachers' Union, founded in 1929, encouraged formal schooling for Malay women. Sexual molestation and harassment of female estate workers were already key issues for protest action in the late 1930s in Selangor and again in 1950, this time in Perak.[2]

Today, feminism has gone beyond its original meaning of fighting for women's rights and legal reforms in education, property rights and suffrage.[3] Its definition has extended to include an awareness and analysis of women's discrimination and exploitation in the family, at work and in society, as well as conscious efforts by all – women and men – who wish to end gender inequality. As such, feminism is a social and political movement for changing women's subordinate position. As a movement, feminism is holistic and inclusive. It seeks to link up with other progressive movements for social and democratic change, and it is not exclusive to women since changes sought are to benefit men as well.

In the early stages of feminist consciousness-raising in the West, there was an assumption that because of a shared identity and experience among women, they would be united towards working and struggling together. That is, as women, they would be able to support one another's anguish and idealism. However, this notion of 'sisterhood' – the belief that women automatically relate to and provide one another with support simply because they share a common sex – proved to be a myth by the late 1970s after Black women criticized women's groups for being elitist, white and middle-class. These groups, it was said, had little understanding or, worse, were condescending of the struggles of Black and poor working-class families.

Later on as the women's movement expanded globally, women in the Third World similarly attempted to develop a more indigenous women's movement, away from the dominance and analysis of the West. Given this fragmentation, when we speak of 'feminism' in this book, we refer to a plurality of feminisms rather than of a unitary, if not false, feminism that binds women together. Certainly numerous types of feminism can be distinguished by looking at their analysis, practices and strategies. As argued by Wieringa (1995: 3–4):

> Feminism is not a one-dimensional social critique, but a multi-layered, transformational political practice and ethics. The transformation is towards feminisation and democratisation on domestic, social and political levels, as well as towards economic levelling and an end to racial discrimination. But in different social and historical contexts, feminists may have other issues to fight for.

Theorizing feminism

Early Western literature on feminist theories focused on several main strands of feminism – liberal feminism, radical feminism, Marxist and socialist feminism, and postmodern feminism (Jagger, 1983; Tong, 1992). However, it is important to remember that in reality the distinctions are not so neat, simplistic and clear-cut, and might even overlap in some areas. A brief summary and critique of these strands can assist us in further delineating the nature of feminist practice in Malaysia, and in understanding why the Malaysian variant has to be scripted based on local experiences.[4]

Liberal feminism

This strand of feminism is rooted in the concept of liberalism which emerged with the growth of capitalism. Basically, liberalism says that all human beings are potentially rational and seek to maximize their own self-interest. Liberals also believe that the state and society should protect the rights of the individual and should allow everyone to maximize their self-interest, and thus their self-fulfilment.

Following this, liberal feminism believes men and women are essentially equal, but women have been discriminated against by laws which need to be changed. Hence there is much emphasis on campaigns for legal reform and equal rights, for example in the areas of education, employment, training and financial management. Ultimately, the belief is that self-interest and rationality will prevail, and equality as a principle will be universally accepted.

However, liberal feminism has been criticised for looking at the individual as a self-sufficient, neutral and abstract entity. Those characteristics are not equally attainable and are unrealistic as a goal since we all belong to particular groups or identities, for example ethnic, class, sex or age groups, and have different personal capacities and needs. In fact, these structures can act as barriers towards achieving self-fulfilment in life. Thus laws might be passed, for example, in relation to equal employment rights, but this will not guarantee that poor women will gain access to these opportunities, as class barriers prevent the poor as a group from acquiring those rights.

Radical feminism

The identification of feminism with radical politics grew out of the women's liberation movement in the United States in the late 1960s, in tandem with the anti-Vietnam war movement. Many of the founders were white, middle-class, college-educated women, some of whom were involved in various New Left groups but became disillusioned by male dominance in such organizations which supposedly preached transformation and justice. Subsequently, these women came together in consciousness-raising groups and discovered that many of them shared similar experiences of male oppression.

This position views that, as a social class, women are oppressed by men. Patriarchy is made possible by the unpaid domestic service of women in the home and by the exploitation of women's bodies through marriage, sexual slavery, pornography, reproduction and rape. In their belief that 'sisterhood is global', radical feminists stress that any woman in the world has more in common with another woman – regardless of class, race, ethnicity, nationality – than she has with another man.

For them, the way to combat patriarchy is through the creation of a culture for women whereby they can reshape their lives outside of patriarchal definitions. For example, lesbian feminism was argued to be a political act to counter the ideological and institutional domination of male privilege. In terms of concrete actions, radical feminists have been active in setting up women's centres dealing with rape, domestic violence and women's health needs. At the global level they have networked rather successfully on issues involving international sexual slavery and human trafficking.

This position, however, has its share of critics, with the main objection being its universalistic and essentialist arguments. As radical feminism does not refer to any historical context – implying that biology is unchanging and given – it has been heavily criticized as falling into biological determinism as well as being 'class blind'. It cannot, for instance, account for the unequal relations and conflict between poor men of colour and rich white women. In this case who is more deserving of 'liberation' becomes a moot question, one which the notion of 'global sisterhood' cannot reconcile.

Marxist and socialist feminism

If radical feminism views gender relations as the primary oppression in life, Marxist feminism – where socialist feminism has its roots – points out that class relations and the capitalist system are the cause of women's subordination. Because of their concern with the pitfalls of the capitalist system, Marxist feminists focus on the exploitative conditions of working-class women. According to this position, once capitalism is overthrown and class society is disintegrated, gender inequality will disappear as well.

Again, this perspective has been criticized as being functionalist, especially for ignoring the reality of women's position in the household. Studies conducted in socialist countries in the 1970s and 1980s pointed out that women remained subordinated at work and at home – a situation that Marxist feminism cannot explain, as it is gender-biased, if not blind.

Attempts to deal with the 'unhappy marriage' between Marxism and feminism led to the birth of socialist feminism whose main objective was to develop a political theory and practice that would synthesize the insights of radical feminism and the Marxist tradition. Socialist feminists argue that class and gender as well as race/ethnic relations of power are all critical in the understanding of society. No single social relation is privileged, that is no one factor is regarded as more important than the other. The struggle then should be equally against capitalism as it is against male dominance in the home as well as against oppression in the workplace and society.

Negotiating the feminist impasse: postmodern feminism

The experiences of the women's movement point out that there are different paths to feminist analysis and practice. Women have proven to be divided, sometimes extremely so on the basis of ideology, class, ethnicity, culture, age or sexuality. For example, some Black women say they have more in common with Black men than with white middle-class women. Women in apartheid South Africa found solace in their families, questioning the Western critique of the family as the first site of women's oppression. Others in the South find that problems of poverty and indigenous women's issues are not the concern of women in the First World.

In recent times, a new strand of feminism – postmodern feminism – has emerged in response to this situation and critiqued the feminist movement for replacing one universal, rational, male subject perspective with another universal idea of 'woman', 'gender' or 'sex'. Hence postmodern feminists reject traditional assumptions about truth and reality and refuse to construct a unitary theory on gender subordination.

While postmodern feminists have been applauded for recognizing diversity among women, they have been equally castigated for being too preoccupied with dissecting and analysing 'truths' and for deconstructing diversity, multiplicity and difference. In turn, as a theory that is meant to inform practice, postmodern feminism has often been criticized for causing paralysis, if not chaos, among activists (Tong, 1992: 232).

The relationship between feminism and the women's movement

The role of the women's movement

The women's movement can take a diversity of forms and interests. Taking off from Wieringa (1995: 7), a women's movement is defined as 'the whole spectrum of conscious and unconscious individual or collective acts, activities, groups or organisations concerned with diminishing gender subordination, which is understood as intersecting with race and class oppression'. It is also true that there might be and have been disagreements among various segments of the movement in relation to agendas, strategies and demands.[5]

To deal with the question of agenda-setting and autonomy, Molyneux (1998: 70) describes three ideal types of women's movements – independent, associational and directed. Independent movements function on the basis of women's self-activity and organization which recognize no superior authority. Associational movements choose to form alliances with other political organizations, while directed movements receive their authority and direction from a higher 'order', typically political organizations or from the government. Feminists are usually more concerned with independent and autonomous organizations where women establish their own goals, organizational forms and types of struggle. In the real world there are and will be shifts and inter-connections among these groups depending on the historical context, and the nature of the issues debated.

A more critical perspective of movements or movement-building is offered by Indian feminist Batliwala:[6]

> First of all a movement is a political process. A movement always has a political agenda and it is a political agenda that is about changing two things. One is the nature of resources and the distribution of resources. Movements are partly about mobilizing and redistributing resources in more equitable ways. And two, I think that movements are about ideologies and policies that flow out of ideologies. Movements are about changing power relations.

In her analysis of the role of women's non-governmental organizations (NGOs), she further argues that:

> The first priority of NGOs should be to catalyse and enable the formation of grassroots women's organisations. We cannot speak of a 'women's movement' without this kind of grassroots base . . . You can have millions of organisations as we indeed do have in South Asia, without them constituting a movement.

Similar caution is underscored by Griffen (2002: 10) who states:

> Despite the inspiring and increasingly diverse forms of women's resistance these many activities do not a movement make. What is meant by 'the women's movement' now needs to be analysed by women, especially with respect to its role, strategies and impact on women's rights in the long run. There needs to be clarification as to whether there is a movement at all or whether 'the women's movement' is now being equated, both externally and by feminists, to the collective of women's NGOs and networks, even if they do not act collectively or organise as a movement.

If one were to adhere to Batliwala's definition of a women's movement, then it is clear that the Malaysian women's movement is not a movement at all, as there is no mass-based women's grassroots movement to speak of – particularly in the sense of the redistribution of resources and the transformation of power, including gender relations in society. But, as will be seen in the following chapters, there have been mass organizations of women as categorized by

Molyneux and there have been various women's NGOs which have acted in collective fashion, as described by Griffen.

At the end of the day what would be useful is to analyse the evolution of these movements, the conditions of their existence and growth as well as their strategies and impact on women's rights in each situation. What is unique in the Malaysian case is also the centrality of Islam and its repercussions on a multicultural polity. This creates a more complex picture of the trajectory of the women's movement, compared with that painted by the commentators cited. To reiterate the points made earlier we have chosen to look at the origins of Malaysian feminism as being influenced by structural and cultural changes as well as upheavals marking the country's transition from one historical phase to the other.

The state and the women's movement: what price?

The notion of the state has received different treatments from various authors. It can be seen from an organizational perspective as simply 'a set of governmental institutions ... making rules, controlling, guiding or regulating' or in relation to its consequences, which is the maintenance of social order by acting as a surveillance system (Dunleavy and O'Leary, 1987: 1–6). In everyday understanding the government is the state and the government has the right to control and coordinate all public activities.

Although the state is meant to be a mediator of the many interest groups in society, it is hardly viewed as being totally neutral, not just in the Malaysian context but everywhere else too. It has been pointed out that in a capitalist society the state's main job is to maintain favourable conditions for capitalist enterprise and capital accumulation so that state revenue can be assured (Macpherson, 1989: 23).

However, the modern state can only survive if it has political legitimacy. Although its primary function is to preserve the continuity of capital accumulation, it must ultimately derive electoral legitimacy, and must to a certain extent give in to popular pressure, even if this may occasionally conflict with economic interests (Boreham et al., 1989: 261–2). In this sense the state functions as a contradictory entity because it is selectively authoritarian and arbitrarily democratic at the same time.

It is in this context that we problematize the relationship of the women's movement to the state, another key theme in the book. As argued by Molyneux and Razavi (2002: 24), 'The central instrument for the protection of rights has been, and must remain, the state.' Whether states protect and/or advance women's rights depends on the political regime and how women's groups engage with such regimes. It has been shown that democratic institutions and procedures are more sympathetic to women's concerns, although there is a tendency for women's groups to become co-opted in the process. Similarly non-democratic regimes also seek to woo women to secure their power base, as in the case of Peru where a large number of women assumed public positions and came into national prominence under the dictatorship of President Alberto Fujimori in the 1990s (Blondet, 2002).

Women's movements engage in the terrain of civil society. Like feminism and the women's movement, the term 'civil society' is a contested concept. This book adopts the definition of civil society as 'the existence of an independent public space from the exercise of state power, and the ability of organizations within it to influence the exercise of state power' (Bernhard, cited in Valte, n.d.). The relationship between civil society and the state, as an arena of political contestation, can thus take varying forms – collaboration, co-optation, resistance and subversion. Women's movements as part of civil society – that space between the individual and the state – cannot avoid engaging with the state, as a site and instrument of power. If the women's movement has been successful in realizing its quest for gender equality at all through its engagement with the state, will it have to pay a price for this? One objective of this book is thus to problematize the relationship of Malaysian feminism with the authoritarian state, particularly the inability of the women's movement to successfully mobilize against state control over its direction.

The crafting of Malaysian feminism

The feminist theories discussed earlier, while useful as a start, have not dealt with multicultural contexts or addressed the problems faced by many countries in the South. In multiethnic Malaysia, situated within the belly of a globalizing economy and driven by an authoritarian state, the women's movement has had to carve a niche for itself to prove its relevance and be regarded as a mover of the democratization process. In this book we attempt to look at how Malaysian feminism has evolved within these contexts.

Distinctive historical moments have engendered many forms of feminist politics and practices. Indeed, the emergence of what we call nationalist feminism, social feminism, political feminism and market feminism have coincided as markers of the country's transformation from colonialism to a post-*Reformasi* state. The latter arose out of the sacking, in September 1998, of Anwar Ibrahim as Deputy Prime Minister. The episode triggered widespread protests among Malays, civil society groups and Islamic youths against then Prime Minister Mahathir Mohamad, stimulating spontaneous calls for *Reformasi* (reform). Anwar's subsequent assault at the hands of the police chief while in custody and a highly questionable trial that convicted him of corrupt practice and sexual misconduct and jailed him for 15 years all fed into this movement.

This is not to say that different historical periods have been marked by a distinctive feminist discourse and practice. All kinds of feminisms may have overlapped and existed in all periods. What is argued here is that the different historical contexts formed the backdrop for the emergence of one dominant form of feminist expression and agency over others.

The issues

By analysing the various women's issues and campaigns, the chapters in this book trace and dissect the engagement of the women's movement with the state in an attempt to understand its relative successes and failures. They discuss problems involving strategies of the women's movement and examine the successes of middle-class women in promoting Violence Against Women (VAW) issues in society in comparison to, say, the failures of working-class women's promotion of labour rights.

Chapter 2 provides some empirical basis as to how 'Malaysian feminism' can be best conceptualized. It presents a broad sweep of the evolution of feminist consciousness in the country's modern history. Instead of using the categories explored by early Western literature on feminist theories, as in liberal feminism, radical feminism, Marxist and socialist feminism, or post-modern feminism, this chapter looks at four phases in the country's historical transformation to place feminism in its Malaysian context. We revisit the phases of its (i) anti-colonial struggles; (ii) post-independence consociationalism; (iii) developmentalism and the rise of identity politics; and its (iv) post-*Reformasi* realignment. Each phase has a dominant feminist consciousness and strategy for mobilization, although some types of feminism can straddle various phases.

This same chapter argues that feminism has been a significant player upon which the identity of the Malaysian state has been carved. Nevertheless, feminist culture has not succeeded in changing the styles of political leadership nor has it been capable of addressing the features of bad governance, such as corruption and abuse of public power. Some aspects of the women's movement may act as a counterforce to mainstream patriarchal ideology. However the appropriation and cultivation of the movement by the state can legitimize the workings of its authoritarianism.

Women's mobilization into male-directed organizations, such as political parties with huge resources, has by far been more successful than their mobilization into autonomous civil movements, especially movements that question the workings of capital and the dominance of a male-centric state system. But the groundwork laid by women's groups of the early 1980s has resulted in the stock phrases associated with feminism – especially the rhetoric on VAW – becoming acceptable in the everyday discourse of Malaysians. These have even been appropriated to justify the relevance of women's role within the male-directed movements. Chapter 2 cautions that numerous and formidable structural impediments still exist in society. In a sense this means that feminism has not really actualized itself as a counter-hegemonic force.

Like many of their counterparts across the globe, independent women activists in Malaysia first came together in the early 1980s in a concerted manner to organize against VAW. To do this, they identified a multi-pronged strategy which included law reforms, public education and improving the provision of services to women who had been violated. Chapter 3 is a critique of a struggle over more than two decades by the women's movement to address this issue. This is done in relation to three specific VAW issues that have been taken up: rape, domestic violence and sexual harassment.

While there are similarities in the approaches adopted in each of these campaigns, there are also differences in the paths traversed. This reflects the difficulties encountered by the women's movement in achieving its objectives to create a violence-free society. For example, in the area of public education, it was much easier mobilizing public support against the crime of rape compared to that of domestic violence or sexual harassment. In the first instance women's groups were able to capitalize on public outrage against violent acts of rape. With the latter, however, they had to first endure reactions ranging from trivializing of the issues or outright hostility, until sufficient public awareness had been generated. The acceptability of each issue was thus contingent upon reactions of the male-dominated society towards these concerns.

Nowhere is this clearer than in the experience of the women's movement with legal reform. Chapter 3 thus focuses its critique on this strategy. While amendments to the laws relating to rape were passed within five years of being mooted to the government, proposals for a Domestic Violence Act took twice as long before they were implemented. In both instances, however, male members of parliament heckled the female ministers responsible for tabling the bills, and made light of these very serious violations.

Indeed, the influence of various arms of the state has been crucial in determining the success of the VAW campaign. Over the years, local women's groups have learnt the hard way that, as civil society, they operate within very narrow confines. This has partly to do with how civil society as a whole has been weakened through systematic dismantling and disempowerment by the state over the years – for example, numerous fundamental human rights have been taken away in the name of preserving national security and stability.

Another explanation, however, lies in the way that women's groups have chosen to lobby for legal reform and better services from the state. They have put themselves in a situation of having to deal with the state's various machineries on its terms. For instance, in the case of the campaign for legislation to combat sexual harassment, women's organizations have finally learnt, after five years of lobbying, that their efforts have come to nought. The government, despite earlier promises of supporting this proposal, has seen it fitter to shelve this idea for an unspecified period of time. Chapter 3 thus raises questions not only for women's groups, but also for others in civil society, as to their choice of future action, given that the experience of engaging with the state has thus been fraught with difficulty.

Chapter 4 takes us on a historical journey in a bid to understand the role and nature of the state *vis-à-vis* its reactions and dealings with women's issues in general and the women's movement in particular. Two main periods are discussed – that of development and the focus on Women in

Development strategies; and the shift towards gender mainstreaming under the onslaught of globalization. The chapter points out the principal factors that influence such engagement – the nature of the political regime together with international and local pressures exerted by civil society.

An important *caveat* to this engagement is the contradiction faced by an authoritarian regime which depends on the electoral process (despite its problems) to be 'legitimately' installed in power every five years. The tensions and ambiguities of such a guided democracy are detailed in the various moves and countermoves made by the state and women's groups as they negotiated with each other in areas ranging from VAW to the general election to the *Reformasi* movement. The institutionalization of VAW concerns through state appropriation spells both success and the death knell for women's groups at one and the same time. This became evident when the Ministry of Women and Family Development – later the Ministry of Women, Family and Community Development – came into being and was played as the gender card for the state's own interest.

This chapter sends a warning to women's groups to be vigilant to avoid a depoliticization process where they become too embedded within the state structures. As noted in the conclusion of the chapter, the challenge as a women's movement is to ensure that its organization and issues are not instrumentalized and co-opted by an authoritarian state – there is a need to maintain autonomy and to engage with the state on it own terms. In the final analysis, women's groups have to link up within the politics of coalition building towards a more holistic transformation of society.

Chapter 5 focuses the discussion on women's groups linked to Malay-Muslim organizations.[7] Several pertinent questions are posed. First, how have Malay-Muslim women's organizations influenced or intervened in state processes involving the role of Islam and women? Second, are there differences among the groups and, if so, how have these contributed to the achievement or failure of social and political reforms?

Case studies of women's involvement in Malay-Muslim organizations are used to illustrate these postulations and questions. We categorize some groups belonging to one end of the spectrum as being feminist, liberal and individualist in character. The other end is occupied by groups that are more communitarian and culturally exclusive in purpose. These organizations have never had a unitary voice but together they act to 'soften' the entrenchment of a monolithic and strident Islam in society. It is argued in this chapter that the combination of a plural political constituency and shifts in state prerogatives, as well as the rising assertiveness of women's voices, have challenged the strength of a conservative Islamic political lobby. Not unlike in authoritarian regimes elsewhere, women's political participation is necessary to safeguard the survival of the political order. Even so, the presence of diverse Islamic women's groups attests to the existence of spaces for the questioning and re-questioning of Islam, even if powerful forces prevail in curbing women's autonomous agency throughout the exercise.

We conclude that there are some issues which have united and divided these groups. The victimization of women through assault on the body as a rallying cry is more successful at uniting women's groups of all shades as opposed to the victimization of women through polygamy, dress codes or unequal punishments (as under *Hudud* or Islamic criminal laws). The fact that Muslim women cannot agree on a common stance or will not necessarily accept the voice of an entrenched religious authority (whether of the state or of other camps) is a reflection of how the invocation of the Islamic literalist tradition by religious authorities and scholars is not always successful. In fact, women in Malay-Muslim organizations with an Islamic agenda can even readily form alliances with other feminists as in the case of the *Reformasi* mobilization.

Chapter 6 asks why, despite their immense contribution to the socio-economic development of the country, women workers' concerns remain relatively unheard, compared to say VAW issues raised by the women's movement. The first section brings out the main problems and issues faced by women workers under the country's march from an industrialized to a 'knowledge' economy in the context of wanting to reap the benefits of today's neo-liberal globalization processes. Several issues are highlighted – from the implications of the shift towards casualization and flexibilization of labour to sexual harassment at work and the low levels of labour mobilization and unionization.

The chapter argues that both state control and persistent ethnic divisions erode an already weakened trade-union movement which is unable to support the mass organization of women workers. A case study of the only in-house union in an American multinational electronics firm shows how, throughout the course of an ongoing 16-year struggle, women workers here have had to encounter various barriers in getting their union recognized. These have ranged from the state protecting capital to the various strategies used by capital to simultaneously contain and coerce labour. At the same time, middle-class women's NGOs have also failed to effectively link up with grassroots groups and to mobilize women workers, caused in the main by the collusion of state and capital to suppress working-class struggles. Nonetheless, it is also argued that women workers' NGOs have also to look into their own organizing strategies as well as attitudes towards the women's movement so that both can work in tandem to advance the rights of women workers.

The chapter ends rather pessimistically in that, unless there is more democratic space for civil society, the voices of women workers will continue to be muted in the race towards unfettered globalization. At a time when key labour issues have yet to be adequately addressed, there are already new challenges for both the women's and labour movements to take up, not least of which are the concerns of migrant and sex workers.

Chapter 7 traces the reactions to attempts by women's groups to raise sexuality rights. This engagement has been shaky at best for various reasons, ranging from a real fear of reprisal from the authorities to the widespread prevalence of homophobia. Nevertheless, in the face of greater regulation of female sexuality today, there is now an increasing awareness of the added layer of discrimination that women face, simply because of their sexual choices, behaviours, preferences and actions. This has led to wider recognition of these issues by the women's movement.

Through several illustrations – the problems experienced by a women's NGO, the All Women's Action Society (AWAM) in attempting to extend the staging of the play *The Vagina Monologues*; the case history of protectionist legislation for women and girls; and the issue of the persecution of a woman who married another woman – this chapter shows how the notion of 'natural', and thus acceptable, sexuality has been carefully constructed by those in power. In this situation, the state has played a key role in two primary ways. One, by demonizing and marginalizing any form of sexual expression, behaviour or lifestyle that challenges dictated 'norms' and, two, by professing to uphold morality and 'protect' society, and, perhaps more accurately, women, from such 'evils'.

Despite the firm grip that the state appears to have over standards of acceptable sexuality, there are still openings that allow challenges to be mounted against its control. As the state is not monolithic – there are allies located within this institution – the resulting contradictions in its actions sporadically provide entry points for engagement. The chapter concludes by highlighting how important it is for the women's movement to continue questioning efforts to control female bodies, even if only to raise an alternative voice to the dominant discourse on sexuality. Better yet, the movement should see this as part and parcel of its efforts to expand democratic spaces in society, which includes freeing women (and men) from all forms of discrimination – legally, culturally and in the domain of sexual choices.

In the concluding chapter we synthesize the three main themes of the book: (i) Malaysian feminism and the women's movement as reflection and outcome of the developmentalist state and its economic project; (ii) the women's movement as an organized entity against and in the furtherance of hegemony and restricted democracy; and (iii) the women's movement as a repository for the discourse and engagement with sexuality. Other issues explored include the rise of market feminism as the new face of Malaysian feminism. However, rather than looking at it as a new practice or movement we have argued that it is more fitting to view it as an appropriation of a feminist practice. This final chapter also puts forward several challenges that the women's movement has to face in order to be relevant in the context of current and future changes. It presents a reflection of the strengths and weakness – and the dilemmas – of the political feminism of the late twentieth century in Malaysia, in conjunction with the opportunities and obstacles for the future of Malaysian feminism.

This book will show that, in the context of an ethnically fragmented post-colonial society ruled by an authoritarian but procedurally democratic – as in abiding to regular elections – state, an autonomous women's movement which began in the early eighties did achieve significant political successes. This is evident in the introduction of new issues such as VAW and sexuality into the sphere of public debate. Further, the nature of political feminism enabled the formation of a trans-ethnic platform for an electoral agenda for the 1999 general elections.

These issues, however, were also readily appropriated by the state and the market, culminating in the 'market feminism' of today. As we trace these developments we seek answers to the question formulated at the beginning of this chapter. How has feminism, as a cultural consciousness or an arresting social and political phenomenon, left its imprint on Malaysian society? Did it constitute a grand political force or merely benign discourses in the public imagination?

2 Accommodating feminisms

The women's movement in contemporary Malaysia

The evolution of feminism in Malaysia has been a result and conflation of many factors. One of these is the establishment of a strong, even authoritarian, national state that is more inclined towards exacting coerced stability than allowing democratic expression. This is sometimes balanced by the opportunity factor brought about by economic transformation allowing for women's employment and organized mobilization. While state priorities have given the women's movement its restrained character, the opportunity factor has allowed it leeway to chart its own course. Malaysian feminism is thus distinct in its origin and political character. It is as much a state project as it is a reaction against statist restrictions and abuses.

Feminism is only one of the many ideological and cultural forces that compete for social acceptance. Like other influences it also attempts to capture a consensual imagination and world-view. Tracing the historical basis of its evolution in Malaysia helps in understanding how its purposes were achieved or thwarted. Women did gain substantially from the strength of a women's movement for gender equality, but these benefits have remained tenuous. They were easily exploited by the state and other institutional forces to further objectives that were even inimical to women's interests. But the contestation between state control and people's autonomy has given Malaysian feminism a sense of dynamism, forcing it to continually respond to changing realities.

The four dominant feminisms discussed in this chapter can be identified by their motives, namely nationalist, social, political and market-driven. We argue that various strands of feminisms underlie the distinct purposes of the women's movement in each phase. The conceptual relationship between 'feminism' and the 'women's movement' is thus in the character of its articulation, the political strategies which it employs and the actors which it chooses to engage with. The complex intertwining of liberal and radical as well as postmodern posturings and motivations will, at the same time as well as at different times, affect how the movement functions. One variable that has exerted an overarching impact has been the authoritarian state, bent on preserving a manageable and quiescent multiethnic populace, thus rendering Malaysian feminism its relatively accommodative and non-confrontational character.

Nationalist politicization

The origins of Malaysia's twentieth-century feminist movement can be traced to the political struggles against colonial rule. Malaysian women of all ethnic origins had their early politicization and leadership training in the tumultuous years of World War II. This critical period spurred various shades of anti-imperialist reaction. The change of rulers, from British to Japanese, had a significant symbolic value. It awakened the local population to the possibility of their own liberation.

In Malaysia's case, nationalist movements against foreign domination simultaneously spawned debates about women's roles in the workplace, their right to formal education and their participation in political organizations (Manderson, 1980; Dancz, 1987; Maznah, 2001). Although such proto-feminist consciousness may have been fuelled by anti-imperialist mobilization it was also a product of a universalizing modernist project of British colonialism. But the colonial administration never had a clear or sustained policy of ethnic integration. Hence, women from different ethnic communities articulated their meaning of nationalism within distinctive, but segregated cultural and historical contexts. In then British Malaya, which did not include the states of East Malaysia, women of Malay, Chinese and Indian origin were all able to actively participate in nationalist movements. But their conception of a future nation state was not forged upon a common ideal and neither were they united in strategy.

The rise of left-leaning Malay political movements soon after the end of World War II was one avenue which afforded Malay women non-traditional roles. For example, the Malay Nationalist Party (MNP) was one of the first political parties to establish a women's wing, Angkatan Wanita Sedar (AWAS – Force of Awakened Women) in 1946. Although women were largely recruited for populist mobilization and expediency, strong and outstanding women personalities emerged from this political strategy. In 1948, the British Military Administration, which had resumed control of Malaya following Japan's defeat, banned the MNP and its women's and youth wings under the pretext that it was pro-Japanese, leftist and militant.

Subsequently colonial administrators cultivated the more moderate, nationalist but British-allied party, the United Malays National Organisation (UMNO). In the negotiation for eventual self-rule, UMNO remained the premier stakeholder. But the fervour of an anti-imperialist movement did leave a mark on women's road to leadership. After the MNP was banned, the three main women leaders of AWAS all took divergent paths with their political leanings:

1   Aishah Ghani, the first leader of AWAS, joined Pergerakan Kaum Ibu (PKI – Mothers' Movement), and became its fifth president and later a cabinet minister in the UMNO-led government.

2   Sakinah Junid, who led the six-mile protest march on the first anniversary of Angkatan Pemuda Insaf (Awakened Young Men's Front) in February 1947, joined the Parti Islam Se Malaysia (PAS – Islamic Party of Malaysia) and became president of its Women's Section.

3   Shamsiah Fakih, joined the Communist Party of Malaya (CPM), carried on the struggle underground, went into exile in China and was only allowed back into the country in the early 1990s.

After the end of World War II, a new Malay women's political organization was formed. The PKI came into being in 1947 to support the male-dominated UMNO. Women's issues were not the main concern to judge by its stated objectives then (Ng et al., 1987: 129).

Nevertheless, the early phase of women's involvement in UMNO was not simply marked by their compliance and acceptance of established structures of male dominance. Among the agitators was Khatijah Sidek, one of the first leaders to question gender disparities within the party. She had been elected head of the women's wing in 1954. Khatijah demanded that more women be represented in party decision-making bodies, that a separate women's youth wing be formed and that there be increased nominations for women to contest electoral seats. But she was chastised for breaching party discipline and finally expelled from the party (Manderson, 1980: 113–14).

As UMNO took over the reins of the post-colonial state, any seemingly radical demands made by women, such as reforming *Syariah* (Islamic) laws, were also swiftly set aside (Dancz, 1987: 161). Soon, women simply acquiesced or were 'naturalized' to the structure of gendered hierarchy within the party. Up until today, the unspoken norm of UMNO's power structure situates the status of its women's wings below that of its all-male youth wing.

During the phase of nationalist uprising, non-Malay women whose ancestors came as immigrants from China and India continued to define their loyalty as largely belonging to their original homeland. Citizenship of their new country, British Malaya at the time, was an ambiguous and fluid notion. Among Chinese women, it was their schooling experience, moulded after the system in China, which played a pivotal role in influencing their specific political involvement. Some joined the anarchist movement and many more became members of the CPM (Khoo, 1994: 1–2).

Some of the most active Indian women in the country joined political movements being fought in India. In 1941, when Subash Chandra Bose formed the Indian National Army, Indian women in Malaya were recruited to be part of the army's Rhani of Jansi Regiment, and travelled to Burma to make their way into India (Khoo, 1994: 3). The first training camp for women was set up in Singapore; Dr Lakshmi Swaminathan, an Indian doctor who practised medicine there, was put in charge of the fighting and nursing units (Forbes, 1999: 212–13). So strong was the fervour for fighting against colonialism (in India rather than Malaya) that even a 17-year-old,

Janaki Davar from Kuala Lumpur, was inspired to sign up as a soldier with the INA despite initial resistance from her parents (Forbes, 1999: 213).

Although it had anti-colonialism as a common defining purpose, such mobilization was still forged along an ethnic-distinct platform and not one which was common to all. The 'nation' was not necessarily the physical ground upon which one stood and the concept of nationalism was akin to liberation of each other's notion of the homeland, rather than a single-minded focus on building a new, united and common entity. It was only after the end of World War II that the political struggles for unity and the building of the Malayan nation actually took off in a concerted way.

This helps to explain why party politics that downplayed ethnic differences were unsuccessful in attracting adherents. The Independence of Malaya Party, set up in 1951 with its membership open to all races, specifically promised equal opportunities regardless of sex. However, it barely survived a year. Another multiracial party, the Parti Negara (National Party), was launched in 1954, promising equal pay for equal work and equal opportunities, including emancipation for women. It too failed to leave a mark in the first general election. The non-communal Pan-Malayan Labour Party committed itself to ensuring women's equality by including a proposal for a 'Women's Charter'. However, it was unsuccessful in garnering mass electoral support.

Malayan women's early involvement in formal politics was only successful if it followed the model of the inter-ethnic consociational 'cartel'. Through this model, nationalism was to be forged based on compromise and accommodation of distinctive ethnic concerns. This type of politics thus overrode all other political projects, such as feminism or labour unionism. Even though nationalists recognized the enhancement of women's rights as an important objective of the nation state, this notion did not become a universal concern. Political mobilization was still based upon ethnic identity and affiliation.

Post-independence consociational politics

It was only in 1963, six years after independence, that a significant non-governmental multiracial women's organization, the National Council for Women's Organisations (NCWO), was formed. This was spurred by the issue of women's unequal pay which was first highlighted by the Women Teachers' Union (WTU), formed in 1960.[1] Unequal pay at the time was an issue which galvanized women's mobilization. The impetus for formation of the NCWO also came from an overall global trend in the 1960s to gain recognition for the rights of working women. International bodies like the Young Women's Christian Association (YWCA) contributed significantly towards the formation of the NCWO. In fact, it was on the YWCA's initiative that a conference of women's groups was organized in 1960. The subsequent establishment of NCWO was boosted by close cooperation from

Wanita UMNO, which successfully organized a Women's Day rally on 25 August 1962 involving many non-governmental women's organizations. 25 August had also been the date of Wanita UMNO's inauguration 13 years earlier in 1949. Then Wanita UMNO leader, Fatimah Hashim (also Malaysia's first woman cabinet minister), saw in the NCWO a formal structure which could serve as an umbrella coalition for these different groups (Dancz, 1987: 139–41). Since then, NCWO and UMNO have kept alive the annual tradition of celebrating National Women's Day on 25 August, rather than International Women's Day on 8 March.

NCWO's leadership structure mirrored the 'ethnic elite accommodation' model of the ruling party. The NCWO leaders were 'deliberately' elected from among women of the three major ethnic groups.[2] What different ethnic women could not achieve through their membership in the women's wings of their ethnic-based political parties was realized within the NCWO. It became the vehicle through which the struggles for legislative reforms for equal pay, women's equal access to public service jobs and marital rights were achieved. Several of the chairpersons were also cabinet ministers. The NCWO was not only a close ally of the government but was a mirror of the 'consociational-democratic' model of the national ruling elite.

Although non-partisan, the identification of NCWO with the government was so strong that representatives from two opposition parties, the Socialist and Islamic parties, withdrew their membership in 1965 (Dancz, 1987: 140). The NCWO tried to overcome the divisions within which multiethnic elite women functioned at party politics level. It played a very important role in encouraging cross-party collaboration among women politicians. However, it was no less a sponsored entity in the sense that it tied its interests closely to those of the establishment. The NCWO selectively engaged in campaigns which either reflected the interests of elite middle-class women or which were not politically contentious. For instance, while equal wages were sought for white-collar professionals, the same rights for equal treatment and remuneration were not sought for women industrial workers. The number of women in the workforce swelled rapidly during the country's export-led phase of industrialization from the 1970s.[3] However, the NCWO steered clear of campaigns related to the issue of unionization of women industrial workers.

The politics of the NCWO set-up and rationale are characterized by inter-ethnic compromise, accommodation and bargaining, much like the Alliance arrangement which was the basis of Malayan independence. The Alliance coalition, which formed the post-independence government, comprised three ethnic-based parties: UMNO, MCA (then Malayan, now Malaysian Chinese Association) and MIC (then Malayan, now Malaysian Indian Congress). All three did their part in sponsoring women's entry into politics. As a result of this, the few women candidates fielded in general elections comfortably succeeded on the strength of party support (Rashila Ramli, 1998). Such a tradition ensured women's unfailing presence in electoral politics but did not allow women leaders to test social limits or to challenge entrenched systems through parliamentary democracy. Since women's wings occupy a subordinate status within their parties, women who were nominated to contest and were elected were inevitably more beholden to their patrons in the party than to their electorate (Kamilia Ibrahim, 1998). Within this *quid pro quo* arrangement, women politicians would choose to tread carefully and toe the party line rather than appease women's rights lobbyists, if the aims of the latter were deemed prejudicial to party interests.

For a long time after independence, women politicians contributed little towards the democratization of gender politics, both within and outside their parties. Even when women's rights legislation and policies were being pushed, it was women's NGOs such as the NCWO which provided the impetus and gentle pressure through behind-the-scenes negotiation, so as to nudge women politicians into action (Maznah, 2001). The NCWO, however, was careful not to push for legislation considered contentious, such as reform of *Syariah* laws. The NCWO's distinctive stance, of which its leaders remain proud until today, is that it has always taken a 'non-confrontational' approach in advancing women's rights.

Reforms to break the vicious cycle of gender inequality within political party structures have not been prominent in post-independent Malaysia. The numerical strength of women voters has failed to translate into a clamour for gender-based reform. Thus the issue of women's representation in parliamentary democracies has remained irrelevant for gender empowerment despite the strong perception that women's role in formal politics can lead to a change for the women's constituency (Rashila, 1998). Conditions in Malaysia are not unlike those in other Asian countries where women's formal representation in national legislatures has been less influential in demanding pro-women policies than the role played by autonomous women's groups (Lee and Clark, 2000).

Developmentalism and identity politics

This third phase of Malaysia's development saw the dynamics of a distinct political era highly charged with ethnic overtones and an assertion of Malay political dominance. At the same time this phase was also witness to an economic strategy that fitted the developmentalist model of capitalist development. First, we shall discuss the political and cultural character of this phase by looking at the significance of the New Economic Policy (NEP) and its subsequent influence on identity politics. Second, we shall describe the economic character of this phase by dwelling on the concept of 'developmentalism' and its implications for gender and ethnic relations and, consequently, the development of political feminism.

On 13 May 1969, ethnic riots broke out in Kuala Lumpur. Popularly dubbed 'May 13th', the incident stands as a critical date in the nation's transition from one distinct phase to another. The episode was used as justification to implement the NEP from 1971, an affirmative-action instrument for redressing economic inequality based on ethnicity.[4] This policy of social engineering through extensive state intervention was justified on the grounds that Malays and indigenous peoples had been unfairly disadvantaged by historical circumstances. After two decades of implementation, the NEP was assessed as delivering both positive and negative results. The socio-economic achievements of Malays have risen and there has been a rapid rate of urbanization among the formerly rural-based Malay population, thus allowing them to enter the modern workforce.

On the downside, the social distributive function of the NEP has been distorted, resulting in the creation of a small class of wealthy Malay capitalists, in tandem with the rise of capitalists in all ethnic groups. Their fortunes were accumulated largely on the back of patronage politics, leading to the attendant consequence of rampant cronyism and corruption within the system. The NEP became the *leitmotif* of Malaysia's evolving social, cultural and political landscape through the decades from the 1970s through the late 1990s.[5]

In this phase the ideology of developmentalism – defined as a discourse which 'valorises improving material standards of living, rapid economic growth, and political stability' (Loh, 2003: 165) – became more entrenched in policies and governance. The concept of 'developmentalism' here is used to describe a particular variant of capitalist development which characterized the experience of East Asian economies (Gilpin, 2001: 305–40). The rapid transition of these economies from an underdeveloped, post-colonial state into Newly Industrializing Countries (NICs) led theorists to proffer an explanation around the role of the state. A developmentalist state plays an overwhelming role in leading the market, instead of the other way around; it also concentrates on a strategy of growth instead of redistribution. Added to this is the curtailment of democratic space and human (especially labour) rights to ensure a trouble-free environment for industrialization and foreign investment. Malaysia, as one of the later NICs (after South Korea, Singapore, Hong Kong and Taiwan), fitted this model of development, but with a slight difference. Although the Malaysian government was focused on industrialization and wealth accumulation, it was able to proceed with a redistribution agenda. Some form of income distribution was affected under the justification of the NEP. Political democratization was not a main priority of the state as it had also implemented the NEP through an 'authoritative *fiat*' in the wake of the 1969 racial riots. The model of export-led industrialization promoted by the state saw a massive influx of a new labour force comprising young women into the urban sector. A majority of this workforce was Malay and rural.[6]

But it was in this phase that Malaysia also experienced highest economic growth. With this came a heightening of identity politics. This can be perceived as rising ethnic differentiation, acting as a form of boundary closure. This marked off the *bumiputera* (indigenous person) from the non-*bumiputera* or, in wider context, the Malay from the non-Malay. Islam as religion was simultaneously incorporated to lend more definitive authenticity to the identity of the cultural Malay or was used to displace the old, maligned 'Malay' characterizations ('the lazy native'), purported to be the source of this group's backwardness. The new 'Islamized' identity adopted by Malays was more assertive, forceful and had strength in a global movement.

Political causes were also formally and informally identified to be the exclusive domain of particular ethnic groups – for instance, Islamic women's rights could be articulated only by Muslims, Chinese education rights taken up only by Chinese political parties, and estate workers' rights only by Indian political parties. As a result, it was difficult to universalize social problems and their articulation as women's issues, labour issues or as issues of civil liberties. This was left to segments of the residual 'civil society' to take up. People either pragmatically acquiesced to the national project (referring largely to a politically disempowered non-Malay constituency), instrumentally accepted it (largely those who had the capacity to benefit from it) or reinforced identity politics through it for the further assertion of political dominance and exclusiveness (largely Malays and Muslims).[7]

Women divided

When the global revivalist Islamic movement swept through Malaysia from the 1970s, it did not take long for a hyper-ethnicized feminine identity (the veiled, modest, maternal Malay-Muslim woman) to take pre-eminence over other identities. Like so many past and contemporary examples elsewhere women quickly become the touchstone of a new project for recasting ideological foundations (Kandiyoti, 1989; Mostov, 2000).

In Malaysia, it was as though women's agency was used to 'rebuild Malay-Muslim identity' (Ong, 1995: 179). The liberty to adopt a non-ethnicized feminist identity became a limited option among large numbers of Malay women. Malay Muslim women sought a psychological as well as pragmatic rationale to justify their choice of clothes, lifestyle and social behaviour. Minimally, the veil was adopted because this was deemed to be the undisputed symbol of Islamization even if piety is exhibited in a marginal way. The project to submerge the identity of a universalized woman took full effect and resulted in a division between 'Islamized' women and others (including non-Muslims) who remained outside the Islamization project. Eventually divisions become naturalized, creating 'other' nations within the 'mainstream/dominant' nation.

The enforced dichotomization between Muslims and non-Muslims also led to a pervasive if erroneous perception that unequal gender relations are only associated with an Islamized social system. Islamic practices were considered to be highly gendered and non-Islamic practices were considered more gender-neutral. As will be shown elsewhere in this book, the discourse of gender inequality and sexism is not only embraced by Muslims but by other communities too.

But more political energies were expended to fortify the *Syariah* laws, while cultural attention was targeted to ensure a distinct dress code for Muslims, particularly women. Thus one finds that in a nation-within-a-nation, robed Muslim men would not be similarly concerned if a scantily clad non-Malay woman were to cross their path. A modestly dressed but unveiled Malay woman would attract much attention, if not disapproval.

The birth of political feminism

Within these circumstances the feminist movement began to take on a more political character. Several new women's organizations, all coalescing around the issue of Violence Against Women (VAW), were formed in the early to mid-1980s. The Women's Aid Organisation (WAO), Women's Crisis Centre (WCC – later Women's Centre for Change), Women's Development Collective (WDC), the All Women's Action Society (AWAM), Sabah Action Women's Resource Group (SAWO) and Sarawak Women for Women's Society (SWWS) were some of the groups that sprouted. These were initiated by middle-class urban women, many of whom had completed tertiary education in the West. Among them were women student activists of the Left, especially those disenchanted by the pervasiveness of sexism within movements which prioritized the articulation of class at the expense of gender interests. At various times, these organizations came together under the umbrella of the Joint Action Group against Violence Against Women (JAG-VAW).[8]

Feminism as a political project could only gain its adherents among those at the political margins. These were women who wanted to articulate their sense of personal and systemic oppression through a language of anti-establishment or counter-hegemony. Many wanted to move away from politics and organizations that were too ethnocentric. Thus, the reach of feminism became quite limited given that ethnicity was still heavily entrenched in all forms of organizational life in Malaysia.

Nevertheless, the appeal of 'feminism' among some non-Malay and middle-class women was that it had the image of being 'non-political'. This would enable them to work in women's organizations without their being seen as partisan. Many middle-class women were eager to work with the new NGOs because these extended help to battered or abused women. They viewed their involvement as 'volunteerism' with elements of altruism and charity, rather than something necessarily oppositional to the mainstream.

However, the underlying principles and philosophy behind the formation of the new women's groups as held by their founders were not simply to confine their activities to extending social services to abused women. It was also about injecting a new ideology of feminism into the conception and origin of women's oppression. One manifestation of this mission was to uncover what was behind women's victimization when subjected to violence.

The issue of VAW was a palpable common denominator in every woman's life, cutting across class and ethnicity. However, women located away from the more developed urban centres had fewer organizational capacities and resources to deal with this issue either at a service-orientation or advocacy level. But VAW was also the only site that did not yet come under the purview of the state. It was an issue that the new women's groups could confidently claim as their 'own'. Thus, for almost two decades, the new women's movement in Malaysia strategically seized upon this issue. The VAW issue eventually became the repository of the many ideals of social change – feminism, liberalism, socialism and even Marxism.[9]

There were also attempts during this period to broaden the movement, both in terms of platform or issues and networking. One of the key strategies of WDC was to annually bring together women activists from both women's organizations and grassroots groups to debate on issues such as ethnicity, class, patriarchy and political participation. It was also a time for sharing the varied experiences on concerns ranging from VAW to issues affecting women workers, estate women, the urban poor and indigenous women in the East Malaysian states of Sabah and Sarawak. As a result of these encounters an initiative called the National Women's Coalition (NWC) was introduced in 1992 comprising about 20 organizations. It included groups like the Sabah Community Group (PACOS) and Institut Pengajian Komuniti (Institute for Community Education), which worked with indigenous women; People's Service Organisation and Alaigal, working with plantation workers; Malaysian Women for Ministry and Theology and Sisters in Islam, working with progressive Christian and Muslim women; and Sahabat Wanita (Friends of Women) and the Peneroka Bandar (Urban Pioneers Group), working with factory workers and the urban poor respectively.

Under the NWC, five commissions were set up – labour, VAW, culture and religion, health and land – to cater to the concerns of the wider women's movement. Despite the existence of grassroots groups, the NWC was incapable of building a mass women's movement, particularly with women workers and (Malay) peasant women – two important bases for an effective movement. In 1996, due to lack of resources and personnel, the NWC unofficially folded after sending a delegation to, and holding a workshop at, the parallel NGO meeting to the 1995 UN World Conference on Women in Beijing, China. Nonetheless, informal networking continued while the JAG-VAW carried on with lobbying and educational activities.[10]

Unlike earlier women's movements built around nationalist struggles, political feminists were not able to make inroads into the rural Malay heartland. In fact, most Malay women who used to be part of the left-leaning Malay nationalist movement AWAS were almost all absorbed into UMNO after independence (Ng et al., 1987: 136). Feminism that was promoted in Malaysia's developmental phase was ensconced within a Western-liberal framework. The notion of women's rights and equality associated with this group was deemed biased towards middle-class and non-Eastern values. The nationalism of earlier years had a more 'indigenous' and 'organic' ring to it. Early colonial resistors emerged from the ranks of marginalized rural and religious movements (Roff, 1967). But long after independence, the priorities of a new economic development policy hived off the Malay community's participation along the concerns of civil society. Hence the women's movement was unable to spread the notion of women's rights and equality as a universal cause in a society that was still divided by ethnicity.

Working-class women

For example, the feminist movement did not build substantive alliances with working-class women. This was despite the massive and rapid entry of rural Malay women into the industrial workforce (Lim, 1978; Grossman, 1979). The 'horrors' of waged-work and cultural dislocation seemed to offer the right conditions for their political mobilization. But this did not happen, for two reasons.

First, laws were enacted to prohibit unionization among workers in the foreign-owned electronic sector. Women were the ones largely hired as soon as the country embarked on attracting foreign investments for its export sector. Second, the 'Malay condition' became the social bulwark against women's mobilization by unions or feminist groups. Since a majority of industrial workers were Malay women, cultural and religious factors operated immediately to distance them from activities that were considered anti-establishment (or a stance that was going against the legitimacy of a 'Malay' government).

In the early years of export-led industrialization, Malay women's involvement in factory work was not looked upon favourably. They were labelled 'morally loose' and considered 'easy sexual prey' by institutional forces which employed sexual metaphors and discourses to affect social control upon the women (Ong, 1987: 183). Young, unmarried, rural women were brought out for the first time from their villages and were housed as a group in the cities without parental supervision – an uncommon practice at the time. As if to redeem their 'sullied' moral identity and to escape the slew of cultural admonishments by representatives of their own communities, Malay women workers situated their loyalty even more resolutely within their ethnicity rather than within their new class of a labouring force.

As though 'assailed by contradictory, unflattering representations of themselves' these women had little choice but to turn to Islam for more guidance and self-regulation which seemed to mesh well with their expected work discipline and asceticism in life (Ong, 1987: 185). Malay women's cultural status thus changed in the complete opposite of their economic status. Despite experiencing a tremendous sense of economic mobility they were pressured to become more 'traditional' and, in doing so, reaffirmed women's role in the reproduction of the patriarchal family. The reality that confronted many social activists at the time was the fact that, ultimately, a majority of the women workers themselves only wanted 'to earn more money, to get married and to be able to leave the factory job soon' (Chan, 1991: 24).[11]

Alliance with rural peasant women

The feminist movement of the 1980s also did not build even the weakest of alliances with rural peasant women. This was because the rural Malay constituency was a domain that was almost completely hegemonized by Malay political forces. These were either representing the ruling coalition or the opposition. UMNO heavily patronized the Malay peasantry because rural constituencies are important to its political survival. Electoral constituencies have been delineated so as to result in the increase of Malay-majority seats. This has given the greatest advantage to Malay candidates who contest on the UMNO ticket. As these constituencies are strategic to UMNO's electoral dominance, the state has maintained tight control over Malay villages.

State Development Committees, although set up and funded by the state, are *de facto* the eyes and ears of UMNO. Resources and subsidies are channelled through these committees in exchange for political loyalty towards the party (Shamsul, 1986). The UMNO government sets up state-sponsored farmers' organizations in different commodity sectors (rubber, oil palm) and, within these, there is usually a women's section. The role of Wanita UMNO is to basically reaffirm or construct the 'traditional' role. The activities of government bodies like *Kemajuan Masyarakat* (KEMAS or Community Development Agency) is one channel through which village-level Wanita UMNO members can win influence. As most of the rural organizations existing today (from rubber smallholders associations to youth organizations) have all been set up under the auspices of the government, it would be impossible for peasants to organize anything autonomously. Even informal village women's networks for *gotong-royong* (traditional communal work), *kutu* (tontines) and *membaca yassin* (Qu'ranic rectitations) – as well as household rites for births and funerals – have all come under the benevolent watchfulness (and control) of UMNO (Ng et al., 1987: 145).

Nevertheless, despite UMNO's rural hegemony, today's main opposition party PAS has succeeded in building its base within the rural enclave. One reason why PAS has been successful is because of the *lacunae* in UMNO's patronage net. Resources are limited and therefore it is not coincidental that some of the poorest villages in the poorest Malay states are also the hotbed of Islamist opposition politics. Economic or social deprivation of the rural poor is easily converted into a cause through the language of Islam. Religion is used to attack the deficiency of the secular and 'morally corrupt' government in that it is accused of not prioritizing policies on social redistribution over more materialistic and grandiose projects intended to showcase modernity. During the pre-independence phase when the state maintained a weaker hegemony over the peasantry, insurgent movements succeeded in establishing their bases in the rural interior. These recruited peasant women into various nationalist movements including that of the outlawed CPM. Its 10th Regiment was specifically set up to recruit, train and encamp Malay members, including women.[12] Today, the more reliable outlet for dissent among rural communities is through their embrace of Islamic opposition politics.

Alliance with Muslim women

By the late 1980s, aware that there were gaps in the reach of the women's movement, some feminist groups began to make efforts to engage with Islam. This activity was initially spurred by international feminist networking, such as initiatives organized by the network of Women Living under Muslim Laws (WLUML). The WLUML was one of the most significant networks which began a global project of feminist dialogue and engagement with Islam (Shaheed, 1994). Many Malaysian feminists (both Muslims and non-Muslims) participated in activities that it initiated. For many, it was through these activities that they were able to meet up with other Muslim women coming from hitherto unknown traditions of diversity within Islam itself.

Out of these experiences, organizations like the WCC, WDC, AWAM and Sisters in Islam found it salient to incorporate an Islamized paradigm in the generation of some versions of an 'indigenous' feminism. This was to counter male-biased Islamic movements that flourished during the resurgence. Sisters in Islam undertook to exclusively focus their agenda on the liberation of Muslim women. The group was formally established in 1993 and sought to reinterpret Islam from a feminist viewpoint. In 1995, the Penang-based WCC also started a research project on Muslim Women and Law to study the impact of *Syariah* laws on women's rights and status (Maznah, 2000). By the early 1990s the WCC had begun offering social and legal counselling for Muslim women.

But there was never any project to challenge the hegemony of Islam *per se.* The groups wanted to engage with Islam (its discourses and authority) by entering into dialogue with it, while deploying its discourses within an 'Islamically' acceptable social framework. Such efforts did not succeed in breaking down the wall of exclusivity which separated the domains of Muslim from non-Muslim women. Nevertheless, the 'secularized' nature of debates over women's rights created an opportunity for Muslim and non-Muslim feminists to find common ground. At the very least, they were able to physically converge at fora to deliberate on various prospects for reform, from *Syariah* laws to the Islamic nation state.[13]

During the the 1980s and early 1990s a large majority of Malay-Muslim, middle-class and professional women remained untouched by the feminist project. If they were involved in organizational work at all, they were to be found largely within Islamic organizations.[14] A majority of Malays, especially their youths were only drawn (either by choice or peer pressure) to Islamic movements. These movements ranged from being fundamentalist-radical, even counter-hegemonic (such as the Darul Arqam), to one which can be characterized as being modernist and having close ties with UMNO, like Angkatan Belia Islam Malaysia (ABIM – Islamic Youth Movement of Malaysia). There were also NGOs such as the Jemaah Islah Malaysia (JIM – Islamic Reform Congregation) which drew a large part of its membership from among Malay students abroad and among Malay professionals, a majority among whom were trained in Western universities. JIM claims to be a movement of 'reform', or drawing people to the Islamic way of life through charitable acts of providing educational and health services to the community. Many women professionals, such as doctors and teachers, are involved in providing such services.

Malay women who constitute a large membership of these movements would keep clear of secular feminist discourses and organizations. The overall project of Islamic movements is to capture the gender discourse so as to fall within the rubric of Islamization. Educated, professional Muslim women within these organizations advocate the principle of gender complementarity rather than equality. Even though the VAW campaign from the 1980s to the 1990s engaged a wide spectrum of women's groups ranging from the mainstream to the (largely non-Malay based) feminist, the absence of Malay women's representatives of Islamic groups was striking. It must be noted that with the exception of Darul Arqam, the main urban Islamic groups which had a large women's membership, particularly ABIM and JIM, belonged to the Islamic mainstream. Like the other hyper-ethnicized civil society, they were also an extension of the state (which portrayed itself to be committed to Islamic governance), and did not identify with labour, women or human rights causes in any prominent way. Even the VAW issue did not provide enough of a bridge to bring middle-class Islamic women and feminist groups together. It was as though the rubric of hyper-ethnicization was resisting the impulse to universalize women's interests and identity.

At this time, in the mid-1990s, the bulk of the Islamist civil society was a 'captured civil society' performing its role as the purveyor of the ideology of separateness and exclusivity. It was only during the political crisis triggered by the abrupt sacking of Deputy Prime Minister Anwar Ibrahim in September 1998 that ABIM found itself on the opposite side of the government led by then Prime Minister Mahathir Mohamad. ABIM had been founded by Anwar in the 1970s.

JIM, which had an image of being non-partisan, almost instantly took an active and partisan role in the *Reformasi* movement that sprung up in support of Anwar.[15] The immediate post-crisis period saw the active participation of women members of JIM in meetings and programmes planned by feminist groups. The impact of *Reformasi* saw women in Islamic organizations becoming more open to speaking the language of feminism. Part of their wider cause of dissent against the government was translated into the struggle to restore democracy and justice.

Post-Reformasi realignment

The East Asian financial crisis of mid-1997 was significant in terms of the economic damage that it wrought on hitherto prosperous NICs in the region. It was at this time that Mahathir's dominance of Malaysian politics began to flounder. A year later, his treatment of Anwar prompted largely Malay-based outrage. Ultimately, the *Reformasi* movement triggered the expression of a host of other reasons for discontent, ranging from government corruption and the emasculation of the judiciary to questionable racial policies brought about by abuse of the NEP. This movement simply referred to as the *Reformasi* essentially evolved to become the all-encompassing counter-hegemonic, cross-ethnic uprising against a perceived anachronistic order.

In 1999, the Barisan Alternatif (Alternative Front) opposition coalition was created, then consisting of four major parties – PAS, DAP, Parti Rakyat Malaysia (Malaysian People's Party) and the newly formed Parti Keadilan Nasional (Keadilan, National Justice Party). The 'rainbow' partnership seized the situation of a weakening state as an opportunity to rebuild and reconstitute the strength of counter-hegemonic forces. This was also a chance for the once residual civil society to stand up to an overpowering state.

Two questions emerged. First, why would the Malay elite in general, who derived clear advantages from the state's affirmative-action policy (the NEP), embrace a cross-ethnic opposition movement after the financial crisis? Second, why would secular feminists as well as the marginalized but autonomous civil society find it necessary to participate in this multiethnic and multi-sectarian coalition?

In addressing these two issues, it must be stressed that it was not the financial crisis *per se* that led to the heightening of *Reformasi*. The early stage of the *Reformasi* outburst was a largely Malay-led movement. Anwar, a charismatic former dissident Islamic activist, was considered an icon of reformist Islam when he was invited to join UMNO in 1982. Hence, his dismissal angered a section of the urban-based, Malay middle-class that had identified with his Islamic aspirations.

By 1998, the NEP had also created the core of a self-assured Malay middle-class who were less dependent on government patronage for upward mobility, and thus had few qualms about being more critical towards the UMNO-led government (Maznah, 2001a). Another reason why a cross-ethnic opposition movement came about was the impending general election of 1999. There was a strong sense that the ruling Barisan Nasional (BN – National Front) coalition government could either be unseated or denied its hitherto unbroken record of winning a two-thirds majority in parliament given the level of disaffection that had been generated, both from its handling of the financial crisis and over the Anwar issue. In many ways, forming a united opposition coalition, whose membership ranged from Islamic fundamentalists to secular democrats, was largely a pragmatic strategy to try to achieve 'the unthinkable' in Malaysia's electoral history (Khoo, 1999).[16]

In 1999, and along the same lines above, seven women's groups, including an Islamic organization,[17] put together a women's charter to be used as a platform of election demands. This was entitled the 'Women's Agenda for Change' (WAC – see Appendix B). A meeting to discuss and debate the charter saw extensive participation of representatives from some 34 organizations who attended a first meeting held in January 1999.[18] Among the Islamic movement, PAS's women representatives did not endorse the document. However, the women's division of JIM readily involved itself in the preparation of the charter.[19]

On 23 May 1999, the WAC, which had 11 demands ranging from land rights to rights on sexuality, was officially launched. These represented some of the more comprehensive demands made by feminists for an election campaign. However, such a display of 'unity' among a disparate set of women's groups was not indicative of a strong tide of newfound feminism among many of the groups. Rather, it was a wave of *Reformasi*-inspired enthusiasm which had brought together a coalition of a plural civil society to counter the political repression of the day. By the time the next post-*Reformasi* national election was held in 2004, there were fewer instances of multiethnic convergences. The other strategy that emanated from feminists during the *Reformasi* fervour was to nominate a woman candidate to contest the election on a gender-issues ticket. A group dubbed the Women's Candidacy Initiative (WCI) was formed and put up a feminist candidate who eventually contested a parliamentary seat as a DAP candidate, but specifically on a 'women's rights' ticket.[20]

Between reforms and restoring the status quo

The appropriation of women's interests for electoral legitimacy was quite successfully used in the 1999 general election. Women's rights have since become an issue to which all political parties are keen to lay claim. Their understanding of women's rights seems to be conveniently left open and inconclusive, a situation which poses interesting questions.

Both UMNO and PAS may handily insist that their conception of 'women's rights' excludes the Western notion of feminism. But contradictions will emerge especially among their women members. Now that the women within UMNO and PAS are encouraged to shoulder greater leadership responsibilities, will they gain in terms of rights too? And why have gender issues become so important to both parties? For UMNO, women form one of the few remaining bases from which the party hopes to recover

some of its legitimacy after the erosion of its moral and economic credentials out of the Anwar crisis. UMNO is also banking on young women
members of the newly created party wing, Puteri Umno, to become its grassroots vote mobilizers.[21]

One way to gain women's votes is to reconstruct women's empowerment
through the tool of religion. The issue of gender 'reformulation' is important
to PAS because it aspires to gain a multiethnic and multi-religious consensus,
which inevitably must address the question of women's nominal rights. By
early 2001, PAS had also come around to recognizing the importance of
women in its future electoral calculations. It announced plans to allow women
to contest the next general election, held in March 2004. The party constitution was amended in 2001 to reserve one of its vice-presidents' posts for a
woman, and to increase the number of women in the party's Central
Working Committee. However, then newly elected leader of the PAS *Dewan
Muslimat* (Women's Assembly), Fatimah Zainab Ibrahim, was also cautious
about appearing too strident on behalf of women, preferring to let the
Majlis Syura (Religious Council) determine the parameters and nature of
women's participation in the party.[22] For all this, PAS has not resolved the
larger issue of gender representation and equality in an envisioned Islamic
state.

The sincerity and ability of PAS and UMNO in addressing some of the
new challenges, specifically creating a united Malay Islamic consensus,
accommodating non-Malay demands and interests and delivering gender
justice and equality, have all been left ambivalently open. Lately, too, there
have been relapses in PASs position of trying to win over the women's
constituency. In 2003, the president of PAS and then *Menteri Besar* (Chief
Minister) of Terengganu, Abdul Hadi Awang, received brickbats for his
unfortunate remark that women were only suitable for specific professions,
given their physical 'limitations' during childbirth, child rearing and
menstruation.

Unlike PAS, UMNO has used a different strategy to cultivate women to
its side. As one response to the *Reformasi* movement, UMNO has tried to
fashion a new identity for young Malay women. This strategy was employed
through the establishment of a new women's youth wing, Puteri UMNO,
with membership from among Malay women below the age of 40.[23] It turned
out that with this as one of its reform strategies, UMNO was successful in
recapturing its Malay support. The 2004 general election delivered a
triumphant win for UMNO with Terengganu recaptured from PAS and
Kelantan being retained only narrowly by the PAS government.

The decline of *Reformasi* zeal occurred soon after 2001. It was most likely
fuelled by the repercussions of the September 11, 2001 terror attacks in the
United States. The issue of the Islamic challenge, and its association with an
unbending agenda, became a looming national concern, especially due to the
fact that PAS had refused to relent on its objective to set up an Islamic state.
Due to this the DAP took the decision to leave the opposition coalition.

Thus by late 2001 the politics of 'alternatives' began to experience a retreat due to many miscalculations on PAS's part. For example, in August 2002, the PAS-led Terengganu government passed the *Hudud* and *Qisas* Enactment, which was deeply controversial and violated many tenets of human rights.[24] By then, the public had become more attuned and informed as to the probable character of the Islamic state that a party like PAS would be fashioning if voted into power. As *Reformasi* was too closely associated with PAS's rise, the fate of middle-ground parties in the coalition, namely Keadilan and PRM, was also sealed with that of PAS's defeat in the 2004 elections. It is difficult to see what is left of *Reformasi* after the 2004 general election, except for the jolt it gave to political parties like UMNO to embark on their own reinvention.

The inability of *Reformasi* politics to bring about substantial change in the political system can be due to several circumstances, such as:

1 the futility of fighting against an overpowering and hegemonic state;
2 the alienation of society from the political process out of both fear and apathy;
3 the redundancy of public politics in the aspiration of personal goals;
4 the lack of any desirable alternative, other than what is already familiar, no matter how flawed it may be; and
5 the end of ideology (or politics) and the beginning of the embrace of the pragmatic.

Whatever the implications may be, we see this fourth phase of Malaysian feminism's development in the post-*Reformasi* era as being taken over by the discourse of the personal. The essence of feminism and its symbols have been appropriated by the market. The image of 'liberation' no longer comes with a subversive undertone; instead its desirability is associated with the freedom to consume.[25] Feminism is looked upon as an ideology that endorses personal choice. It can range from choosing a political stance (or not choosing to have any), to asserting extreme consumerist sovereignty. This is the era of personal-choice feminism, leading to a paradoxical sense of individualism. One can even have the liberty to adopt a group identity that is ultimately inimical to individual freedom.

But at this current juncture we are also seeing more women keen to make a foray into electoral politics. In the 2004 general election, 97 women were fielded to stand either in state or parliamentary seats. Both government and opposition parties increased their number of women candidates compared with the 1999 election when women contested 63 seats. However, unlike in 1999, the campaign strategies in the 2004 election made little use of the gender card. This was partly because PAS had taken the sting out of its 'anti-women' image by fielding 10 women as candidates; after not allowing women to do so since 1959. Altogether 56 women won their seats out of a total of 724 seats contested – a meagre 7.7 per cent women's representation in the Malaysian legislature.[26] This latest election was not about reforms, whether human or gender rights, but about endorsing the new prime minister and a continuation of the *status quo*, and about accepting or rejecting political Islam. A preference for the 'good life' (as purveyed by the BN) and the rejection of the 'grim life' (as conveyed by PAS) was the message which won the election and gave the BN its overwhelming victory.

In the next and final section of this chapter we reiterate the phases through which Malaysian feminism has evolved and constructed its identity. But it must be emphasized that it would be erroneous to assume the presence of any single, unitary feminism at any one phase of Malaysia's historical transformation. But if looking at trends demands a more essentialist or reductionist clarity, then it is possible to view four distinct phases in Malaysia's gender history which willy-nilly correspond to four varieties of feminism.

Four phases, four feminisms

Nationalist feminism

In the first phase of Malaysia's modern history, women's elevation as political, social and economic agents of emerging nation states was integral to the struggle for national autonomy. Women were granted rights of advancement not as 'victims' of patriarchy but as 'victims' of foreign colonisation and an obsolete traditional system. There was much faith in modern institutions, particularly formal schooling and the legal system, as a way of bringing progress to women. The solution for addressing women's inadequate representation in these institutions was to break down formal barriers against their entry into professions and public office.

Social feminism

In the second phase, or the phase of post-independence consociationalism from 1958 to 1969, the nationalist essence was translated into more pragmatic purposes. Women become the objects of new legislation, which sought to grant them equal rights in employment and suffragist issues. The major beneficiaries of feminist politics during this period were women in white-collar occupations and women who received formal education. Many among the latter ended up as modern homemakers. Some of these elite participated in women's organizations, many of which were set up as welfare and charity bodies to benefit women of the less privileged class.

The NCWO was one of the most important women's organizations during this time. It was the first umbrella movement for women's organizations and was instrumental in providing a distinct 'feminist' thrust in the imagination of the period. This was based on the founders' perception that women's rights were largely neglected because of the absence of modern institutions and laws to provide the necessary corrections. Hence, the NCWO's goal was not to doubt, let alone challenge, modern and state institutions but to make them effective for women's benefit. Some scholars have labelled this type of feminism as social feminism, in which women make no distinction between themselves and men in the experiences of deprivation (Forbes, 1999: 158–9). Nationalist liberation and nation-building, once achieved, is thought to be able to solve the problems of inequality brought about by colonialism. Social feminism is also welfaristic in orientation and in keeping with the norms of women's propriety at the time. Social feminists operate within a rubric that is socially acceptable and in tandem with a post-colonial modernizing project of nation-building.

Political feminism

The third phase in the evolution of feminism in Malaysia occurred from the early 1970s until the late 1990s. After 1970 Malaysia entered a uniquely new phase involving a drastic change in governing policies. The implementation of the NEP is considered a watershed moment in Malaysia's history. There was an emergence of politics centred on identity questions largely because the project for equity was already subsumed under the NEP and framed by an ethnic discourse. By then a movement like the NCWO had to face new contenders for control over the discourse on women's rights. A majority of Malay-Muslim women retreated into Islam and cultural conservatism. At the same time new women's groups, which sought to deal with the gender inequality issue from a more structural perspective, were formed. The leadership of some of the newer women's organizations pushed for a fresh perspective on the 'woman question'. New conceptual ideas were introduced to revisit the roots of gender inequality. Terms such as 'women's subjugation' and women as 'second sex' were used widely. Questions about the origins of women's structural and personal subjugation were likewise raised and debated.

By the early 1980s, feminists saw in almost every societal structure the stamp of patriarchy (Ng and Maznah, 1988; Rohana, 1994). The notion of 'patriarchy' was academically as well as popularly touted as constituting the origin of gender inequity in society.[27] The term was both ambivalent as well as convenient in the naming of an 'enemy'. The advocates could construct and model their organizations around some of these definite premises. The result was the setting up of autonomous women's groups not directed by a larger purpose such as nationalism, modernism or socialism. They shunned any associational linkage with a parent (or male-led) organization.

Besides a new vision, new modes of strategizing were thought of. However, the concern to mobilize women in a massive way via a directed organizational structure, such as that used by political parties, was less important, if not impossible. Patriarchy as the root cause of women's oppression and inequality was a popular idea to disseminate. Through such ideas the new movement took on a more discernible characteristic. The initiators focused on problems that were universally experienced and applicable to a majority of women on a cross-ethnic basis. Social feminists before this had focused their attention on doing welfare work and making women visible in the public sphere and in gainful employment. Although social feminists fought for the recognition of women who were denied political and economic mobility due to male-biased prejudices, they had no intention of changing the structure of the modern state.

In contrast, feminists in the 1980s sited their struggles within very specific concerns, the main one being VAW. This was perceived to be a universal wrong and inevitably inflicted upon women by the logical implication of a patriarchal order. It was asserted that violence could be specifically gendered and all women could potentially be the victims of this ill. Not only was violence considered to be the social symptom of patriarchy, but patriarchy was also the basis which led to other grave problems faced by women in their struggle for recognition as equals to men.

The women's movement also evolved as a purveyor of 'politically correct' norms. Public education, considered essential to changing outmoded perceptions of gender relations, was one of the main activities pursued. The movement also supported institutions that inherently mitigate male biases and prejudices. Gainful work among women to stimulate economic development was already in full swing. This was a project which was unequivocally backed by the state. The emerging feminist movement also rode on this wave. Political feminists acted to obstruct new modes of patriarchal control from taking root, such as the implementation of *Hudud* laws, and to negotiate reforms with the state.

Also during the 1980s, the term 'feminism' began to take on a more globally popular and widespread usage. This new movement could be considered to represent the most politically radical phase in Malaysian feminist history. It was political because women's issues were presented as a human rights agenda, hence making them an obligatory public concern and requiring the commitment and intervention of the state for the deliverance of not only social services but also mechanisms for human rights compliance. It was also the most political phase because women's groups were more vociferous in voicing their position as a separate political lobby rather than as being part of a larger, male-directed organizational structure.

In this third phase women were no longer mere objects of legislation, but had become lobbyists and prime movers of specific legal reforms. Perhaps because of this, it became necessary for the movement to continue engaging with the state, as social feminists had done earlier. The feminist movement of this phase fought to stress the obligatory role of the state to legislate for women's protective measures and combat the deleterious manifestations of patriarchy, in this case violence. A male-biased system was seen to be the root cause of VAW, of gender-biased laws and of women's low occupational status, as well as of women's inaccessibility to positions of leadership and power. In this phase some of the more crucial laws such as the Domestic Violence Act 1994 were passed and critical amendments were made to laws related to rape.[28]

The ideology of developmentalism had also become more entrenched in policies and governance. In this distinctive political phase, the rate of women's participation in the labour force rose rapidly. The Malaysian developmentalist state pursued a policy of aggressive export-led manufacturing. There was a conflation of a condition of stridency by the women's movement together with the phenomenon of women's visibility in employment, enabling feminists to exert some influence over the state. However, although women constituted a critical component of the growing economy, their political role could still be contained by the state. Ironically, this has predisposed the state to become more receptive to some of their demands.

The historic coming together of women's groups and a wide spectrum of civil society was achieved in 1999 through the launching of WAC during the *Reformasi* period. The ideas and demands contained in WAC had a symbolic value which the government wanted to capture. By giving tacit support to it the government was able to promote its own commitment to women's rights, thereby winning the votes of those who otherwise would have supported the PAS-led *Reformasi* movement then.[29] WAC gained prominence but only for a short duration. As the ruling BN coalition consolidated itself after winning the 1999 election, and as the effect of *Reformasi* ran its course, the momentum to sustain WAC also came to a halt. WAC was essentially the last hurrah for political feminism in this third historical phase.

But the economic success of the developmentalist era resulted in women actually having many lifestyle choices at their disposal. They could continue to be involved in welfare work, to provide social services to women who were victims of male abuse, or to commit themselves to advocacy work for legal reforms and consciousness-raising against the harms of patriarchy. In entering the twenty-first century, fewer women would experience discrimination in education or employment. Women's groups have been relatively successful in getting the state to intervene in matters related to laws and enforcement on domestic violence, rape and sexual harassment. To a certain extent, much of the goals of social and political feminists had already been 'mainstreamed' as the country entered its post-*Reformasi* phase.

No doubt all these achievements were, at best, half-way measures and, at worst, only minor challenges against a discriminating system against women. Incidents of gendered-violence remain high, perhaps even more prominent. Women continue to retreat into their cultural community and become even stauncher defenders of patriarchal virtues such as the glorification of motherhood, domesticated lifestyles and polygyny. What happened at this time was that the new discourse about women's rights began to be modified to suit the ambit of economic liberalization and notions of bourgeois consumer 'freedoms'.

Market-driven feminism

The fourth and latest phase of Malaysian feminism's evolution into a market-driven entity is ushered by a post-*Reformasi* phase of national economic resuscitation. The denial of democratic space and the violation of human rights by the state continue to be conditions that impede the growth of a civil society. At the same time the present government also attempts to create an image of its own willingness to inject reforms into the system.[30] But freedom engendered by the market – and one complemented by a functioning mass-consumer culture – works to depoliticize many of the issues related to reforms, and reinforce political apathy in society.

Some women's groups which originated as the fountainhead of political feminism have now carved their legitimacy around the dispensation of welfare services such as providing counselling, shelters and legal assistance to women in crisis. At best, they continue to function as social feminists by concentrating their efforts on inserting legal and institutional correctives into the system so that women can be protected from all forms of gendered-harm. They also continue to agitate the state and society at large to remove formal barriers against women's recognition as equals in the public realm. In this context the single most important role of more advantaged (middle- and upper-class) women would be to mediate between the state and marginalized women, for the latter's benefit. Among the more privileged women, the syndrome of 'victimhood' by the state has now become less of a personal threat because of their ability to become economically empowered through the workings of the market.

How is this happening? Women's increasing participation in the job market has meant greater consumer power for them. It is perhaps because of this, rather than political mobilization *per se*, that feminism as a social movement and consciousness has gained greater mass appeal. The message of feminism can also be subjected to the logic of the free market. Many feminist activities during this phase have been fashioned by market dictates. For example, in 2002, even department stores were contributing towards women's empowerment. A club set up by a department store in Kuala Lumpur organized many consumer-oriented activities for women, presumably for their personal development.[31] By 2004, this trend had gone further – the management of a shopping centre in Kuala Lumpur became involved in promoting awareness of preventing violence against women and children.[32] Commercial enterprises have to be credited for showing a 'caring face' behind their hard-nosed drive for profits. But this sensitivity towards women's issues is also a reflection of a commercial sensitivity towards women as a growing and an important niche-market to capture.

Conclusion: recapitulating the Malaysian experience

In our discussion and analysis we explained the evolution of feminism by relating it to the onset of notable historical transitions and phases. Four political moments were identified, closely corresponding to the rise of new feminist trends. Generally, we can discern the existence of four dominant feminisms in Malaysia's history – that of the nationalist, social, political and market-driven variations. These often straddle more than one historical period and should not be taken as movements that are fixed and non-continuous in flow. These trends may be summarized as:

1   *Nationalist politicisation.* This phase marked the beginning of Malaysia's modern history, or the period of anti-colonial struggles culminating in the formation of the nation state. The kind of feminism which took the lead in defining the terms of justice for women was largely conceived around the achievement of self-rule rather than human rights or personal autonomy. This is the period in which nationalist aspirations predominate as the basis for women's emancipation.

2   *Post-independence 'consociational' politics.* In the second phase, of post-independence ethnic bargaining, the nationalist essence was translated into pragmatic purposes. Influential women's groups such as the NCWO tailored their goals to be in consonance with the agenda of the new governing elite. We refer to the dominance of this type of feminism during this phase as being social in nature.

3   *Developmentalism and identity politics.* The third phase saw the implementation of the NEP. Alongside this was the emergence of politics centred on identity questions. New contenders for control over the discourse on women's rights also entered the scene. During this period too, the ideology of developmentalism defined governance and policies. Women's groups, meanwhile, lobbied the state to intervene in matters related to laws and enforcement against domestic violence, rape and sexual harassment. The influence of political feminism on civil society and governance reached its height, as seen in the prominent role played by political feminists in *Reformasi* politics and their conception of WAC. The latter left an impact on the electoral process, albeit briefly.

4   *Post-Reformasi realignment.* This phase in the evolution of feminism into a market-driven phase is apparent in the post-*Reformasi* period. Women are still confronted by a multiplicity of issues, such as the demand for political and economic equality, but this situation is juxtaposed against their increasing participation in the job market, which gives them the power to consume. Commercial interests have since taken up the promotion of women's issues to tap a niche market formed by economically independent women. However, it also means feminism is subjected to market conditions at the expense of its original spirit for autonomy and political representation. A collective delusion is being cultivated that freedom of the market and an unfettered mass-consumer culture are good enough measures to exact personal autonomy and power. The idea has won the day as shown by trends in the latest national electoral exercise which saw voters voting in the direction of developmental goals.

The notion of feminism, as well as its trajectories and political motivations, has been extremely fluid. If there is a common denominator among all the trends charted, then it has to be the continuing struggle of women to be incorporated as players in any reform movement. In each period, women have succeeded differently. The discourse over women's rights has evolved from being elite-centred to gender-centred and being ambivalently centred between self and community as the power of the marketplace overwhelms even that of the state. However, the feminist agenda has been important enough at every level of history to be incorporated as a statist concern.

In the next chapter we look at a period of political feminism's manifestation in the history of Malaysian social movement. The VAW campaign was one example. This has become one of the major markers of political feminism's foothold in society. In the following chapter, women activists' prolonged engagement with the state through the legal reform campaign is discussed. This period demonstrated a triumph of civil society negotiation rather than confrontation, hence ensuring circumscribed successes for the women's movement but great gains for state legitimacy.

3 The Violence Against Women campaign

A never-ending story?

The Violence Against Women (VAW) campaign is an unfinished agenda of the Malaysian women's movement. Despite efforts by activists to address this phenomenon for over two decades, crimes related to VAW continue to rise all over the country and are seemingly unstoppable.[1] Almost daily, newspaper reports relate stories of women and girls being violated and assaulted, sexually or otherwise. Such crimes reveal a disturbing pattern where, among other things, the profile of rapists and rape victims is getting younger (as evidenced in the rise in date-rape and gang-rapes by youths). At the same time the severity of violent acts is also on the increase with a growing number of rape-murder cases being cited in recent times. Apart from these, there have been more and more incidences of incest, as well as custodial rape, and rape by persons in positions of authority.[2]

This chapter evaluates the strengths and weaknesses of the strategies that the Malaysian women's movement has employed to address the issue of VAW. While a range of approaches has been utilized – mainly public education, training, services and advocacy – we focus on the movement's lobbying and advocacy efforts for better laws to address VAW. Such emphasis is warranted because this is an area which has posed many challenges to activists, and contains important questions for those contemplating future action against VAW. In examining the legal reform campaigns that have been organized around rape, domestic violence and sexual harassment, we seek to show what the movement has gained and lost in this twenty-year struggle. Before entering into this discussion, however, a brief explanation is given on how the whole VAW discourse surfaced, and what are the drawbacks of this approach that anti-VAW advocates and activists need to be aware of.

When the term VAW first appeared in various parts of the world, at different points in time from the late 1970s onwards, it gave a name to acts that were far from new – rape, domestic violence, sexual harassment, incest, female genital mutilation, honour killings, forced pregnancy, sexual slavery, etc. These had prevailed for the longest time ever, but remained invisibilized in most contexts largely, but not solely, as a reflection and consequence of the unequal relations between men and women in society.

According to Margaret Schuler (1992), the rise of activism and research on issues related to women's status marked the end of this silence. Bringing the subject out into the open, however, was no easy feat. Rape and domestic violence survivors, for example, had to overcome the stigma of shame in order to speak out against their perpetrators and give a face to these acts of violence. Since the dominant view at the time also deemed such acts as private, this made it all the more difficult to bring them out into the open. Nevertheless, since this process of unveiling started, there has been no shortage of efforts worldwide to understand the nature, forms, extent and consequences of VAW. In turn, new doors opened up, allowing previously unspoken acts of VAW to be recognized as crimes, and for redress measures to be forwarded and instituted.

In many regards, then, VAW has been a successful and significant rallying point for women. To some extent too, this subject has yielded positive responses from most quarters, including from within institutions that otherwise have been oppressive to women – the family, religion and the state. Indeed, in the name of combating VAW, all kinds of programmes, activities and even funds have come into being. Some of these have gone into public education campaigns; others into the setting up and running of shelters and counselling services. Financial support has also been made available for training, advocacy and legal reform initiatives. In some contexts, even, anti-VAW efforts have been mainstreamed with policies and the like being established by the state, eager to show its sincerity to improve women's lives.

While all this is well and good, one of the original intentions of feminist activists in bringing to the fore VAW issues appears to have been sidetracked along the frenzy of activity. Apart from equality and freedom for women, feminism has also stressed women's empowerment, something which clearly appears lacking in many of the anti-VAW efforts that are currently in place. Rather than operate through processes that would facilitate women's empowerment, these attempts have, in the main, stressed deliverance of tangible results such as the enactment of laws to punish perpetrators.

Also problematic has been the absence of a mass movement-led campaign against VAW; in many parts of the world the work still appears to be headed by a small group of dedicated but predominantly middle-class women. Given this, one could ask: how successful can an anti-VAW campaign be if more women themselves are not empowered to contribute towards stamping out this scourge?

Last but not least, the attention that VAW issues have steadily attracted for over two decades now – particularly with it being mainstreamed by the state – has also come at a cost. In many countries, Malaysia included, money flows more easily into women's groups working in this area as these issues are perceived as more legitimate compared with those like women's land rights or women workers' rights. Although VAW is indeed a concern that cuts across class, ethnicity, sexuality, location and other such determining factors, the marked imbalance in resource distribution between groups working on VAW and non-VAW issues is also something that needs to be questioned.

Origins of the VAW campaign in Malaysia

In the early 1980s, a group of about 20 women aged between 20 and 30 came together in Petaling Jaya, Selangor, to discuss issues related to the status of women in Malaysia, as well as the women's movement of the 1960s and 1970s. Some of the women had just returned from studies abroad and been exposed to various social justice movements such as the anti-Vietnam war and the civil rights movement; others had been involved in different causes locally. All had in common a desire to improve the lives of women in Malaysia. After a year of informal meetings, the group decided to consolidate its efforts by linking up with more Malaysian women. Through this, they hoped not only to increase public awareness of women's subordinate position in society, but also to expand their activities beyond middle-class and urban-based women.

Which issue, however, was suitable for realizing the above purpose? With several women belonging to organizations that were already involved or in the process of getting involved with VAW issues, this theme was proposed and accepted as the main focus of the group. Apart from being based on needs at the time, this choice was also influenced by other factors. These included the belief that these issues could potentially unify women across class, geographic location, culture and religion, and the fact that, globally, VAW was gaining importance as an area that warranted redress.

This was the beginning of the formation known today as the Joint Action Group against Violence Against Women (JAG-VAW). The original grouping comprised individuals who were either non-aligned or affiliated with organizations which agreed to be part of this entity.[3] They were the Association of Women Lawyers (AWL), Malaysian Trades Union Congress (MTUC)-Women's Section, Selangor and Federal Territory Consumers Association-Women and Media Section, University Women's Association and Women's Aid Organisation (WAO).[4]

The first significant public activity of JAG-VAW was a two-day workshop and exhibition, held in a workers' community hall in Petaling Jaya, to commemorate International Women's Day in March 1985. Four main issues were highlighted: physical violence (rape, domestic violence and sexual harassment); portrayal of women in the media; prostitution; and the law. Preparations for this event took about a year. The process was intensive yet empowering and exhilarating for the hundred or so women and men involved. Together, they came up with creative presentations ranging from role-plays, poems, songs and dances to a mock rape trial, slide shows and an exhibition of 150 posters. Significantly too, the feminist slogan 'the personal is the political' was practised with the group consciously adopting a non-hierarchical and collective decision-making process, and men taking charge of childcare during the event.

The event was a major success. Helped by positive media coverage, it drew around 2,000 people from all walks of life, an unprecedented response at a time when it was not common for VAW issues to be articulated publicly. Buoyed by this experience, this JAG-VAW initiative was taken on a nation-wide road-show – from Ipoh and Penang to Sabah and Sarawak – leading in turn to the formalization of several new women's groups.[5] With the fledgling movement in place, there was no turning back.

The anti-rape campaign: first victory?

The workshop-cum-exhibition activity in March 1985 was important not only because it was the first time in Malaysian history that the subject of VAW had been raised for public scrutiny, but also because it sparked a campaign to improve legal protection for women. Following this, JAG-VAW teamed up with the National Council of Women's Organisations (NCWO) – then an umbrella organization of around 50 women's groups – to hold a public workshop on how the law impacted on women in Malaysia. Out of this emerged a joint memorandum calling for reform of all laws that discriminated against women. This was submitted to the government in early 1986.

Although the memorandum contained demands related to various areas of women's concerns, JAG-VAW decided to prioritize the issue of rape,[6] identified as the most pressing concern then. Legal reform was adopted as one of several strategies that the group would use to combat rape. Women activists, increasingly aware of the different dimensions of problems faced by rape survivors – ranging from under-reporting of this crime and insensitive investigation and trial procedures to the stigmatization of those raped – also sought to:

- lobby for the establishment of new or improved services for rape survivors in the form of one-stop crisis centres in major hospitals, as well as special rape investigation squads consisting of trained female police officers to handle sexual assault cases;
- carry out continuous mobilization through education and training for women both at the urban and rural community levels;
- generate publicity through the media, street theatre and exhibitions in shopping malls and supermarkets; and
- network with other organizations, particularly the NCWO and women's wings of political parties, to lobby for relevant amendments to the Penal Code.

The anti-rape campaign gained pace in 1987 when the media highlighted a spate of gruesome rape-murders of children. One of them involved nine-year-old Ang Mei Hong, raped and brutally murdered on her way home from buying breakfast.[7] Following this, the Women's Development Collective

(WDC) initiated a coalition of NGOs called Citizens Against Rape (CAR), which went on to organize a mass demonstration outside the coffee-shop where Mei Hong lived, located along a major road in Kuala Lumpur, the capital city. This, being the first major demonstration on what was perceived to be a 'women's issue', caught the attention of the media, particularly since both men and women were seen as equally outraged. As noted by a major daily: 'Carrying placards in several languages and distributing pamphlets, the group denounced the public, the police and other authorities for turning a blind eye to the increasing cases of rape and sexual violence against women and children.'[8]

Unfortunately, political events overtook the VAW campaign when, in October 1987, the state clamped down on what it saw as increasing opposition to its policies. A police sweep code-named *Operasi Lalang* was enforced and the country cowered in fear as the police arrested more than 100 people and subsequently detained 40 of them without trial under the Internal Security Act 1960. Of these, four were women, including three who were activists in the movement against VAW.[9] Energies were then divided between, on the one hand, securing the release of the detainees[10] and, on the other, continuing the campaign against VAW. This was even more difficult to organize because of the overall fear and lack of trust that *Operasi Lalang* had instilled among certain non-governmental organizations (NGOs). Despite this, the All Women's Action Society (AWAM), which had been functioning since 1986 – although its application for registration only received approval from the Registrar of Societies in February 1988 – managed to carry on with training, lobbying and advocacy efforts against VAW, in particular rape.

Finally, in March 1989, after four years of mobilizing by women's groups, parliament passed a bill on reforms to laws relating to rape.[11] The struggle, however, was to last right up to the very end with the then Deputy Minister in charge of Women's Affairs under the Prime Minister's Department, Siti Zaharah Sulaiman, having to present the amendments amidst heckling from some of her counterparts in the male-dominated Dewan Rakyat (House of Representatives). More significantly, only some of the amendments forwarded by the women's lobby were accepted:

- imposing a mandatory jail term of at least five years – including whipping – for convicted rapists;
- raising the age of statutory rape from 14 to 16 years;
- allowing for abortion if a medical practitioner deems this necessary to safeguard a rape survivor's mental and physical health;[12]
- prohibiting in court the cross-examination of a rape survivor's past sexual history unless it is connected to the accused; and
- raising the jail term for sexual molestation from two to ten years.

What failed to make the cut were demands to expand the definition of rape to include non-penile penetration;[13] and making it a criminal offence for police officers not to record complaints of rape; and also for the media not to publish or broadcast the identity of rape survivors or their families. The proposal for *in camera* rape trials was rejected,[14] as was an amendment to make it illegal for a person in authority to take advantage of his position to elicit sexual favours from any woman under his power, and the proposal to shift the burden of proof from the survivor to the perpetrator.[15]

Although the 1989 amendments brought about some improvements in legal protection against rape, there remained a number of loopholes in the law because women's groups were unable to push through all their demands. Not surprisingly, within ten years an even more disconcerting picture had emerged, reflected by an increase in cases of gang rape, date rape, custodial rape and incest.

Appalled at this trend, the women in AWAM decided to revive the anti-rape campaign in 1999.[16] They started by commissioning research to determine the efficacy of laws relating to rape in providing justice and protection to survivors. Through this, the organization was able to identify a new list of recommendations that was presented to the Attorney-General's (AG) Chambers the following year. When this was met with silence, AWAM set up the Anti-Rape Task Force, bringing together other NGOs, namely PS the Children, Women's Centre for Change (WCC), WAO and Sisters in Islam.

Since its inception in August 2001, the Task Force's main focus has been on pushing through another set of amendments to the laws relating to rape. Specifically with regard to the Penal Code, the group is seeking, amongst other things, to widen the definition of rape, make marital rape an offence, introduce the concept of aggravated rape and penalties for this, as well as have specific punishment for repeat rapists. It also wants the Evidence Act to be further amended so that a survivor's sexual history, regardless of her relationship with the accused, will no longer be relevant.[17] At the same time the Task Force is proposing that the government sets up a body which will provide financial compensation to a rape survivor.[18]

Up to the end of 2003, there was little progress in having these laws amended. The situation improved marginally in 2004 when, as will be discussed later, the rape and murder of two girls forced some change. Similarly, the setting up of a Parliamentary Select Committee on amendments to the Criminal Procedure Code and the Penal Code has been a positive move as well. However, it is too early to determine what the Committee's impact will be and, more importantly, to what degree demands of women's groups will feature in its final recommendations. To be sure, the state still appears very much as having the upper hand in dictating what the reforms should be.

Critique of the anti-rape campaign

The foregoing account suggests that the women's groups, while doing well to kick-start a slow process of reforming laws relating to rape, have also been unsuccessful on several fronts in their campaign. They have managed to make public an issue hitherto considered taboo and private, and, even more commendable, succeeded in having this taken on and mainstreamed by the state. Yet they have failed to invoke significant change in societal perception of this phenomenon as evidenced by the state's capacity to reject certain demands in 1989, and its ongoing resistance to efforts to further amend the laws relating to rape.

What accounts for this inability of the women's movement to effect real change? In the simplest terms, it boils down to a lack of political strength, resources and a clear vision.

To begin with, women's groups do not wield enough bargaining power to pressure the government into giving priority to their demands. This problem, however, is related to how civil society as a whole is given very little space in which to operate. There is an array of laws which restrict the freedom of Malaysians to organize and express their opinions openly. Without the ability to mobilize public support, interest groups – including women's NGOs – have very little or no control in determining the effectiveness of their lobbying. Their political strength is compromised if they cannot ensure that the recommendations to the government are adopted in a timely manner. Indeed, the government is resistant to various forms of advocacy and, in most instances, pursues *its* agenda. The introduction of new legal provisions pertaining to the offences of incest and child sexual abuse, initiated by the then Minister of Law, Rais Yatim, rather than civil society groups, attests to this.[19]

Looking at the list of what was accepted out of the amendments proposed in 1989, it is clear that the government's interest in protecting women rape survivors went only a little way. Measures involving dramatic punishments that were also easier to implement and could demonstrate results were favoured over those that threatened existing power relations. Thus proposals to raise jail sentences and introduce whipping were acceptable, whereas those calling for the punishment of men who used their positions of authority to coerce women into having sex with them were not.

One may argue that the state was genuinely interested in protecting women and saw punitive action as the solution to deter potential rapists. Whether or not punitive action would have the desired effect is debatable. However, what is clearer – as demonstrated by attempts to impose the death penalty for convicted child rapists – is that the state does not always know and do what is best for its citizens. In this instance, the then Minister of Law reluctantly retracted his proposal only after a huge outcry by certain NGOs who correctly pointed out that this measure would impede the reporting of such cases, thereby rendering it pointless and leading to exacerbation of the incidence of child sexual abuse.[20]

By January 2004, however, public demands to punish rapists with castration or the death penalty resurfaced following separate incidents involving the rape and murder of two girls aged nine and ten respectively within the space of two weeks. Even as courts immediately handed out stiffer sentences in rape trials being concluded then, the cabinet gave the green light for the mandatory death sentence to be imposed on rapists who kill their victims. Consequently, calls for amendments to impose harsher sentences for rape, ranging from life imprisonment and whipping in public, to the mandatory death sentence, were heard all over again. Women's groups reiterated their stand that re-education of society – not knee-jerk reaction – was the way forward. Their rationale remained the same, that victims would be reluctant to report rape by family members if the outcome was imprisonment for life or worse, execution, and that such crimes would be driven underground as a result.

In 1989, the state gave in to the minimum demands of the women's movement, not because it was sincere in creating safer spaces for women or because it was giving in to the feminist lobby, but because of the groundswell of public opinion. The media played an important role in this, generating widespread publicity on the proposed amendments to the laws relating to rape, and prior to that, highlighting the prevalence and problem of rape. Despite this and strong public empathy with this issue, women leaders in the movement did not seize the opportunity to mobilize resistance against the state's rejection of certain demands. Instead, they appeared to choose the path of least resistance, accepting what was given, particularly since this was viewed as a milestone compared to the experiences of Southeast Asian counterparts who had accomplished far less in the area of protective legislation for women.

At the same time, the women's movement in Malaysia suffered from not having enough legal expertise that could have helped expedite the process of reform. It remains unable to garner much support from the legal fraternity even though pockets of activist lawyers exist and have assisted in other ways.[21] Current attempts at plugging loopholes in the laws relating to rape have had the benefit of the services of a small team of lawyers. However, exactly how much the members of this team are able to contribute is questionable given the various constraints under which they operate, not the least being a lack of necessary perspective, time and practical experience. Under normal circumstances it could even have been more effective if women's groups had pushed for the establishment of an independent law reform commission or committee to consider its demands. Not only would this body be better placed to review laws relating to rape, it would also be better placed in persuading the government to accept its proposals. Sadly, this option was never considered because of a not unfounded lack of faith in the independence and autonomy of such entities in Malaysia.

It can be said too that in their eagerness to obtain better legal protection and justice for women and girls, the anti-rape campaigners adopted a somewhat short-sighted approach in addressing this issue. Rather than formulating a more focused and systematic response that could tackle all acts of violence against women in one swoop – that is, going beyond rape to include domestic violence and sexual harassment – women's groups adopted a piecemeal approach starting with the amendments to the laws relating to rape. While this strategy may have provided more immediate relief to rape survivors, it also meant that the same obstacles that were confronted during the rape campaign had to be confronted all over again with the domestic violence and sexual harassment campaigns. This has further taxed the already limited energies and resources of women's NGOs. Such a situation could have been avoided if the move for comprehensive legislation against sexual assault had been taken up from the very beginning.

Unintended consequences

Whether it was due to charting new terrain or a lack of political clout, expertise or experience, the anti-rape campaign in the 1980s has resulted in several negative consequences that were unforeseen by its advocates.

The first of these stems from the introduction of whipping as a penalty. When women's groups agitated for this in the 1989 reforms, it was largely a gut reaction to the increasing atrocities surrounding rape. While the idea to whip rapists was mainly motivated by anger rather than a holistic analysis or clear framework, there were also those who believed in corporal punishment and did not see this as problematic within the larger framework of human rights. In fact, then, unlike now, the discourse on human rights among civil society was fairly weak which meant that few considered their actions as violating the fundamental human right to be free from torture. Taking this position was also inconsistent – particularly given the indivisibility of rights – with their premise that every woman has a right to be free from violence. Put differently, one cannot legitimately argue that a person has a right to be free from violence if one advocates violence against other persons, even if this is being proposed as a form of punishment.

In today's campaign to further improve laws relating to rape, many in the Anti-Rape Task Force will agree that earlier calls by women's groups for whipping were a mistake. Taking this stand more than ten years ago has weakened the position of the present women's movement *viz* the government's attempts to introduce the death sentence for convicted child rapists. Although most women's groups have been resolute in their opposition, it has been difficult for them to justify this stand given their track record of having approved another form of corporal punishment (namely, whipping).[22]

Secondly, increasing the age of statutory rape from 14 to 16 years has had the effect of criminalizing consensual sexual activity between adolescent boys and girls. Instead of being used to penalize older men who sexually exploit teenage girls, the law has had an adverse impact on an unintended group, one whose actions do not cause harm and hence should not be punished.[23] This problem could have been avoided if the wording of the provision left room for judicial discretion and mitigating circumstances. But it does not. Perhaps then, women's groups were too hasty in making this recommendation. It is a classic situation of how protectionist measures are not always good, particularly when those meant to be protected are not adequately consulted or when the full ramifications of proposals are not taken into account.

Thirdly, unlike the legal reform campaign against domestic violence, which is discussed later, those in the anti-rape movement did not present the government with a draft bill. Instead they forwarded a memorandum with a list of recommendations. In part, this was because there already were existing provisions related to rape and women's groups chose to amend these rather than forward a comprehensive proposal that dealt with the range of sexual crimes against women. Further, unlike today, anti-state sentiments were stronger then. Women activists preferred to channel their energies into mobilizing activities such as public protests, rather than engaging with the state. There was no concept of wanting to integrate gender concerns into state laws or institutions. It simply was not terrain that activists wanted to enter. The AG's Chambers thus had greater leeway to interpret their demands and consequently, in wording the amendments that were eventually tabled in parliament.

Consequently, in their efforts to persuade the state to widen the definition of rape to include non-consensual anal and oral sex, women's groups actually prompted the *explicit* criminalization of these forms of sex regardless of whether they were consensual or not. Originally, the law under the old Section 377 of the Penal Code was generally worded to read: 'Whoever voluntarily has carnal intercourse against the order of nature with any man, woman, or animal, shall be punished with imprisonment . . . and shall also be liable to fine and to whipping.' When this law was amended in 1989, Section 377 was revised to refer only to 'Buggery with an animal', while the newly introduced Section 377A 'Carnal intercourse against the order of nature' spelt out exactly which sexual acts would be deemed as such. Ironically, thanks to the inability of the lawmakers to conceive of any sexual activity not revolving around the penis as sex, the proposal by women's groups to explicitly criminalize non-consensual cunnilingus fell out of this picture. Instead, Section 377A defined as illegal 'the introduction of the penis into the anus or mouth of the other person, whether it was consensual or otherwise'.[24] Considering that the state rejected another similar demand by women's groups – to expand the legal definition of rape to include object rape – the choice of these provisions is reflective of what is considered sexual acts, namely those only involving the penis.

Equally disturbing is the potential of Section 377 to be used against those who engage in consensual anal sex, particularly those in male homosexual relations.[25] While it is necessary for the law to criminalize non-consensual anal sex – just as it should with any other form of non-consensual sex – the problem in Malaysia is that, as a whole, Section 377 has become a tool to be used against the homosexual community instead of serving as a deterrent to men who commit anal rape against women.[26] Many members of this community thus live in fear that the manner in which they conduct their private sexual lives as consenting adults could result in their imprisonment.

The campaign today

It has been more than ten years since the laws relating to rape were amended. Judging from the government's ability to repeatedly politicize issues for its benefit, and the persistence of similar problems that hindered the first anti-rape campaign in the late 1980s as described, it appears that women's groups will face another uphill battle to secure what they want this time around. Even with greater public concern about the rise in violent – and in some instances unsolved – rape cases, NGOs have not been able to mobilize action to demand better protection for women by the state.

In 2003, an attempt by AWAM to organize a street rally to highlight the problem of rape and to call for more effective measures to ensure women's safety in public spaces[27] met with complete resistance by the police.[28] Interestingly enough, even though the event had the support of the then Ministry of Women and Family Development, the arm of the state that had the final say was the male-dominated police force. Sadly, this reflects the true state of gender relations in Malaysia. When it comes to the crunch, women's needs are sidestepped if the interests of powerful men are questioned.

This notwithstanding, one could ask what AWAM wanted to achieve by inviting the Minister of Women and Family Development, Shahrizat Abdul Jalil, to officiate at the event, as well as by giving a police representative a platform to speak.[29] The choice of finally holding a 'gathering' within the confines of four walls – over what was to have been an open and independent rally to demand that the state be accountable in ensuring safe spaces for women – is extremely telling. Certainly, the approach chosen this time was in stark contrast to that of the CAR initiative of 1987, indicating perhaps the differing contexts and factors at play. In other words, while the issue of rape remains as pressing as ever, the tightening of spaces in which civil society can organize and make demands to the state has caused organizations like AWAM to adapt its strategies accordingly. Yet, is working within limits imposed by the state the way forward?[30]

To conclude this section, it is worth mentioning the on-going difficulties that women's groups have had in getting marital rape outlawed. Unlike the other demands forwarded by JAG-VAW but rejected till today, marital rape as an issue stands out as the most contentious and publicly debated proposal. Even with evidence of this phenomenon existing in the country,[31] efforts to seek redress have persistently been rejected on religious grounds. A typical response would thus attribute Islam as saying that a woman is obliged to obey her husband, even in matters relating to sexual intercourse. Others go even further and argue that marital rape is only relevant to non-Muslims. The irony, of course, is that while it is criminal for a man to beat his wife in Malaysia (under the Domestic Violence Act 1994, DVA), it is not an offence to rape her. Despite this continued opposition, it should also be highlighted that support for efforts to criminalize marital rape has grown in recent years with the National Human Rights Commission (SUHAKAM) being the latest key player to lend its voice in August 2004.[32]

Fighting domestic violence: the long and winding road

Like the campaign against rape, a big part of efforts by Malaysian women's groups to address domestic violence has been through legislative reform. This grew out of concrete experience of the failure of the law to protect women who had been battered. These efforts simultaneously sought to deter husbands from abusing their wives. As the law stood prior to 1994, no specific provisions against domestic violence were written into the statutes. This posed several problems.

It meant that police officers were not obliged to assist a woman who had been assaulted by her spouse. Worse, they were sometimes known to instruct these women to return to their unsafe homes. If a woman wanted to escape her husband's abuse, her only recourse was to obtain a Protection Order. However, this was available only after she had filed for divorce or legal separation. Apart from the difficulties in securing a divorce at the time, this option was also restrictive because it ignored the social stigma that female divorcees carried. Neither was it cognizant of how these women might be economically dependent on their husbands, nor their fears that divorce might cause them to lose custody of their children. In any event, those who sought injunctive relief could only find it via the High Court, located in the major cities. This involved both time and money, and due to poor enforcement, was still no guarantee that the beatings would stop (Tan, 1999b: 52–3).

Given these shortcomings, JAG-VAW, together with NCWO, had included in their 1986 joint memorandum on laws that discriminated against women, a proposed bill against domestic violence. Although the idea was mooted then, it was only in 1989 – after the laws relating to rape had been amended – that this agenda was pursued, largely because resources had been extremely stretched. Furthermore, as suggested earlier, the choice of taking up rape first also had to do with timing, given the spate of brutal rapes and murders that had occurred.

Not wanting to make the same mistakes as the anti-rape campaign, women's groups under the new JAG-VAW formation[33] reworked the bill to present parliament with a comprehensive document that would lead to the enactment of a DVA. It took almost three years of further research, negotiation and drafting before the bill was ready for submission to the government. During this time various advocacy campaigns were conducted, like the Mother's Day workshop 'Confronting Domestic Violence' coordinated by AWAM in 1989, and the postcard signature campaign run by WAO in the same year that collected some 14,000 signatures. This culminated in a media event in 1992 where around 300 members of the public and the NGO community witnessed the then Minister for National Unity and Social Development, Napsiah Omar, also then the minister in charge of women's affairs, officially receive the draft bill on behalf of the government. Despite the Minister's assurance that the government was concerned about the plight of battered women, another two years went by before she managed to get the bill tabled in parliament.

The delay had to do with the government fundamentally disagreeing with the bill proposed by women's groups. Even though state representatives saw value in supporting the move for legislation against domestic violence, they disputed the definition proposed by JAG-VAW, and the way in which legal protection would work for Muslim women. Essentially, JAG-VAW was introducing a quasi-criminal law, which it believed would make it easier for all abused women to claim protection, as well as settle related issues such as divorce, maintenance and custody of children. It was a solution forwarded out of consideration for battered women, to ensure that bureaucratic obstacles did not deter them from seeking and obtaining relief.

The government negotiators, however, felt that the JAG-VAW proposal was untenable given the implementation of a dual legal system in Malaysia. Under this, all matters pertaining to family affairs of Muslims – including domestic violence, divorce, maintenance and custody of children – fall under the purview of state (*Syariah*, Islamic) laws. Yet this was precisely why JAG-VAW had proposed a quasi-criminal law in the first place: so that anti-domestic violence legislation would cover *all* Malaysian women, and not just non-Muslims. In the subsequent lobbying and negotiations, Sisters in Islam worked hard to put forth arguments from the Qur'an to support the call for a law that included Muslim women.[34]

Finally, to avoid a backlash from those who might perceive the JAG-VAW proposal as an encroachment into the jurisdiction of *Syariah* laws and also to pacify the women's lobby and gain mileage through the enactment of a domestic violence law, the government came up with a counter-proposal. In this, the DVA would be attached to the Penal Code and become part of criminal law, thus making it applicable to both non-Muslim and Muslim women.

Problems with the government bill

The problem with the bill proposed by the government was that it distinguished between 'seizable' and 'non-seizable' offences. This meant that women would only be able to seek relief if they showed physical signs of battery, but more specifically, suffer injuries where the skin had been broken (e.g. cuts, bleeding wounds). The law would not offer protection to those hurt or suffering from 'non-seizable' offences such as emotional and psychological abuse – often more crippling than physical abuse – because under the Penal Code the police were empowered only to investigate 'seizable' offences. Therefore, even when a woman has been badly beaten up and has swelling and bruises all over her body, the police would not be able to arrest the offender (Tan, 1999b: 65).[35]

Even though JAG-VAW argued that such an approach would render the legislation 'toothless', the bill finally made its way to parliament. By then, however, it had been further watered down, causing unhappiness among women's groups about the additional deficiencies.

Firstly, the bill was still not explicit in stating that domestic violence was a crime and, as such, encouraged the belief that there was no hurry to deal with it. Also, as pointed out, not calling it a crime with corresponding penalties meant a failure to send out the message that such acts of violence would no longer be exempt from public scrutiny, and that the full force of the law would be behind the victim. Hence, the government-sponsored bill did not have the impact of deterring abusers or potential abusers.

Secondly, the bill further legitimized marital rape,[36] one of the more common forms of abuse against women in domestic situations. It defined domestic violence as an act '. . . compelling the victim by force of threat to engage in any conduct or act, sexual or otherwise, *from which the victim has a right to abstain*' (emphasis added). This meant that there were certain situations in which a woman did not have the right to say 'no' to sex with her husband, as this is widely believed to be his prerogative. Such a decision not only represented a blatant disregard for the right of a woman to exert control over her body and live free from violence, but also had grave consequences in the age of HIV/AIDS and other sexually transmitted diseases.

Thirdly, domestic violence survivors were not automatically entitled to a Protection Order. Instead, this was made contingent upon whether or not criminal proceedings had begun. This meant that a battered woman could wait for several months, if not years, pending the completion of police investigations before seeing any action taken. Such a move went against the entire JAG-VAW campaign which sought to ensure that all survivors – regardless of class, ethnicity or location – had access to fast, effective and affordable relief. Protection had to be given irrespective of whether a criminal complaint was filed or an investigation was in progress.

Finally, the bill did not have a provision on compulsory counselling which women's groups saw as part and parcel of the relief package to be offered to battered women. Nor did it specify police procedures which increased the possibility of further delays in granting protection to survivors. All this, claimed JAG-VAW, made the long-awaited Domestic Violence Bill ineffective. The group feared that the proposed law would be nothing but a 'mere document with limited impact on the lives of women'.[37]

Despite this, the bill finally became law in May 1994, almost ten years after the idea was first raised by JAG-VAW. Even then, the passage of the 'Cinderella Act' – so named because it was passed just before midnight by the Dewan Rakyat (House of Representatives) – was almost thwarted by misogynistic members of parliament. Its passage quite possibly could have been derailed if not for the determination of the minister who tabled the bill.[38]

Critique of the DVA campaign

By and large, women's groups agree that the enactment of a law against domestic violence, even though fraught with difficulties, was a step in the right direction. At minimum, and due to this having been a long drawn-out campaign, there were numerous opportunities for JAG-VAW members to raise public awareness on the importance of addressing this issue. Indeed, even while there are still some in society today who believe that women who are beaten by their husbands probably 'deserved' it, there is also much greater consciousness that such acts are an offence precisely due to the efforts of JAG-VAW.

Likewise, more people today know that there are different avenues of relief for women in abusive domestic situations. For some battered women the law was empowering as it gave them increased hope of escaping the violence. Perhaps the biggest coup was how this campaign resulted in women's groups stealing some thunder from the *Syariah* courts. In uniting Muslims and non-Muslims under one banner, the law transcended the jurisdiction of *Syariah* laws over Muslim family matters where domestic violence was concerned, something that was unprecedented in Malaysia.

Nevertheless, that the women's movement took almost a decade to achieve what they wanted speaks volumes of the difficulties that plagued the campaign. As it was, all the groups in this coalition were operating on very limited resources.[39] Worse, however, was their decision to pursue the path of legal reform which inevitably put them at the mercy of the state. For most of their engagement with the state, these groups showed little capacity to pressure the government into tabling the bill sooner. And as we have seen, neither were they able to have the final say on the contents of the new law.

At no time during the long wait for the Domestic Violence Bill to be adopted did women's groups successfully mobilize public pressure. Although workshops and fora were held to raise awareness on this proposed legislation, this had little impact on the nation's lawmakers. For example, an attempt by AWAM to gauge how many members of parliament supported the bill showed that only 19 out of 180 of them were in favour of it.[40] There were no public demonstrations like those organized by the CAR campaigners in the mid-1980s.

Yet such action may have been exactly what was needed to prod the cabinet along, as JAG-VAW eventually discovered in 1996. After having been subjected to a two-year delay in the implementation of the DVA, women's groups coordinated by AWAM staged a successful protest on 8 March to draw attention to this matter. After photos of this event made the front page of several national dailies, the minister responsible, Zaleha Ismail, announced that she would look into the matter immediately. Even though it took several more months before the legislation was finally implemented,[41] there is little doubt that the collective action had an impact. Regrettably, JAG-VAW learnt this lesson rather late.

As has been suggested, the whole process of discussing and negotiating the contents of the bill with the state was fraught with difficulties. For example, JAG-VAW did not get very far in trying to have the law apply to all persons who had been violated in their home. The state's refusal to extend protection under the act to any woman in the household meant that domestic workers could not obtain protection even though they lived under the same roof as an abusive employer. The state was even more adamant that it would not endorse sexual relations outside the 'traditional' family unit. It was very clear about its margins of acceptance and so narrowly defined 'spouse' as to exclude those who were not in legally recognized marriages. Lai (1996) has argued that this situation arose because all the state was interested in doing when it passed the law was to provide safety for children in violent homes, as well as to create some breathing space for spouses until they could reconcile their differences. In other words, it was never the intention of the state, as it was of JAG-VAW, to unconditionally free women from abusive domestic situations.

Even the decision to accept the government's criminal law approach to domestic violence has been queried. Quite apart from leaving the state to decide what provisions would be accepted under the law, was the overriding desire to have an act that covered all women – as opposed to only non-Muslim women – worth the extremely compromised version that resulted? Was it worth giving up a good piece of legislation – as exemplified by the original bill proposed by women's groups which included all forms of violence as well as marital rape and not just 'seizable' injuries – so that Muslim women could equally benefit and obtain protection? Without insisting that the original bill include Muslim women, would it have been possible for it to have been passed in its entirety and therefore benefit *some* women fully rather than *more* women inadequately? The answers to these questions may never be known but they reflect the real dilemmas facing women's groups within a multicultural setting in their pursuit of women's equality and non-discrimination.

In 1999, the WCC noted the deficiencies of the DVA in a 20-point memorandum to the government. Many of its grievances were related to poor implementation of the law. However, it also called for both the definition of domestic violence and the scope of protection under the law to be widened. In so doing, the group was putting up for debate the same concerns that the government had rejected previously in 1994. These points were echoed and expanded in another paper by WAO in 2001, which drew attention to the inconsistent, lengthy and bureaucratic procedures in obtaining Interim Protection Orders. It also pointed out how the continuing lack of resources and training for police, court and welfare officers explained why women still encountered unsympathetic representatives of these bodies when seeking protection and support from the system. Having highlighted these shortcomings to the authorities, WAO and WCC, together with other women's groups that want to see the law do its job for battered women, continue to press on

with demands for changes to be instituted. Unfortunately ι
well, they are forced to play a waiting game for action to be ta

Eradicating sexual harassment: the learning continues

Although sexual harassment has only assumed greater signifiᴄ
campaign issue from the mid-1990s, women's groups and trade
especially the MTUC – have been lobbying for policies and legislatιon since
the 1980s.[42] The earliest signs of the struggle, however, can be traced as far
back as the 1930s when the Klang Indian Association organized a strike
against the sexual harassment of female workers by Europeans and 'Black
Europeans'. And in 1950, long before sexual harassment was publicized as a
workplace issue in the West, more than 100 male and female rubber-tappers
in Perak went on strike against sexual harassment (Rohana, 1988).

Unlike rape and domestic violence, however, sexual harassment has only
recently been articulated and recognized as a social problem. This is largely
due to the differing perceptions of this subject and to the existence of
various definitions of the term. Simply put, it is more difficult to draw the
line between consensual (e.g. flirtation) and unwanted sexual behaviour and
attention.

Nonetheless, as more women enter the labour force, sexual harassment at
the workplace is now acknowledged to be a serious form of misconduct.
Such recognition has also been the result of relentless advocacy by women's
groups and trade unions at the international level. As more studies on sexual
harassment come to the fore in both the developed and developing countries, research data shows that women, often those younger, experience a
disproportionately higher rate of sexual harassment by their male peers or
supervisors, compared with men.

In view of the increasing incidence of sexual harassment in Malaysia, and
due to lobbying by NGOs particularly AWAM and MTUC, the Ministry of
Human Resources launched the Code of Practice on the Prevention and
Eradication of Sexual Harassment in the Workplace in August 1999.[43]
AWAM and MTUC were the only two civil society groups invited to sit on
the technical committee that drafted this policy.

More than six years have lapsed since the introduction of the Code of
Practice. However, the response of employers towards adoption of this
policy, and in establishing internal mechanisms to combat sexual harassment, has been dismal. By 2001, only roughly 1 per cent of employers – or
4,500 companies out of the 400,000 registered with the Social Security
Organisation – had adopted the Code of Practice for their workplace.[44] Such
a poor response has given rise to debate about the commitment of the
private sector to protecting employees; and since adoption of the Code of
Practice is voluntary, its effectiveness has been seriously questioned as well.
Much of this debate on the policy's lack of 'teeth' to confront sexual harassment has been featured in the media. In any case, the Code is also

problematic because it does not contain an appropriate grievance procedure for this misconduct. As such, 'many victims either remain in untenable situations or resign from their employment' (Zarizana and Marrison, 2001: 5).

It was only in 2000 that the call for legislation against sexual harassment became stronger. The catalyst came from a case taken up in early 2000 by six women, all former management-level staff, against their expatriate general manager in a leading international hotel in Penang. Instead of conducting a domestic inquiry against the manager, the hotel management subjected the six women to this procedure, at times questioning them about the incident till the early hours of the morning. Fearing that they would be victimized further, the women approached WCC for assistance. However, when WCC contacted the hotel management, they were told that neither they nor the Labour Department had the jurisdiction to intervene in this matter.

Quite predictably, after the domestic inquiry was over, the women were charged with raising false and malicious allegations. They were suspended from their jobs and later dismissed. Following this they lodged a police report, and the case is now being heard under Section 354 (outrage of modesty) of the Penal Code. To reach this stage was not easy either. It was only after WCC raised much publicity via the media to pressure the police into taking action that this actually happened.

It was this context of impasse and frustration over existing procedures against sexual harassment that prompted WCC to initiate a campaign for legislation to be enacted, in particular, calling for 'friendlier' and more approachable mechanisms to resolve sexual harassment incidents. JAG-VAW was resurrected in the same year.[45] Thus began the campaign for a law against sexual harassment in Malaysia. Two main strategies were utilized. One was public education through research, training and signature campaigns; the other was direct engagement with the state. For example, in May 2000, WCC started a petition to garner support for this campaign. In just over a month it managed to collect 12,000 signatures and obtained the endorsement of 64 civil society organizations. The signatures and endorsements were then handed over to the Minister of Human Resources, Fong Chan Onn, in June 2000. AWAM and WDC also pitched in by embarking on research to gauge the extent of sexual harassment and to evaluate the effectiveness of the Code of Practice by examining the experience of the pioneer companies that had adopted this policy.[46]

Campaign for law against sexual harassment

While the campaign for a comprehensive law against sexual harassment is still under way, there is scope for reflection on the strategies chosen and lessons learnt so far.

Firstly, because JAG-VAW was not confident that the state would draft a law – more so, a law that would consider all its views – its members spent almost a year drafting a bill. They presented it to the then Deputy Minister of Human Resources, Abdul Latiff Ahmad, in March 2001. From then until mid-2002, a series of dialogues between JAG-VAW and relevant ministries took place to discuss the proposed bill. The coalition also felt the need to obtain international support and so, in May 2002, with WCC as the coordinating body, JAG-VAW organized a regional expert group meeting to listen to the views of other countries that had enacted legislation on sexual harassment.

At the meeting, the proposed bill was again discussed, at times heatedly, by both the NGOs and government bodies represented. Various recommendations were then made and taken up, including the one calling for the then Ministry of Women and Family Development to sponsor the passage of the bill through parliament. In a sense, this three-day meeting, which brought together NGOs and government representatives and allowed them to debate the contents of the bill together, was a significant intervention in fostering ownership by all parties involved.

The bill proposed by JAG-VAW attempted to overcome the limitations posed by existing legislation and policies that covered sexual harassment. It addressed two fundamental points. First, it required employers to prevent sexual harassment, and, second, it provided victims with timely and meaningful access to legal recourse. In line with these objectives, the proposed bill required employers to create in-house mechanisms to address the issue – those who did not comply or who did not act upon complaints would be held liable.

Also significant was the decision of JAG-VAW not to criminalize sexual harassment, a lesson learnt from past experiences with the police and courts. Instead, the bill proposed the creation of the post of a director who would assist complainants, and investigate and attempt to resolve such complaints through a process of conciliation. However, if conciliation is not appropriate or fails, an independent tribunal would look into the matter and an inquiry, if necessary, would be held. With specific timeframes stipulated, this system of reconciliation was designed to provide a safe and sensitive response to sexual harassment complaints.

Another important and forward-looking contribution by this JAG-VAW effort was the redefinition of work and work relationships. Current labour laws such as the Employment Act deal only with those in strictly legal work situations. Previously, anyone who fell out of this traditional definition – for instance, those in contract and subcontract work, voluntary work, as well as those involved in servicing clients, guests or patients – was excluded from protection. Quite often, members in the service sector are more vulnerable to sexual harassment and yet would have no recourse to action. As such, the proposed bill sought to provide a more comprehensive definition of work, broadening both the concept of work and the notion of a workplace. The global shift towards more informal and electronic modes of working, much of which present insecure employment especially for women in the middle- and lower-income groups, means that definitional boundaries of sexual harassment need to be expanded so that all workers can be adequately protected.

A final progressive dimension of the bill was how it proposed to deal with sexual harassment in public spaces by using the legal concept of 'vicarious liability'. This passes on liability to a third party for acts done by a person because of a certain relationship between the third party and the latter. For example, if a woman takes a bus and is harassed by the conductor or another passenger, she will have the opportunity to lodge a complaint with the bus company and demand that action be taken against the offender(s). This is because under this bill, the company would have been obliged to take responsibility for providing an environment that is free from sexual harassment.

All this notwithstanding, the campaign also encountered its share of stumbling blocks. Many of these were similar to the experiences of the campaigns to enact legislation against rape and domestic violence, for instance the lack of resources. However, unlike in the past where the state was reluctant to back the demands of women's groups, key officials in the then Ministry of Women and Family Development were initially sympathetic to the proposed Bill. Instead, in this case, there appeared to be a 'new' enemy: capital.

From the start, employers' bodies such as the Malaysian Employers Federation (MEF) consistently maintained their opposition to the bill, arguing that the voluntary Code of Practice was more than sufficient; it resisted being 'forced' into compliance. Part of the problem was that women's groups lacked experience in dealing with this entity since all their previous experience had been around engaging with and questioning the state. In addition, whereas the state has had some vested interests in accommodating NGOs, employers have little compulsion to do the same.

Still, even after the results of the AWAM-WDC research clearly showed the limitations of the Code of Practice, and a survey on the proposed bill demonstrated overwhelming public support, the state continued to drag its feet. It claimed that it needed the support of all parties to enact the bill. The ensuing impasse was due to the fact that the MOHR felt that the proposed bill was too broad, and that the MEF was unwilling to budge on this issue.[47] In a situation where the state had to choose to back NGO demands or support capital, it appeared that the latter commanded greater say. This is certainly a problem because by giving in to capital the state would be compromising the interests of women, particularly women workers, whom it is supposed to protect.

The limitations of relying on the then Ministry of Women and Family Development to push for the tabling of the draft bill became clearer in 2004 when the Minister's interest in this issue showed signs of waning following the expansion of her portfolio to include community development matters. By 2005, JAG-VAW's worst suspicions were confirmed when the Ministry announced that the enactment of an anti-sexual harassment law would be shelved indefinitely.[48] Clearly, then, as a 'junior' player in the government, it would appear that the Women's Ministry had to give in to the male interests of both cabinet and capital. Meanwhile, JAG-VAW has been left in an unenviable position of having to return to the drawing board.

Conclusion

In less than 20 years, the women's movement in Malaysia, through the JAG-VAW campaign, has done well to move one of its agendas forward: the creation of a violence-free society. Not only have the various anti-rape, domestic violence and sexual harassment advocacies made public these previously private (and stigmatized) issues, but they have also succeeded in getting these mainstreamed and institutionalized by the state. The introduction of female police officers to handle sexual crimes and the creation of the One-Stop Crisis centre in public hospitals in each major city are examples of these achievements. Even though much of the news coverage on such issues continues to have a predominantly sensationalist slant, this has been able to raise the profile of such phenomena as crimes that should not be tolerated. Most of all, as pointed out elsewhere, the success of the women's movement in mainstreaming gender issues has been such that when the opposition Parti Islam Se Malaysia (PAS) wanted to introduce *Hudud* (Islamic criminal) laws in the state of Terengganu, the provisions related to rape incurred the wrath of *all* women (Khoo, 2002). This included women in PAS who joined others to condemn the bill for defining rape against the interests of female victims.[49] This joint action across political and religious affiliations is important and augurs well for the future of Malaysian women.

What is interesting about the Malaysian experience is how women's groups have managed to achieve all of the above largely through a process of negotiation with the state. Unlike elsewhere in the world, there has not really been a mass movement behind the demands forwarded by women's groups here. Instead, there is latent but steady support. Without visible public backing, however, the women's movement has been more reactive in its approach to eradicate violence against women. Operating within a framework of tight state controls, it is not yet strong enough to adopt the range of strategies that *should* be available to any actor in civil society who seeks change. Precisely because there is an inherent fear of being persecuted by the state for speaking out, there is no history of mass mobilization for human rights, let alone women's rights, in Malaysia. Thus women's groups have had to use what they perceive to be the next best strategy: dialoguing and negotiating with the state, while using the media as an ally to expand public support.

By engaging with the state, however, the movement has exposed itself to the vagaries of party politics, and the consequences of having its agenda manipulated and appropriated. For example, the mainstreaming of gender issues in state institutions serves to give the state more credibility as defenders of public interest. The next chapter elaborates on how the state functions in relation to issues promoted by the women's movement and also examines the responses of the movement to the different forms of state intervention over the years. The analysis is situated from a feminist perspective in the context of changing local and global realities.

4   An unholy alliance?

Women engaging with the state

The establishment of the Ministry of Women and Family Development in early 2001[1] may have given rise to the public impression that women's groups have a rosy relationship with the state. This is in contrast to the almost adversarial stance of the state to other NGOs, particularly groups involved in human rights issues and community organizing which are perceived as critical of government, or 'anti-government'. Admittedly there is now more government rhetoric on the need to advance women's status and discuss gender issues with the concomitant pledge of funds to women's non-governmental organizations (NGOs), accompanied by much publicity and fanfare.

Moreover, the 1995 United Nations (UN) Fourth World Conference on Women in Beijing played a positive role in putting up for greater public scrutiny the concerns of the women's movement. Accordingly, the meetings and the processes around the Beijing event and the post-conference activities allowed more public awareness and debate, with the global women's movement putting pressure on their respective governments to fulfil their commitments to the 1979 UN Convention on the Elimination of All Forms of Discrimination Against Women (CEDAW).

The question is, to what extent is this perception of women's non-conflicted interaction with the state accurate? What has been the relationship of the women's movement *vis-à-vis* the state? To what extent has there been consensus and/or conflict, and when have alliances been forged or compromises made? Who are the winners and losers in this negotiation with the state?

This chapter attempts to respond to these issues by taking a historical perspective of the relationship of the women's movement with the post-colonial state, which, in Malaysia, has been far from democratic. The lack of such democratic space will inevitably affect the processes and outcome of the agenda of any progressive women's movement seeking gender and social justice. The chapter tries to delve into the underlying roles and motives of state action and the tensions that have emerged when engaging with women's groups. It ends by challenging the women's movement to be more critical and constantly vigilant in their engagement with, and expectations of, the state.

Feminist theorizing of the state

The state is seen as a set of institutions with the authority or power to make rules which govern society. As an arbiter of democracy, it is also considered the most important political organization in the global system. Feminist theorizing of the state, to date, has been generally limited. However, recent writings reflect a rethinking of the state which is seen as a more complex entity rather than essentially patriarchal and/or capitalist, and serving the unitary interests of men or capital (Tan, 1996). Post-structuralist feminists have stressed that the state should not be regarded as a monolithic institution but 'as a many-layered organisation with internal tensions and contradictory agendas where competing political actors speak in different voices' (Rai, 2000: 12). As argued by Pringle and Watson (1992), the state is not a unitary force nor is it a structural given. They argue that it is not necessary to conclude that the state will act uniformly to maintain capitalist or patriarchal relations or that this is its 'purpose'. Hence, the state should be seen as erratic and disconnected; the outcome of its policies will depend on the range of discursive struggles from one moment to another.

In an interesting article, Connell (1994) points out that gender plays an important role in influencing how the state is organized. He says that the 'state is constructed within gender relations as the central institutionalisation of gendered power. Conversely, gender dynamics are a major force constructing the state, both in the historical creation of state structures and in contemporary politics' (*ibid.*: 148).

In deconstructing the state as a historical process and as a structure of power, Connell argues that since it is a site of political struggle, it becomes a focus of interest group formation and mobilization in sexual politics. Subsequently, the concern of feminism to capture a share of state power is a necessary response. He then notes, '[the question] is not whether feminism will deal with the state, but how: on what terms, with what tactics, towards what goals?' Furthermore because the state is constantly changing and its position on gender politics is not fixed, it allows for gender dynamics to intervene in its development. He further points out 'crisis tendencies develop in the gender order which allow new political possibilities' (Connell, 1994: 159–60).[2]

These writings elucidate that there is a need to examine the historical practices that construct the state and that it is in the process of engagement that specific interests are articulated, regulated and re-constituted. However, it is clear that dealing with a Western liberal democratic state – which is the context of the writings cited – is rather different from interacting with an authoritarian regime. These debates have focused primarily on Western nation-states and their processes. How does one theorize a repressive state with democracy as its showcase, in a Third World, post-colonial context?

Democratic institutions of statehood (for example, an independent judiciary, a free press) were poorly established in most Third World countries in which the European state system was imposed on post-independence states, without the historical struggle, ideas and experiences of 'civil society' evident in Europe. The type of civil society in post-colonial states was weak as the political regime was in the hands of the elite who often imposed authoritarian rule on the people, repressing those who challenged its hegemony (Saravanamuttu, 2002b).

The nature of the relationship between civil society, including women's groups, and the post-colonial state is a new and ongoing debate. Since the tension between resistance, engagement and cooptation is never fully resolved, Rai (2000: 12) argues for an 'in and against the state' position which 'allows feminists to build on their own mobilizations in civil society to engage with state institutions from a position of relative autonomy'. And it is not always that both parties do this with clear intent or in unified ways.

With this framework in mind, the following sections examine the nature of women's engagement with the Malaysian state by discussing various factors which contribute to that relationship – the nature of the political regime, the international scenario, and the extent of democratic space that allows the full or retarded functioning of civil society in general and women's groups in particular. As a by-product of political struggles, what have been the experiences and lessons of the women's movement with respect to engaging with the state in terms of making it more democratic and gender sensitive, if not feminist?

We examine two main historical periods – the era of developmentalism and Women in Development (WID); and the current reign of globalization and gender mainstreaming, particularly in the context of the post-Beijing World Conference on Women. We start with a general analysis of state formation in Malaysia before going to the specificities of the two periods in terms of the responses of the state regime and the nature of women's engagement therein. Such a methodology will allow us to better understand and contribute to the current debate on women, feminism and the state.

The state of Malaysian democracy

While Malaysia formally practises parliamentary democracy, scholars have variously described its political regime as being 'repressive', 'quasi-democratic' or 'authoritarian'. As argued by Crouch (1992: 26–7):

> . . . Malaysia's democratic institutions have been little more than a façade disguising effective authoritarian rule. The ISA [Internal Security Act 1960], various restrictions on public debate, effective control of the press, intimidation of the judiciary and the emergency provisions combined to block the emergence of an effective opposition, thereby enabling the Malay-dominated elite to rule continuously. In this context, elections provided little opportunity for opposition parties to effectively challenge, let alone replace, the government. Critics were tolerated only

to the extent that they did not actually pose a political threat to the ruling elite.

This is a rather pessimistic analysis, giving little hope to civil society to freely develop and mature. Indeed, as noted by others, this type of social control is made possible by the classic 'carrot and stick' tactic within Malaysia's ethnicized political system, where the electoral and political processes have been successfully manipulated along ethnic lines (Saravanamuttu, 2001). However, some have pointed out that it is also possible to push the boundaries of this democratic space. In describing Malaysia as a 'statist democracy' – and while not denying the ability of the state to weaken if not incapacitate civil society groups – Jesudason (1995: 340) points out that the state is 'also sufficiently based on electoral support that the ruling coalition experiences pressures to perform adequately to get the requisite support'. In short, the state since independence has utilized a wide array of policies and mechanisms to be both coercive and dominant, and yet can co-opt issues and groups where it sees fit. The history of civil society in Malaysia has always been to resist or engage within these set parameters, sometimes to the peril of their members and their organizations.

It is in this context that the struggle of women's groups *vis-à-vis* the state has to be understood in the discussion that follows.

Development, NEP and WID: 1970s–early 1990s

The pre-WID period

From the time of independence in 1957 until the early 1970s, women's issues were not of particular significance to the state, which was bent on building its project of modernity within an ethnic-based political system. This period saw the state attempting to use the Western economic development model of import-substitution, without paying too much attention to wealth and income distribution. This resulted in about half of the population, particularly in the rural areas, living below the poverty line.

Welfare and related associations nurtured and sponsored by the colonial state continued into the post-colonial era. New organizations were also formed with the acquiescence of the state, and sometimes with the participation of those in political power. One such group was the National Council of Women's Organisations (NCWO), formed in 1963 and which acted as an umbrella organization of women's groups including the women's wings of the ruling parties. Except for the struggle for equal pay for women in the public sector,[3] the relationship between women's groups and the state in the 1960s was muted and was not transparent as most negotiations were 'whispered' in government corridors and through private conversations among the elite on both sides. Such intimate liaisons were possible as the NCWO was an example of a 'statist' women's organization, that is the non-governmental version of 'consociationalist' politics.[4]

State intervention and WID

The ushering in of the New Economic Policy (NEP) in 1971, partly born out of the ethnic riots in 1969, saw a major reversal in the role of the state in economic development. Political scientists have noted the interventionist nature of the Malaysian state then – one which was more concerned in the 1970s and 1980s with the ethnic question (Loh, 2000). This shift resulted in the enhanced role of the state in capital accumulation, especially for elite *bumiputera* (read UMNO) interests. State-sponsored economic institutions and enterprises were established to promote *bumiputera* participation. Whoever stepped in the way and/or questioned the outcome of these policies was swiftly stopped by detention under the ISA as seen in the spate of arrests in the 1970s of student activists, academicians and political leaders, and the 1987 police sweep code-named *Operasi Lalang* when more than 100 people, including human rights and church activists and politicians, were arrested.

Export-led industrialization became the new focus of development policy, with the state beckoning foreign capital with various incentives to invest in Malaysia. Free-trade zones became the order of the day as the need for workers in the newly buoyant electronics industry coincided with the interest of the state to balance the ethnic ratio in the cities. What was unusual, however, was the influx of young rural women workers to work in these first-generation factories which deployed a combined patriarchal-cum-capitalist strategy in hiring cheap but pliant and docile workers to manufacture chips in the expanding electronics sector.[5] Thus in the 1970s and 1980s, the state's main interest in women was from a purely trade and investment perspective; women's concerns and rights were deemed secondary to their primary ability to be employed by foreign capital in the nation's march towards modernity.[6]

At the same time, at the global level, the momentum of second-wave feminism was emerging in the late 1960s and early 1970s. Women in the industrialized West were fighting for equality before the law and greater access to education and employment. Interest in women in the developing countries was catalysed from the pioneering research of Boserup (1970), which disclosed that not only had women's position deteriorated as a result of colonialism, but also that modernization had excluded and, worse, bypassed women. However, Boserup also concluded that development was fundamentally good and non-discriminatory and thus the best way to improve the status of women was to integrate them into programmes consciously planned for them.

This was the period of Women in Development (WID). In 1970, the UN General Assembly emphasized the importance of the 'full integration of women in the total development effort' as part of the International Development Strategy of the Second Development Decade (Tinker, 1990). The main thrust of this package was that planners should increase women's

involvement and productivity in the modern sector by providing the necessary education to change attitudes, as well as the legal and administrative
changes to ensure that women would be better integrated into national
economic systems.

The call of WID at the global level fitted well into the development
agenda of the Malaysian state. After all, both were interested in making
women more efficient and productive, particularly by ushering them into the
modern industrial sector. In July 1976, the National Advisory Council for
the Integration of Women in Development (NACIWID), was set up under
the Prime Minister's Department as a response to the call of the UN
International Decade for Women (1976–85). Consisting of government and
non-governmental male and female appointees, its objectives were to serve as
a coordinating, consultative and advisory body to the government to ensure
the full integration of women in national development, and to enable women
to develop their potential capabilities to the maximum.

However, the lack of interest of the state in promoting women's potential,
whether legally or administratively, was clear. NACIWID was only an advisory body without any decision-making powers. Moreover, its members were
by and large political appointees and came mainly from the upper strata of
society, hence its concerns for ordinary women were minimal and detached.
Institutionalization of women's concerns only came about seven years later,
in 1983, with the establishment of the Secretariat for Women's Affairs
(HAWA), located at the Administration and Finance Division of the Prime
Minister's Department, and accountable to a Deputy (and junior) Minister
of Women's Affairs. Again, the lack of resources and personnel provided for
HAWA retarded its effectiveness, and revealed how insignificant the 'woman
question' was to the state throughout the 1970s and 1980s.

Nonetheless, prodded by national and international pressure, particularly
the growing momentum of the women's movement in the 1980s, the state put
forth a National Policy on Women in 1989, and for the first time it had a
chapter aptly termed 'Women in Development' in the Sixth Malaysia Plan
(1991–5). The NCWO played an important role by organizing consultations
with its members, recommending to the government that the policy goals
should ensure greater sharing, equality in access to resources, information
and opportunities for all women and men.

However, despite the language of equality, the National Women's Policy
and the WID chapter were still framed within a mainstream development
perspective, where women were perceived as economic resources rather than
as citizens in their own right. In addition, women were still seen as key to
family development and stability. In its own telling way, the last but one
chapter of the Sixth Malaysia Plan concluded that:

> The Government is committed towards increasing the effective involve-
> ment of women in overall national development. In recognition of the
> crucial role women play in family development and their increasing

participation in economic activities, the Government will continue to support programmes that strive to facilitate the role of women both within and outside the family. As women constitute a vital economic resource, the Government's goal is, therefore, to integrate women as equal partners in nation building.

(Government of Malaysia, 1991: 427)

There was hardly any objection, even from the NCWO, about the limitations of the WID framework, which was already being critiqued from the late 1970s. The basic disagreement with WID was that it accepted the status quo of the current development process without questioning the power relations in society or the structural relations between men and women which obstruct the realization of women's access to resources. What was needed was a transformation of the entire development processes, structures and socio-economic strategies, as well as the uneven and dependent relationship between developed and developing countries. It was within this context that the Gender and Development approach was conceived as a critique and alternative to WID, but this approach never really took root in the gender mainstreaming discourse in Malaysia. As will be discussed, in effect only the term 'gender' was appropriated with its real contents left untouched.

Nonetheless, it can be said that the National Policy on Women was significant because, among other things, it highlighted the importance of increasing women's participation in state decision-making processes, and the need for all data to be sex-disaggregated so that women's contributions could be seen and acknowledged. To an extent, this in turn has encouraged and legitimized the inclusion of women's views and needs into any project planning, as well as strengthened the role of women's affairs liaison officers (called gender focal points) already placed in every government ministry and agency (Tan and Singh, 1994: 26). More importantly, this document became the basis of the chapter on 'Women in Development' in the Sixth Plan, ensuring that state funds were allocated in recognition of women's contributions to the nation. Since the previous five-year national development plans had made only passing or no reference to women's contributions to the nation, this was considered major progress.

New women's groups, autonomy and the state

Women were by no measure an open political force to be reckoned with in the 1970s, but by the late 1980s, the state was being pressured to engage publicly on women's issues by the emerging non-governmental women's activist groups formed earlier that decade. While they were autonomous in organization and perspective, there were two streams of thought in the new women's groups – one saw the need to engage with the state due to the demands for legislative change around Violence Against Women (VAW) issues; the other, being more grassroots-based, did not see the state as its ally due to its patriarchal and class interests. However, the initial mood was confrontational in nature, as seen in the nature of an anti-rape campaign in the mid-1980s and the launching of the 'Women's Manifesto' in 1990.[7] By the early 1990s, the women's movement became more open to engagement with the state.

The 1980s saw the emergence of progressive NGO groups taking up a series of issues from squatters' rights to protests against the building of dams and the dumping of nuclear waste – issues critical of the nature of development in the country. Women activists were also part of such actions and protests. In line with this trend, the horrendous cases of rape reported in the media pushed women activists in the VAW campaign to mobilize and lead an anti-rape campaign through a coalition called Citizens Against Rape (CAR). However CAR was short-lived as the emerging civil society movement became an opportune target of the state's repression when a political crisis within UMNO erupted, leading to *Operasi Lalang*. Among those detained were women activists, accused of being Marxists who were mobilizing workers and women to overthrow the state.[8]

The state became more authoritarian and political repression was the order of the day. For example, in 1988 the Executive held closed-door tribunals and removed the then Lord President, Mohd Salleh Abas, and two other Supreme Court judges when the former directed that the controversy regarding the legality of UMNO be heard by the entire Supreme Court.[9] It is within such a political context that reforms to the Penal Code regarding rape were made in 1989 – as a political concession to the demands of women's groups, and to win back the support the state had lost. To be sure, as a humanitarian issue, it did not cost the state much to pass such reforms even though these only came four years after the initial demand. Moreover, not all the demands for reform were met. While the slow pace of state response reflected the lack of clout of the fledging women's movement, the fact that women's groups were able to exact a response at all underscored their ability to mobilize and organize public consciousness and opinion. According to two independent observers:

> The success of the (rape) campaign was because while the NGOs' initiatives on the legal drafts were going through the proper state channels, the NGOs were also continuing the education and conscientisation campaign throughout the country, generating the groundswell of popular support and mass media coverage which then fed back to the state.
>
> (Tan and Singh, 1980)

By the early 1990s, through their various educational, services and advocacy programmes, women's groups had established a stronger presence. Nevertheless, their efforts at lobbying the state continued to yield mixed results. By this time the state was more prepared to engage with women's groups, as can be seen in its involvement of women's groups in the discussion leading to the passage of the Domestic Violence Bill in 1994. Another reason that contributed to this was the then proactive minister who was sympathetic to women's rights and issues and open to listening to women's NGOs.[10] As a result, a more confident women's movement was receptive towards such an engagement with the state. Nonetheless, the state still dragged its feet in gazetting the Domestic Violence Act (DVA). It was only two years later, after the All Women's Action Society (AWAM) organized a public demonstration, that it was finally enacted in 1996. As reported in a newspaper:

> Three years ago, in an episode so unusual for placid Malaysia that it made headlines, women activists marched across a hotel lobby chanting 'Act now, right now' and confronted a startled Cabinet Minister. The tactic worked: A law to protect battered women was implemented after 11 years of lobbying.[11]

At another level, lobbying efforts did not have the same success. In the run-up to the general election in 1990, several women's groups, mobilized by the Women's Development Collective (WDC), came together to formulate the 'Women's Manifesto for the '90s: Questions for our Politicians' (see Appendix C). Like the National Policy on Women, this document was premised on the recognition of women's roles in development; however, it was different in that it was critical of the development process which, it claimed, had widened the gap between the rich and the poor as well as damaged the eco-system. Subsequently, its proponents strategized for women to influence national policies by making their votes count at the forthcoming elections.

For the first time a political statement was being made, with the Manifesto deploring the fact that:

- race and religion continue to divide Malaysians;
- several amendments to the Constitution have eroded many fundamental human rights;
- women are still being discriminated against; and
- the fruits of development have been inequitably distributed.

The Manifesto contained questions for all politicians, focusing on seven issues: women and work; the law; VAW; development; health; corruption; and democracy and human rights. When launched, however, only 11 groups endorsed the statement. Those who did not support the Manifesto, including women's groups, said that human rights and development were not women's issues and that the document was too critical of the government. It is interesting to note that the women's groups which did not support the Manifesto included both the 'old' women's groups and some recently established autonomous groups, reflecting the different political stances.[12] Later, however, parties in the opposition coalition *Gagasan Rakyat* (People's Force) included the Manifesto demands in their campaign pledges in the run-up to the 1990 general election.

Gender was thus not a critical issue; women's votes *qua* women's issues were not significant as there was no gendered political constituency to speak of. All this was to change significantly from the mid-1990s when women's issues, for various reasons discussed in the next section, became slowly appropriated and instrumentalized by political forces, and the gender card was thrown on the table for better or for worse. It became another and different ball game for women's groups – a game where the process of engagement with the state became more complex.

From Beijing to the post-crisis state: towards gender mainstreaming

Globalization, crisis and Reformasi

The beginning of the 1990s saw the country bouncing back from the global recession of 1986 as it pursued an aggressive policy of economic and financial liberalization. Globalization was the order of the day as the economy steadily picked up to near double-digit growth by the mid-1990s.[13] From 1987, the economy grew at an average rate of 8.5 per cent annually. By early 1997, unemployment stood at 2.9 per cent with the poverty rate successfully held down to 8 per cent. Malaysia, keenly locked into the global capitalist system, became one of the 20 largest trading nations in the world.

However, the opening-up of the economy to unregulated financial capital led to widespread speculation in the non-productive sectors, particularly the construction industry and the capital market, leading to a bubble economy which eventually burst in August 1997. This occurred close on the heels of similar problems in Thailand and Indonesia. All of a sudden the Asian economic miracle became a debacle; Malaysia's currency depreciated about 30 per cent of its value to the US dollar and the stock market plunged to an all time-low.

Before it could recover from the blow, the country was hit by another crisis – this time the meltdown was between the then Prime Minister, Dr Mahathir Mohamad, and his deputy, Anwar Ibrahim, who was unceremoniously sacked in September 1998. Anwar, who put up a tough fight, was subsequently detained and the Malaysian public saw a display of Machiavellian politics unprecedented in the nation's history.

Women's agenda for change

With globalization pushing not only economic restructuring, but also linking civil society at the global level, the fortunes of the Malaysian women's movement in the mid-1990s had already taken a turn for the better even before

Reformasi. By then it was not possible to ignore the larger goings-on in the international arena, which were a culmination of ongoing efforts in the previous two decades. The UN Fourth World Conference on Women in Beijing had a decidedly marked impact in this regard. This meeting, more commonly known as the Beijing Conference, was a follow-up to the 1985 Nairobi women's conference – and in many respects the result of seeds sown by the global women's movement at the time – and contributed to greater recognition of women's issues in Malaysia in several ways.

It influenced the media into opening up more space for women's groups to voice their concerns publicly. This was evident in the widespread media coverage on women's issues before, during and after this event. As an example, women's groups came up with their '11-point Agenda' and presented their demands to the then Prime Minister's wife, Dr Siti Hasmah Mohd Ali, who was leading the Malaysian delegation to Beijing. In turn, the publicity gave the local women's movement a higher profile and, accordingly, more legitimacy in the eyes of the state. The different preparatory activities leading up to the conference also appeared to give the Malaysian government a final push to ratify CEDAW just before its official delegation arrived in Beijing. Out of the actual conference itself, the government endorsed the Beijing Declaration and Platform for Action, thus reinforcing its intentions, at least on paper, to advance the status of women in the country.

These gains notwithstanding, it is important to note that at no point during the Beijing process did the state give its unqualified backing for women's issues. In fact, it was careful never to state its support in terms of advocating women's rights. For example, the Malaysian government placed several reservations to CEDAW, particularly when it perceived the treaty's articles as contravening the position of women under *Syariah* (Islamic) laws. As noted in its 1995 reservations:

> The Government of Malaysia declares that Malaysia's accession is subject to the understanding that the provisions of the Convention do not conflict with the provisions of the Islamic *Syariah* law and the Federal Constitution. With regards thereto, further, the Government of Malaysia does not consider itself bound by the provisions of articles 2 (f), 5 (a), 7 (b), 9 and 16 of the aforesaid Convention.[14]

The Malaysian state was also not supportive of the entire range of reproductive rights for women, one of them being the right to abortion. Instead, it made it a point to distinguish itself from what it perceived to be the agenda of feminists and Western-influenced women's groups at Beijing. Thus it held up the interests of women so long as this applied only to their roles in national development – the WID position did not alter. While this position reflected the government's sentiments, it was also meant to placate the more conservative elements in Malaysian society who otherwise may have objected to the state's uncritical adoption of the Beijing outcome.

Obviously the message was also targeted at the local women's movement to keep them and their activities in line with 'national interests'.

However, the women's movement was not so easily restrained and, as the 1997 financial crisis unfolded and the *Reformasi* movement gathered momentum, four key women's groups[15] and several individual activists initiated the Women's Agenda for Change (WAC) with the objectives of further raising society's awareness of the position of Malaysian women; strengthening the political participation of women to work towards a just and democratic society; and intensifying the network of women's organizations and NGOs in the country. It was also envisaged as a lobbying tool for the general election due to be held by the end of 2000.

The idea was the same as with the 1990 'Women's Manifesto' – to pressure political parties, including those in government, to pay attention and be committed to women's concerns in return for votes. The issues and demands were either similar or additional to those made in 1990. Yet the response to this new document, launched in May 1999, showed startling progress compared to the 'Women's Manifesto'. Compared to the 11 endorsements that the first initiative had received, 76 NGOs supported this second effort.[16] It was a political *tour de force* as it commanded the support of a wide diversity of civil society, ranging from consumer and environmental groups to religious-based bodies. And for the first time Muslim women who represented welfare-based Islamic bodies joined the women's movement in their call for reform. Surprisingly, the NCWO endorsed the politically charged document as well, although the Minister of National Unity and Social Development was also then its chairperson. More interestingly, the main women's wings of the ruling coalition Barisan Nasional (BN – National Front) gave their backing, with the government later even going so far as to project it on national television as *their* initiative.

The vastly different reactions to the 'Women's Manifesto' (of 1990) and the WAC (of 1999) can be explained in several ways.

One has to do with the internal cohesion of the movement as a whole. In 1990 feminism and women's rights were not yet in vogue, but more importantly there was a striking distinction between state-endorsed and autonomous women's groups. The former tended to be reluctant to support issues that they did not perceive as 'women's issues'.[17] They disagreed with the demands for greater transparency and accountability from the state, as well as the call to repeal all repressive laws such as the ISA. At the time too, the autonomous women's groups stood on the outside of the periphery of government, trying to forward women's interests without engaging too much with the state. They were, in many ways, looked upon with disdain and suspiciously perceived as anti-government, if not militant. By the time the WAC was put forward, however, this situation had changed. Having had more experiences and opportunities to get to know each other and collaborate on projects, women's groups and other civil society organizations had built a level of trust that had not previously existed. This helped to garner support for the WAC.

Another key factor was the drastically changed economic and political climate in the late 1990s. Originally a few women's groups and individuals got together to discuss their responses to the 1997 financial crisis and to draw up advocacy plans in anticipation of the 1999 general election. However, before any concrete proposals could be formulated, Anwar was arrested and the *Reformasi* movement took to the streets. This upsurge against the government's repressive measures opened new doors for women's groups as well as other civil liberty NGOs, and strengthened their leverage with politicians. Thus from a document that was initially conceived as a reaction to the financial crisis and to prepare for the general election, the scope of the WAC was successfully extended to political advocacy.

For the first time in the history of the autonomous women's movement, members of the WAC Organizing Committee[18] were approached by at least three different factions within Wanita UMNO, the women's wing of UMNO. Such courtship resulted in a meeting with the women's wings of the main parties in the BN. The meeting was chaired by the head of Wanita UMNO in the presence of the Deputy Prime Minister. Pledges that task forces would be formed in line with the 11 issues of WAC were given to the WAC Organizing Committee members present. Their overnight popularity can be attributed to the way that events surrounding the sacking of Anwar had destabilized the traditional Malay support base of the government. Ensuring women's support in this politically volatile environment was thus seen as paramount.

It soon became apparent that the government had backed the WAC primarily for show. There was no concrete follow-up to the promises made to the WAC Organizing Committee. Even more revealing was how, when this document was sent to every Member of Parliament (MP) for personal endorsement, only 13 responded positively – four from the ruling coalition and nine from the opposition. Undaunted, WAC widely publicized this poor response in the form of a report card of the MPs, resulting in their taking this media blitz unkindly and accusing WAC of being arrogant in demanding such undertaking. It was even seen as an opposition-inspired document. Another advocacy activity was to present the demands for reforms at meetings with the MPs in parliament.[19] The WAC Organizing Committee met with MPs from both the ruling coalition and opposition.

Notwithstanding this the government continued to use every opportunity to play the gender card in the run-up to the general election of November 1999. In fact, the elections saw a record number of women being nominated to contest. This included a candidate put up by the Women's Candidacy Initiative – a group of independent women advocating gender representation in formal politics (Tan and Ng, 2003: 115–18). In the elections, 20 women candidates were voted into power, making it the first time in the nation's history that women comprised more than 10 per cent of MPs in the Dewan Rakyat (House of Representatives). Whenever possible, the government-controlled media was also used to deprecate the policies and stance that the

LIVERPOOL JOHN MOORES UNIVERSITY
LEARNING & INFORMATION SERVICES

opposition party Parti Islam Se Malaysia (PAS – Islamic Party of Malaysia) – by no coincidence the main political rival to UMNO – adopted on women. This included their position that women were not allowed to run for public office.

While not an issue in previous elections, all of a sudden, women's concerns became highlighted in campaigns, with one government politician remarking that his trump card in winning the elections had been to woo the female electorate. As observed by Maznah (2000: 14), 'the run-up to the country's latest elections is seeing a marked politicization of women's issues. The entry of Wan Azizah [Wan Ismail][20] as a leading icon of opposition forces . . . is feeding into the imagination of the public that gender may count after all'.

Even though the general election comfortably returned the BN to government, its leaders were not content to rest on their laurels. As women were considered loyal and consistent in their voting patterns, the government sought to both cement existing female support and win over new voters. In this, the Prime Minister surprised the nation in early 2001 by announcing the creation of the Ministry of Women's Affairs. While women's groups had on different occasions in the past called for the government women's machinery to be strengthened, none had anticipated that their calls would be met this way. Put differently, although most welcomed the new ministry, it wasn't the most important item on a long list of demands that they would have insisted on getting at that juncture.

Entering the third millennium: between appropriation and resistance

The new millennium began with the BN in control of the government although it had to reckon with a reduced majority and, additionally, having lost the east coast state of Terengganu to PAS. Hegemony had to be regained by rebuilding both the economy and winning back support from the *Reformasi*-type Malays through the 'carrot and stick' method. Key leaders of the youth wing of Parti Keadilan Nasional (Keadilan – National Justice Party) were detained under the ISA, leading to a vacuum in its organizational capacity. As the economy began to slowly recover from the 1997 financial crisis and the fire of *Reformasi* dampened, an odd normalcy took over the nation.

In 2001, when the Democratic Action Party (DAP) broke away from the BA because of a disagreement with PAS over the Islamic state issue, there was much disillusionment over the opposition's potential to effect any change at all.[21] Civil society, caught in the middle, had a difficult path to tread as religion, swayed by politics and enmeshed by race and culture, divided the country once more.

Another card played by the ruling party was to continue to win over women, a tactic used with some success in the 1999 general election, especially in counter-posing the government as modern opposed to an archaic

PAS which discriminated against women. The appointment of the rather feisty and savvy Deputy Minister of Women's Affairs, Shahrizat Abdul Jalil, was a test and an affirmation of the importance of women as a political constituency. Shortly after being made a full minister, she changed the ministry's name to the Ministry of Women and Family Development in 2001 to gain approval and support among the powerful but male-centric factions within her party, UMNO. This later caused confusion for women's groups and child rights activists as it blurred the boundary between her ministry and the then existing Ministry of National Unity and Social Development which oversees family issues.[22]

Nonetheless, to prove her mettle and to legitimize her position she set herself doggedly to the strategic task of gaining the support of the now more experienced women's movement, particularly activist groups under WAC, which she perceived as anti-government. In fact, through her efforts the state has been intent, at least at the level of rhetoric, on institutionalizing and appropriating women's issues. Gender mainstreaming, UN-style, thus became a reality in Malaysia as the national machinery for women changed gear.

One of the minister's first tasks was to personally visit various women's NGOs and to call for dialogues, including with the WAC Organizing Committee. The strategies used to build linkages, or to control the women's NGOs, depending on how one sees it, were varied. One was by offering them funds, which were much needed by the resource-starved women's groups. Another was by setting up various task forces under the ministry and inviting women's groups to either be members or to chair such task forces and/or committees. And finally, there was the appropriation of VAW issues – a campaign which the women's movement had been spearheading for the previous 20 years. But the hasty and haphazard appropriation led to some tension and confusion between the two parties.

In November 2000, Shahrizat, as Deputy Minister of Women's Affairs then, established and chaired a National Steering Committee on VAW, in which women's NGOs were invited to participate. This committee had grandiose plans and, to accomplish these, four subcommittees – co-chaired by representatives from women's NGOs – were created, *viz* Implementation of Law and Policy; Research and Development; Strategy and Action Plan; and Management and Coordination.[23]

Women's groups welcomed the National Steering Committee as a good opportunity to intervene in and influence policy. It became an avenue for them and government agencies to jointly discuss issues affecting women, and to gain greater recognition among public bodies like the police, Welfare Services Department and Jabatan Kemajuan Islam Malaysia (Department of Islamic Development Malaysia). In short, the National Steering Committee opened new doors for women's groups, enabling them to build better contacts with these agencies, and in the long run to enhance the services that they provide to women.

The sub-committees functioned initially but in less than a year only one was still operating – the Implementation of the Law and Policy sub-committee, co-chaired with the Women's Aid Organisation (WAO). It did a good job of coordinating amendments to further improve the DVA and submitted, in May 2003, a comprehensive memorandum to the minister. The other three subcommittees were put in cold storage. This included the Strategy and Action Plan sub-committee which was supposed to launch an awareness-raising campaign on VAW. However, the campaign was over-turned and renamed WAVE (Women Against Violence; *OMBAK* in Malay), triggering the ire of the women's groups.

The demise of the three subcommittees has been attributed to the intro-duction of a new structure in the ministry in early 2001 – the Technical Working Groups (TWGs), all of which were chaired by the minister. As before, women's NGOs were invited not only to be part of this set-up, but to head the various subcommittees. In total there were TWGs on eight issues – law; religion; media and communications; decision-making; health; job marketing; economy; and education and training. To a certain degree, these TWGs duplicated the work of the sub-committees of the National Steering Committee on VAW. For example, the TWG on law was further sub-divided into four components – Law Reform, *Syariah* laws, Family Court and VAW – some of which were already under the National Steering Committee.

However, given that the terms of reference were not clear, these sub-committees could not deliver results because technical support was generally not forthcoming from the ministry. Instead, the functions of the National Steering Committee on VAW and the TWGs became increasingly ambiguous as substantive women's issues were sidelined and replaced by the sound and fury of large-scale public events such as the *Nur* (Light) and *OMBAK* campaigns instead.

Organized by the Ministry, *Nur* was intended as an annual event show-casing women's achievements, comprising multiple events such as seminars, award ceremonies, exhibitions and keynote speeches by the Prime Minister and male political figures. These have been held as glittering ceremonies in grand venues. Unlike the subcommittees which gave NGOs more scope to participate in decision-making and influence policy, these activities were, in the main, for short-term public education and publicity purposes dictated by the whims of the minister, a fact that eventually led to some women's groups boycotting the *OMBAK* campaign.

Originally, the Strategy and Action Plan sub-committee under the National Steering Committee had been planning since late 2000, a national-level awareness campaign on VAW. The minister then decided to commission an advertising agency to design an appropriate theme to launch the campaign. In the initial stages, women's groups under the subcommittee, particularly WAO, had assisted the advertising agency. However, at a certain point, the minister overturned the VAW campaign into *OMBAK*. It was conceived as a public event primarily to profile the ministry via a media, education and training campaign associated with the messages of VAW, including the issuing of membership 'cards' to those committed to its objectives.

In May 2001, the Ministry invited selected key NGOs to obtain their views on the *OMBAK* materials prepared by the advertising agency. At this point, the groups objected to the way the campaign angle had been switched from one that was meant to address VAW, to one that emphasized women's roles in ending all forms of violence. They tried to point out that not only was this against the original spirit of the Steering Committee – that is, set up specifically to address VAW – but also did women a great disservice by making them solely responsible, once again, for maintaining peace and harmony in their communities and in society.

In early July 2001, in their letter of withdrawal from the *OMBAK* campaign, three women's NGOs pointed to the lack of perspective of the issue as well as to the lack of transparency in the decision-making process.[24] Their protests fell on deaf ears. The *OMBAK* campaign was launched by the prime minister on 23 July 2001 to mark the first year of the establishment of the ministry. Women's NGOs boycotted the event, and the campaign was implemented with mixed results.

Caught in the cross-fire and with the press following up on this controversy, the minister had to appease her constituency and hurriedly agreed to take up the constitutional amendment on gender equality, one of the demands put forward by WAC in 1998. And this the minister successfully did by having the prime minister announce – during the launch of the *OMBAK* campaign – that gender inequality would not be tolerated.

Within a week, on 1 August 2001, the minister sponsored a proposal to parliament to amend Article 8(2) of the Federal Constitution to add that there should be no discrimination based on gender. On 14 August the amendment was passed by the Dewan Negara (Senate), while Royal Assent was obtained on 6 September. It was gazetted on 27 September and enforced with effect from the next day. The incredible speed and the manner in which this amendment was accepted were not due to the 20 years of lobbying by women's NGOs. Rather, political expediency dictated the move – the importance of sustaining the support of the female constituency and the wider need to combat PAS showed that the state was not motivated by any real feminist concerns.[25]

Consequences of engaging with the state

At one level, it has been felt that maintaining good relations with the ministry puts NGOs in a better position to receive funds for their work. This relationship is at best tenuous, as NGOs are basically at the mercy of the ministry for a financial handout; even when they are lucky enough to be recipients, the amounts are determined by the ministry rather than based on the needs of the NGOs. Such a situation could also lead NGOs to be less critical of the government in case funding is decreased or cut. In some cases, NGOs that link up with ruling political parties to seek funds have seen more favourable results than those who approach the ministry on their own, thus suggesting that the relationship between the ministry and NGOs is extremely unequal.

To make matters worse, by virtue of receiving funds for service provision (e.g. counselling, shelters), NGOs are now being criticized whenever the public perceives that the work is not adequately done or that women's rights are not sufficiently being upheld. Instead of placing the onus on the state to do this, the public has come to expect NGOs to play this role. NGOs will always be a poor substitute, given their lack of resources to fulfil such a role.

It has also been said that by working with the ministry women's groups gain greater legitimacy among the citizenry. This is true to the extent that better contacts have been established with certain government agencies. Yet it is debatable whether this legitimacy can only be gained by working with the ministry. For the amount of time and energy that has to go into maintaining good relations with the ministry – for example, by sitting in various committees and working groups, and providing the ministry with information and expertise that it lacks – it would seem that there are far more disadvantages than benefits.

At the same time, a depoliticization process seems to have occurred whenever women's NGOs are embedded within state structures without any long term and systematic vision (as seen in the duplication of activities and ineffectiveness of the National Steering Committee on VAW and the TWGs) to genuinely advance women's rights. Recognizing the folly of being too deeply implicated within the state, the women's groups under the Joint Action Group against VAW (JAG-VAW)[26] decided in early 2003 that they would not be part of state structures, and that they would withdraw from chairing the TWG sub-committees.

The alternative proposal was that these be headed by ministry officials themselves, thus throwing the burden back to the state to be responsible for its own goals. However, women's NGOs agreed to serve as deputy chairpersons, as internal 'watchdogs' of the effective functioning of these groups. This proposal was brought up to the minister in May 2003 and, at the behest of the women's NGOs, she officially disbanded the National Steering Committee on VAW and agreed to look into the restructuring of the TWGs. It remains to be seen how effective these structures will be and how women's groups contest the powers-that-be within such state boundaries.

Further engagement: general election 2004

In anticipation of the next general election, WDC under its Women Organizing Network programme, initiated several meetings in 2003 and 2004 for women activists to discuss the nature of their engagement in the electoral process. Several different strategies were put forth, including a boycott of the elections; campaigning for, and monitoring of, candidates; and standing as candidates. The different paths revealed the past experiences of the women's movement, although what was interesting this time around was the call to boycott the elections. This sentiment reflected the distrust in the electoral process which had previously smacked of gerrymandering, state control over media coverage, and the lack of democratic space for opposition or independent candidates to explain their manifestos.

As speculation on the polling date built up from early March, an abrupt decision on the polling date was anticipated again, which would give candidates, especially those from the opposition ranks, very little time to mobilize their campaign. Nonetheless, activists felt that it was important to use the event to continue making the public more aware and critical of gender and social issues that would be used yet once more to woo voters. Given the energy, time and resources available, women activists decided that monitoring the candidates was the most realistic way to give gender issues a high profile over the usually short campaign period. The Women Monitoring Election Candidates (WoMEC), an informal network of the JAG-VAW, was launched in a press conference on 9 March.

True to form, the government moved swiftly to fix Nomination Day on 13 March and polling on 21 March. It was the shortest campaign period in Malaysia's electoral history, at less than eight days. WoMEC, coordinated by WDC, was forced to respond just as quickly to meet its objectives:

- To ensure that issues and concerns of citizens (in particular those of women) claimed centre stage in the election agenda; and
- To get candidates to commit to upholding citizens' issues and to make them accountable to their promises after the election.

To do this WoMEC decided to monitor and evaluate the manifestos of the political parties in relation to issues of gender equality and democracy as well as to obtain the commitment of candidates on the nine issues identified by WoMEC. These were similar to the unfulfilled demands from the WAC document and included safety and security, reform of laws that discriminate against women, and abolition of repressive laws. Given the short time at its disposal, WoMEC had to scramble for its views to be heard in the media. It came up with several press statements, most of which were published in the print media. In addition WoMEC members were featured in the press (of all languages) and were profiled in feature articles before and after the general election.[27]

Conclusion

Within the context of an authoritarian, non-feminist regime, which at the same time needs to seek legitimacy through an electoral system, the politics of engagement between the women's movement and the state is fraught with tensions and ambiguities. On the one hand, the state has to show that it has to safeguard and promote women's rights, whether symbolically or in real terms. On the other, during times of political instability, and if it feels sufficiently threatened, it is capable of using both coercion and manipulation of the gender card. In the final analysis the state, although needing to legitimize itself and notwithstanding the existence of 'femocrats'[28] within its ranks, will only give in to the pressures of the women's movement, both locally and globally, when it sees fit to do so, particularly where civil society is weak.

In the Malaysian case, such ambivalence and lack of a coherent direction is clearly seen in the following instances or outcomes:

- the government's various task forces on women's issues are not effective;
- reform of the laws relating to rape and domestic violence, and demands for legislation against sexual harassment have been put on hold for several years now;
- the government's CEDAW report is more than eight years late;[29] and
- the promises made to the WAC Organizing Committee are now shelved.

Indeed, it has been generally observed that while the national machinery has been entrusted with, and is responsible for, gender mainstreaming, it has by and large proven to be ineffective in advancing women's rights, particularly for poor and working-class women. There are structures of power within the state which are major impediments to effectively address women's issues and rights. Some of the obstacles include the lack of good governance, the lack of commitment to women's rights issues, poor resources and compliance with a neo-liberal economic model which views women as objects of 'development' (Griffen, 2002; Rai, 2002: 177–82). And even where the state is more benevolent and open to feminist demands, mainstreaming gender is an activity that is embedded in bureaucratic and political contexts.

Despite this uphill struggle, it can be seen that the women's movement in Malaysia has succeeded in putting the VAW agenda in the public domain – it is now visible, institutionalized and mainstreamed. However, where other apparatuses of the state are concerned, for example the government and the police, women's issues are not viewed as challenging the status quo. If contentious aspects are raised at all, as for example with marital rape, the institutions have successfully rejected these demands and placed their interests first. The lack of women's representation as a strong political constituency has not helped either. This sheds further light on why it was possible for the government to drag its feet over enactment of the DVA, something that most advocates expected at the outset of the campaign to take less time to secure than the amendments to the laws relating to rape.

The challenge then is, as an autonomous movement, how does it ensure that its organization(s) and issues are not co-opted by a repressive state? How does it engage with the state on its own terms? Pushing the boundaries (for example, in going beyond VAW issues) will have implications when the state's repressive arm is activated against those perceived to threaten its political and economic existence. What does an 'in and against' the state position mean, particularly when the government is a strong supporter of neo-liberal globalization?[30]

In order to contest the state on its own terms, the women's movement has to continuously and consistently open and enlarge public discourse and debate. It has to deal with a multi-class, multiethnic, multicultural society in a way in which differences can be respected and resolved without bringing disunity to the movement. It has to bridge the divide between older and younger generations of women. This means building trust and respect, being less judgmental and having an attitude of openness among various groups.

The vision of the women's movement must include the struggle towards gender equality, justice and democracy. Women's groups should thus link up with like-minded groups in civil society, work at coalition building and towards a more holistic transformation of society. Thus a shift in strategy is the call of the day. Too much time and energy has been spent on lobbying for legislative reform. It is critical for the women's movement to move beyond its predominantly middle-class base and expand and strengthen its political constituency through various channels, such as movement building, electoral participation and advocacy so that it has a stronger foundation and can improve its negotiating power. However, it must also anticipate that the politicization of religion and culture will be used to overshadow the importance of feminist demands. The women's movement must therefore tread carefully to negotiate the political minefield of being 'in and against' the state.

As will be shown in the next chapter, women in Malay Muslim organizations had to manoeuvre between the will of the state and the various competing forms of Islam within society. In this process feminist groups have had to enter into an unavoidable alliance with the state in order to mitigate the rise of an Islam that could be retrogressive to women.

5 Negotiating political Islam

Women in Malay-Muslim organizations[1]

In Malaysia, many organizations limit their membership to a particular ethno-religious community, while eschewing any religious purpose to their existence. Lately, among Malay-Muslims this has changed. In this chapter we discuss the nature of women's involvement in organizations that have an exclusive Malay-Muslim membership.[2] Many did not start out as having an Islamizing agenda, in the sense of having the political intention to spread the influence and word of Islam.[3] But with the advent of Islamic resurgence in the late 1970s, women in Malay-Muslim organizations have been invariably drawn to imbue some of the aims of this resurgent movement. As they confront the discourse and practical outcomes of an assertive political Islam, women have become significant as victims, pawns, beneficiaries or agents of the movement.[4]

This chapter will focus on the political role that Muslim women play in negotiating with state and Islamic forces for their communal or personal gains. It specifically looks at how Muslim women who belong to Malay-Muslim organizations have influenced or intervened in national processes involving women's issues. We discuss how they have helped or hindered the promotion of the Violence Against Women (VAW) campaign and the struggle for gender equality laws and policies. Only some of the organizations in which Malay women participate started out as a direct response to Islamic resurgence. Indeed, the diversity and tensions among women within each group have framed gender reforms as a slow and incoherent process. Nevertheless, it was precisely because of this conflicting diversity that Islam was unable to rigidly fashion women's role.

In this chapter, we see feminist politics and mobilization as playing an overwhelming role in mitigating the rise of patriarchy through the guise of political Islam. The discourse of women's rights has become critical in the national agenda, especially in the preservation of the state's secular character. But it must be stressed that the presence of an ethnically plural political constituency and expedient shifts in priorities asserted by an authoritarian, developmentalist state are even more important in tempering the ascendance of any strongly ideological, anti-market and inclusively ethnicized movement.[5] The shifting purposes of Malay women's engagement with Islam and the state will also leave us to wonder if Malay-Muslim women's organizations can exist as autonomous agents of change.

Origins of women's politicization through Islam

Malay women's involvement in a political civil society can be traced to their involvement in nationalist politics of the early twentieth century (Maznah, 2002). With the onset of the Islamic resurgent movement from the 1970s, they played a central role in its ascendance as well. The recruitment of women into Malay Islamic movements is quite similar to that of the early period of nationalist mobilization. Women were heavily courted as participants and movers of these movements for two main reasons – consolidation of a new communitarian identity and mobilization of a mass following inclusive of women, youth and children. This is not to say that they did not join these movements voluntarily and wilfully. No doubt, these women also identified with the goals of Islam's resurgence and felt that they could be more empowered through it (Sharifah Zaleha, 2000). In a general but comprehensive sense, the aims of the Islamic or *Dakwah* (preaching) movement, as it is popularly referred to, was to achieve and embody the following:

> The non-separation of the religious, legal, and political spheres is affirmed. The household be the source of law as well as the norm for individual behaviour, both for the sovereign and for the simple believer. The definition of an autonomous political space, with its own rules, its positive laws, and its own values, is prohibited. Finally, the state is never considered in terms of a territorialised nation-state: the ideal is to have a power that would rule over the entirety of the *umma*, the community of the faithful, while actual power is exercised over a segment of the *umma* whose borders are contingent, provisional, and incomplete.
>
> (Roy, 1999: 13)[6]

Women's participation was highly crucial for the Islamization agenda to succeed. Many women founders saw their decision to be part of the movement as an act of defiance against the 'establishment' Islam then. The latter was considered too restrained in pushing for a greater degree of Islamic governance in society. Islam as a religion, although traditionally and deeply implanted in the social existence of Malay life, can still be reinterpreted in radical ways to impute a new meaning to the Malay political identity. During the resurgence it became the voice of dissent instead of conservatism. For instance, society at the time did not look kindly on Muslim women's decision to wear the veil, frequently taunting those who did have the courage to do so as *hantu bungkus* (shrouded ghosts) (Khalijah, 1996). But in no time, women's veiling took on the proportion of a 'symbolic capital' for the movement's ascendance around the world (Gole, 1996).

Most of the movements were urban-based and were initiated by young and highly educated Malays, many of whom received their tertiary education abroad. A formal qualification and the prevailing New Economic Policy (NEP) as affirmative action for Malay advancement guaranteed future well-paying and well-placed careers.[7] This ensured that women within the movement (who were also beneficiaries of educational subsidies and scholarships) would not lose out economically in spite of a strong social force to domesticate their role. The paradoxical outcome for these women was assured upward economic mobility while imbibing a secondary social role to that of males. The emblematic trappings of 'domestication' in the form of veiling and subdued conduct were at the same time combined with a new sense of economic empowerment.

The legitimization of the newly founded resurgent Islamic organizations was dependent on the credentials of their membership. It was important that the movement could be backed by the support of highly educated women. At a period when Malays were trying to assert their sense of economic competence, this was a significant projection. Hence, it was never possible to neglect the need for women's leadership no matter how pervasively the discourse of domestication was being disseminated. Women were actually shielded from the risk of real subjugation as there was still a gap between theory and practice, between discourse and reality, and between what was aspired to and what was achieved by the resurgent movement. In Malaysia, there were two contradictory agendas: an ethnic and a religious one. The NEP was aimed at creating a class of successful and assertive Malays (to a certain extent cutting across gender), but the Islamic agenda was heavily geared towards subduing women's public role. Thus, no matter how theoretically rigid some of the Islamic interpretations on women's roles were, women still existed in a practical world that allowed them leeway to escape from the manifestations of dogmatism.

Furthermore, even in the midst of a rising tide of Islamization, the essence of modernity was never completely substituted. The Islamic resurgence itself was a modern movement, in which procedural and organizational structures were heavily utilized to realize its goals. At first blush Islamic fundamentalism[8] may appear to be a movement against modernization, but it is in fact a manifestation of modernization (Gellner, 1994; Brown, 2000). One familiar thesis about why Islamic fundamentalism is readily embraced is because it allows members of newly urbanized, socially disintegrated societies in the wake of rapid modernization to find cultural refuge and preserve their identity through an assertion of a familiar heritage, which is Islam (Esposito and Voll, 1996: 127).

In this thesis Islam is assertively embraced as a way of softening the disruptive and alienating effect of modernization. But this reinvention requires a process of dipping into imagination and memory. The focal points of most political Islamic movements are the 'original' years of Medina (of the seventh century) and the reconstitution of the political community in the form of a pan-Islamic *umma* (transnational community) from the late nineteenth century, in reaction to Western colonial hegemony (Mandaville, 2002: 69–82). In Malaysia, despite state support for Islamization to permeate many public institutions, modern foundations were kept intact due to the country's multiracial composition and Western-centric capitalist development model which the state relentlessly pursued.

Organizational diversity

Given such contradictions, the major Malay-Muslim women's organizations inevitably took on a variety of characteristics. These range from being pragmatist to centrist to communitarian and liberal feminist in essence. We term these groups as being either pragmatists, communitarians or Islamic feminists. What are their characteristics? How have they engaged and negotiated with Islamic powers, discourses and symbols to carve out their own path for survival and legitimacy?

The pragmatists

We define pragmatists as those who are expedient players and answerable only to their political constituents. They do not have definite or inflexible agendas and are not dogmatically committed to a set of unchanging ideals. In Malaysia, the ruling Barisan Nasional (BN – National Front) coalition's component parties operate on an understanding that only a multiethnic consociational arrangement would be able to obtain the widest voter consensus. In this 'social compact', the Malay-Muslim party United Malays National Organisation (UMNO) is, however, the dominant partner. There is also the unwritten but unchallenged understanding that the country's highest leadership will be Malay-Muslims from this party. It can be said that the main ideal of the party and its wings (youth, women and young women) is to ensure that a majority Malay support is sustained in order to reproduce and enforce the notion of Malay political dominance. Hence women's organizations within this rubric function as a supportive network to sustain the larger goals of the parent organization. But if the larger goals of the main body undergo change, women's groups will then accommodate this change accordingly.

The communitarians

Communitarians see themselves as aspiring towards a specific goal of building an alternative moral, social and political order. Individual liberties and humanist prerogatives are subsumed in the interest of building a communitarian ideal. In the Islamic case it is the idiomatic *umma* that is idealized as a focus for reclamation. There is an explicit rejection of outward manifestations of 'Western decadence', including the freedom of women to

LIVERPOOL JOHN MOORES UNIVERSITY
Aldham Robarts L.R.C.
TEL. 0151 231 3701/3634

partake prominent public roles. The euphemism 'gender-complementarity' is touted in place of the notion of 'the primacy of male authority', as being the more morally correct principle of achieving justice in gender relations.

The Islamic feminists

Islamic feminists comprise Muslim women who start out as being liberal feminists. As they realize that they cannot afford to disengage themselves from the resurgent Islamic world-view, they became more open to this paradigm. Failure to do so would alienate Muslim women of faith from accepting any of the ideals of feminism. Hence, to participate within the fold of their community's acceptance, Islamic feminists must inevitably address salient issues. Institutions and practices of Islam such as the *Syariah* and its implications for women, as well as interpretation of Qu'ranic texts on women's status, are crucial focal points of engagement for the Islamic feminist. We thus define Islamic feminists as those who accept from the outset that Islam is a system of belief that is democratic and just to women. In line with this, they uphold and promote the principle of *ijtihad* (reasoning) and *ijma'* (decision by consensus) to reclaim Islam for women. Some of the specific goals of Islamic feminists are to reform male-biased aspects of the *Syariah* and to counter patriarchal authority by highlighting the gender-justice essence of the Qu'ran. It must be stressed that Islamic feminism could only thrive as political feminism. This is because feminists who choose to struggle within a religious framework must inevitably engage with the actors of political Islam, in a terrain which is highly politicized and beyond the boundaries of the merely cultural or social aspects of the faith.

Malay-Muslim women's organizations in a spectrum

Wanita UMNO, Puteri UMNO and Wanita Keadilan as political pragmatists

Wanita UMNO (women's wing of UMNO) was formed on 25 August 1949 in Butterworth (now Seberang Prai). The main party itself had been formed three years earlier. The original name of Wanita UMNO was Pergerakan Kaum Ibu (PKI – Mothers' Movement) but the name was later changed to attract the participation of young women and the professional class.[9] Although Wanita UMNO's ideological position with regard to women is not always obvious, its practical aims are clear. It functions to coexist with, and be supportive of, the party's wider agenda – to dominate the BN as the unquestioned 'first among equals' of the component parties. In this larger scheme, there is no ambivalence about the niche carved out for the women's wing. It is a vote mobilizer, specifically among women but increasingly among all voters, especially the rural constituents.

In appealing for women's votes Wanita UMNO does not promise to only serve women's interests, but also party interests. Its underlying mission is to preserve Malay political, economic and cultural pre-eminence. Party workers employ the cultural approach of spreading goodwill through house-to-house visits to build a rapport between local party members and the village community. Wanita UMNO members say they have to consistently project a caring face by visiting households for weddings, funerals, births and numerous other social events. Since the UMNO network is very extensive, with membership at the state, division and branch levels, each member is given a number of households at the branch level among which to befriend and cultivate supporters. They must also be vigilant for any swings in the political mood at the grassroots. In tandem with this, members are periodically gathered for training and refresher courses at various locales around the country, the trip and occasion being akin to an all-expense-paid holiday.

UMNO still depends on this personal mode to retain its supporters and gather new ones. However, the *modus operandi* only works well in the rural setting where intrusions into the sanctum of private households are tolerated, and where such social doting is accepted as part and parcel of a communal lifestyle. This is the *forte* of the women's wing, whose members are able to strike up personal rapport with female members of the community. They appeal to voter sentiments by assuring the continued dominance of UMNO in BN. Voters' support is in turn solicited to ensure that UMNO's role as the main representative of the Malay consensus will remain intact.

However, with the increasing rate of urbanization among Malays and a shrinking of the rural population, Wanita UMNO finds it much harder today to use this tried and tested approach. For one thing urban constituencies are much larger and households are less willing to be visited by any party worker who is a stranger. In this context, Wanita UMNO will be pressured to find new ways to reach out to voters. It can no longer rely on goodwill visits but must also be in tune with the more sophisticated civic concerns of urban dwellers. It is not surprising then that its role has been overshadowed by the emergence of Puteri UMNO, a new wing whose membership base consists of women under the age of 40.

Despite Wanita UMNO's historically significant role in gathering a Malay consensus to sustain the political model centred on Malay-dominance, there is still a limit as to how much it can achieve today. Control of the wing by an older generation of women has caused the organization to lose touch with the sentiments of young women. UMNO's poor performance in the 1999 general election and the crisis of credibility arising from the sacking of the party deputy president and Deputy Prime Minister, Anwar Ibrahim,[10] fuelled some questioning about the gap which could not be filled by Wanita UMNO (Maznah, 2003). A whole section of Malay youth felt they had been alienated from the party's influence and reward structure. They felt they were not obliged to provide ready support for the party, especially with the resounding call of *Reformasi* ringing in their ears.

Winning back their support was UMNO's priority, and this was indeed achieved when the party regained its Malay votes in the 2004 elections.

Perhaps UMNO also knew from the 1999 elections that women are more loyal to the party than men. It was almost as if women are the more reliable source of 'credibility' capital when the authoritarian regime is shaky. Elsewhere women have been known to be fiercely loyal to their patrons without expecting much pecuniary benefits in return (Blondet, 2002: 303).

It was out of such a situation that the idea of the formation of Puteri UMNO (literally, UMNO's Princesses), the young women's wing, came to fruition. This grouping had hitherto been an untapped political force in UMNO. Young women had either been neglected as a political entity or publicly acknowledged for all the wrong reasons. Much media attention for example has been directed to the question of their sexual vulnerability and to the protection they would need from sexual predators. UMNO's newfound positive attention towards women as political agents was thus greeted with much approval by the progressive section of society.

So great was the need to regain Malay support that party leaders saw in Puteri UMNO their best hope for a turnaround. The idea was to focus on Malay women and youth to win them over as supporters. From a pragmatic point of view young women supporters could also be harnessed for a front-line role in election campaigning. Puteri UMNO's eventual formation was dependent on the backing of strong party patrons. If not for this Puteri UMNO's first elections held in November 2002 would not have had a good start. The *pro-tem* head, Azalina Othman Said, was not only challenged by several contenders but was also alleged to have committed acts of corruption as well as accused of being a lesbian. All of these were never substantiated. These insinuations were eventually quelled because detractors were unable to win the support of the party leaders, namely the president and his deputy, to pursue the charges to any length.

Forming a new women's wing to draw in more women supporters for UMNO was also meant to deal a blow to Parti Islam Se Malaysia (PAS – Islamic Party of Malaysia). As PAS's policies are most easily challenged when it comes to women's rights, Puteri UMNO was to serve as the contrast to PAS's notion of women's political participation. Instead of treating women as silent party workers, UMNO would be the opposite of PAS. Young women within UMNO would even be the beacon of its reform agenda. Instead of 'scaring away' women with stern Islamic reprimands, Puteri UMNO would present itself as the caring face of freedom for women. Furthermore, it would not only be given equal status as the other wings, it would be showcased as evidence of UMNO's success at embracing reform. It even became necessary for UMNO to invent an image of the 'new Malay woman'.

When Puteri UMNO was in its early stage of formation, silent and subliminal propaganda through popular novels and films was heavily used to sway the Malay subconscious into accepting this new portrayal.[11] It also quickly appropriated the ideals spelled out by feminist NGOs. It liberally adopted the Women's Agenda for Change (WAC) initiated by women's NGOs as its mission, by stating that it is 'our agenda together as women' (Puteri UMNO, 2001: 12). The three approaches of Puteri UMNO were spelt out as education; service and health; and wellness. Under education, almost the whole of its mission is carved around the adoption of WAC. This may even go against the grain of its stated vision and manifesto, which is largely to limit the wing's membership to Malay women and more importantly to 'help UMNO in all elections and ensure Malay dominance in Malaysia'.[12]

Both Wanita UMNO and Puteri UMNO are concerned about projecting an image which highlights their responsiveness to Islam. For example in 2001, Wanita UMNO even had to state in print that one of its aspirations was to create a society that will have a national administrative system based on the sovereignty of laws based on the Qu'ran and *Hadith* (Sayings of the Prophet).[13] Whether it is purely rhetorical rather than practical, UMNO as a party is cognizant of the need to place Islam in the foreground of its political agenda. Similarly, Puteri UMNO uses the Islamic justification (words of the Qu'ran and *Hadith*) to encourage its members to do charity work.[14] Increasingly the party measures its survival by the extent it is able to counter the claims and practice of Islam touted by the Islamic-based opposition party PAS. But the 2004 general election proved that PAS has had to take the UMNO route by fielding ten women candidates.

Wanita UMNO did not start out as a religious movement but found itself adapting to a changing circumstance brought about by the gradual but forceful influence of Islamizing forces. For example, in line with UMNO's backing of an Islamization agenda, the women's wing had to incorporate this factor into the reconstruction of its image. Not unexpectedly, the issue of veiling eventually became a controversy. At UMNO's 10th General Assembly in 2000, pressures from the prevailing Islamic 'upper hand' forced a resolution to make it mandatory for Wanita UMNO members to wear the headscarf (though not necessarily full veiling) at all party annual meetings.

Resistance still remains strong among some diehard 'modern' members. Ironically, the one who seems most recalcitrant in abiding by this directive is the wing's leader, Rafidah Aziz. In official photographs of Wanita UMNO committee members, she is the only one who has remained unveiled. This contradiction can be interpreted in many ways. Among these is that there is really no inflexible conception or prescription as to who can rightly lead the women's group. However, lip-service to the norms of a pervasive Islam is observed for political expediency.

While modernization and economic progress has been the staple mission of UMNO, it has had no choice but re-fashion its image around Islam to win the support of its predominantly Malay-Muslim constituents. Still, as the leading component party of the ruling coalition, UMNO must also be seen to accommodate non-Muslim interests. Puteri UMNO was meant to convey such a picture – the embrace of modernity and religiosity in a complementary way among the young was emphasized. Party pragmatism led to the use of the message and symbolism of a resurgent Islam in tandem with liberal feminism which could be used to 'reinvent' an old power base.

Further down the spectrum of pragmatism lies the opposition political party Parti Keadilan Nasional (Keadilan, National Justice Party). It was formed as a counterpoint to UMNO at the height of the *Reformasi* movement, by those sympathetic to Anwar's plight including supporters who defected from UMNO. The core member-groups were from two big Islamic NGOs, Angkatan Belia Islam Malaysia (ABIM – Islamic Youth Movement of Malaysia) and Jemaah Islah Malaysia (JIM – Islamic Reform Congregation of Malaysia). The Keadilan founder-members, however, wanted a multiracial party with a dominant Malay base. The party's principles were couched as imbibing universal social justice and Islamic democracy. Given its need to obtain broad-based multiethnic political support, Keadilan was cautious about being identified as an Islamic party, although it would never go far as to proclaim itself a secular party.

In 1999, it joined three other political parties to form the opposition coalition, Barisan Alternatif (BA – Alternative Front). However, in late 2001, the fabric of BA unity was torn when the Democratic Action Party withdrew due to differences with PAS over plans to implement an Islamic state in Malaysia. As a consequence of this, as well as public fatigue over the inability of the BA to effect change over the Anwar issue, the appeal of Keadilan as a viable 'middle' party began to wane.

Another of Keadilan's problems was related to its leadership. The experience of having to build coalitions and alliances with core member groups with divergent interests was something that its leaders never had to attempt previously, hence now resulting in tensions and crises. Since the party was founded on a multiracial platform it was not possible for the two main NGO member groups, ABIM and JIM, to function as they did before. The whole question of Islamization had to be reconceptualized, given that Keadilan's aim was to try to solicit cross-ethnic and cross-religious support. The fallout of *Reformasi* had already forced many of the member groups to think beyond confining their struggle to a mono-ethnic constituency. But to adopt this principle at a pragmatic level was much harder than what was envisaged.

At the first party election, the ABIM and JIM camps competed for control but this ultimately resulted in the ABIM faction withdrawing. Feminist women, meanwhile, found themselves in an ambivalent position; they had to comply with a conservative Islamic stance on women (promoted by the Islamic NGOs within the party) as well as support a more liberal and moderate Islam (to appease the non-Muslim constituents).[15] But unlike UMNO, Keadilan was not able to conjoin the two conflicting interests to its advantage. There are many reasons for this. The structure of the authoritarian state has cut off just about any outlet for such a possibility. Lack of resources, limited access to the media and judicial intervention, and police action against its campaign to win supporters have all been affected to deny the party a democratic space to compete equally with parties such as UMNO. Ultimately all of these disadvantages crippled its ability to sustain the support of voters and resulted in Keadilan's dismal performance in the 2004 general election. The party only managed to retain one parliamentary seat, which was contested by party head, Wan Azizah Wan Ismail.

Keadilan's contribution to UMNO's revival has been to serve as a wake-up call. When Keadilan was formed at the height of *Reformasi*, it attracted the support of large numbers of youth. At the time Anwar's teenage daughter, Nurul Izzah, was centre-staged as a prominent political icon. In no small way she and her mother, Wan Azizah, became the focus of attention for the mobilization of youth and women into the party. UMNO read this as a 'danger signal' and responded very swiftly by concentrating its reform strategies upon youths. The formation of Puteri UMNO can be read as a specific manoeuvre to steal the thunder from Nurul Izzah and Wan Azizah.

UMNO's material resources paved the way for Puteri UMNO's rapid entrenchment in society. Within a year of its launch in 2001 it was already able to establish branches in every state (except Sarawak) where UMNO has control. It does not come as a surprise that young women have been drawn into the party – for reasons ranging from direct monetary and social rewards to guarantees of future employment, as well as belonging to an institution that has renewed its call for ethnic pride. The early initiators of Puteri UMNO were hopeful that young people hitherto detached from UMNO's historical promise of *Ketuanan Melayu* (Malay Dominance) would rediscover the appeal of this slogan.[16]

Helwa ABIM, Wanita JIM and Dewan Muslimat PAS as Islamic communitarians

ABIM, among the earliest Islamic NGOs to spearhead the Islamic resurgence in Malaysia, can be described as a communitarian-oriented movement. It was registered in 1972, led by Anwar in its early years and exerted strong influence over Malay youths in the 1970s. This rising tide of Islamization among educated youths and the urban middle-class drew attention and support away from UMNO's archaic brand of Malay-nationalist politics. Later on, trying to ride the crest of the wave and appropriate the success of the movement, UMNO leaders successfully persuaded Anwar to join UMNO in 1982.

Anwar rose swiftly within the ranks, culminating in his being considered the premier-in-waiting until just months before his fall from grace in 1998. The rise and fall of Anwar is perhaps an iconic reflection of the shifting concerns of elite political actors within the ruling structure. At the time of Anwar's incorporation into the ruling system there was a need to reinvent the relevancy of Malay leadership. Then, Malay nationalism could only be powerfully expressed if it could be couched in alternative symbols. The movement to mitigate or undermine the force of modernization and Westernization provided much of the answer. As such, infusing Islam in politics was an effective national strategy. By the time Anwar was ousted from UMNO, the issue was more than just the question of leadership rivalry between himself and the then party president and Prime Minister, Mahathir Mohamad. That the sacking was done without much injury to the current regime suggests the shifting or waning influence of Islamic idealists and nationalists within the ruling system.

The original structure of ABIM included a women's wing known as Helwa ABIM. One of the first things that occupied its members then was to get Muslim women to adopt the veil, over the objections of some quarters during that period (Khalijah, 1996: 94). Women's early and main role in Helwa ABIM was also to establish a system and network of pre-school education emphasizing Islam in its curriculum. Women ran day-care centres and Islamic kindergartens (TASKI), the first of which were set up in 1975 (Md. Sidin, 1996: 97–8).

By 1974, ABIM had started to lobby the government to reform the education system so that this would be in line with its goals towards Islamization. ABIM's main concern over the education system at the time was that it lacked a moral component and that there was a separation of religious knowledge from the other branches of learning. Hence, it proposed that:

- the subject 'Islamic studies' be made compulsory for all Muslims and non-Muslims in school;
- the number of religious teachers be increased;
- school uniforms for Muslims be changed to reflect an Islamic outlook (from skirts to *sarong* for girls and short pants to long trousers for boys); and
- an Islamic university be eventually established.[17]

It can be said that ABIM was quite successful at getting the government to establish almost all of the programmes above. The degree of Islamization within the system was increased manifold from the early 1980s. Anwar's political ascendance was both the source as well as the symbol of this 'successful' Islamization.

Within the same end of the spectrum occupied by ABIM is a seemingly similar organization known as JIM. It was founded by students mainly in the science fields who had completed their tertiary education abroad under government scholarship. JIM may actually be seen to rival ABIM in terms of membership as both were then soliciting support from among Malay middle-class professionals. However, by the late 1980s ABIM had come to be considered a mainstream organization. Subsequent spurts of Islamic youth idealism and radicalism could not, therefore, be accommodated within its structure. The formation of JIM filled this political vacuum. JIM has a global network of support, drawing inspiration from the struggles and writings of the proponents of Jemaat e-Islami of Pakistan and the Muslim Brotherhood of Egypt.

JIM advocates say they are building, nurturing and creating an alternative community based on the principles of Islam. The organization is very formal with branches at the central, state and local level, and includes the women's and youth sections. A large proportion of the leadership consists of professionals trained in the medical sciences and engineering. A prime goal is to advocate an Islamic way of life which accommodates modern, progressive values. Hence educational and career pursuits for women, especially in the science and medical fields are viewed with pride.

The ideal of an Islamic community that is in tune with contemporary trends and is innovative in its endeavours for renewal is the principle consistently drummed into JIM members (Mohamed Hatta et al., 2000: 5). In a brochure, the women's wing Wanita JIM expresses 'hope to produce a workforce of *du'ats* who are responsible and caring citizens through welfare work and social service'. The *dakwah* (preaching and missionary work) is done by reaching out to every level of the community with social and educational services. JIM sees itself as building a supportive infrastructure that includes administration, consciousness-raising and study groups, and finance and information technology (for dissemination and networking). JIM aims to make its women's wing prominent at the national level, resulting in a national coalition of Islamic women's groups and networks with other important women's groups. There is also an emphasis on building a corps of specialists in various fields such as health, law, *Syariah* laws, education and entrepreneurship (Mohamed Hatta et al., 2000: 5–10).

Wanita JIM, formed in 1993, functions as an important component of the central organization. It claims to take on an '*umma*-centric' rather than a 'group-centric' approach (Harlina, 2000: 109). The emphasis is on the role of women as an 'integrating' force within families. But the committee makes it a point to highlight that its members are all highly qualified professionals.[18] Much of the advice, counsel and prescription for Muslim women is about being Islamic and modern at the same time. For example, there is concern with achieving discipline through time-management, and with balancing career and family life without sacrificing one for the other (Aliza, 1994: 99–103). The head of Wanita JIM, Harlina Haliza Siraj, explains that the struggle of women in the movement is neither to perpetuate patriarchal systems nor to aspire to a feminism that advocates total liberation. However, she insists that women must nevertheless seek empowerment in the form which existed during the Prophet's time (Harlina, 2000: 107–8). In a way, JIM has come to the realization that it would be futile to stop women from exercising some of their more important rights, notably the freedom to pursue a career.

We now move on to looking at a very important player in the politics of Islamization. PAS as a political party has been in existence longer than JIM or ABIM. It is also clearly more communitarian. As a political party it went through several phases of development. It started out with a nationalist-socialist tradition. It evolved to become more radically fundamentalist when control of the party shifted to Young Turks who were inspired by the Islamic resurgence of the 1970s. Unlike UMNO which is flexible in its pragmatic accommodations and responses, PAS's goals are still confined within a starkly communitarian ideology. It translates Islam in a more rigid way than UMNO would have done. Hence, we use the label 'communitarianism' rather than 'pragmatism' to describe PAS's trajectory, despite it being a political party.

The PAS Dewan Muslimat (Women's Assembly) was formally established on 3 January 1953. This idea was proposed by Haji Zabidi Ali at the party's 1952 Annual General Meeting held in Butterworth (now Seberang Prai). The purpose was to complement the earlier establishment of the party's Dewan Pemuda (Youth Assembly) and Dewan Ulama (Religious Scholars' Assembly). The mission of PAS women is, simply put, to 'build a society of high morals in all spheres of human life and to be the upholder of true Islamic teachings' as well as to 'spawn a generation of *mujahidah* (fighters with a cause) women who are knowledge, charitable, worshipful and will function as the *da'ie* (preachers) of society'. But the main vision is also to 'build an Islamic state in Malaysia through the efforts of Muslim women'.[19]

PAS women's membership in 1992 stood at 11,000 (Dewan Muslimat PAS, 2001: 7). Until recently, all the women leaders had their formal training in the field of Islamic education. The early women leaders received their higher education from Islamic institutions either locally or in Sumatra, Indonesia. Unlike women leaders of the newer Islamic movements such as JIM and ABIM, PAS women did not receive their political education in the West. Just like their male counterparts, their political activism was bred out of a stronger indigenous tradition. However, an increasing number of professional women (including those educated in the West) are now joining and leading the party. The Dewan Muslimat has also established an international network, including links with the International Islamic Women's Union, which has its headquarters in Sudan.

Despite the reticence of PAS women in supporting women's rights, the party as a whole assumed a new sense of importance with *Reformasi*. This was spurred by the realization that women do count in politics, especially in electoral politics. In contesting the 1999 general election, UMNO and its BN partners were left with few strategies to win except by discrediting PAS, their main rival. UMNO used the campaign strategy of painting PAS as unsupportive of women's rights. This immediately put PAS on the defensive. Not only did it have to disabuse voters of the BN allegations, but more importantly it had to demonstrate that its women members were not playing second fiddle within the organization and hierarchy. It was at this point that PAS began to project some of its women leaders in a more prominent way. Those who received the most attention from the media were highly qualified professionals; they had none of the traditional religious qualifications and credentials of the party's previous women leaders.

Two women leaders who gained prominence in the post-1999 period were medical doctors, Lo' Lo' Mohd Ghazali and Siti Mariah Mahmud. At the 2001 PAS Annual Meeting, they were both elected to the Central Committee, with Lo' Lo' also elected as an executive committee member. Going by their public statements they can easily be considered feminists at heart who have chosen to empower women through the route of religion. While this has resulted in a positive image for PAS, the women leaders still face a dilemma when it comes to defining women's role in the party. For one thing, a higher profile for women leaders has brought out the potential divide between Islamic traditionalists and modernists. Both groups profess that their purpose and vision for change is consistent with the professed goals of Islamization as exhorted by the party. However, over several issues, such as on women and *Hudud* (Islamic criminal) laws, the modernists are less prone to take a dogmatic and inflexible line.

There are two areas of potential disagreement between the traditionalists and modernists. One has to do with leadership style within the party. The struggle to get women to be equally recognized within the leadership hierarchy has been reduced to a seemingly petty battle, such as whether or not to allow women to sit on stage alongside male leaders during party conventions. Lo' Lo' spoke openly about this at the 2000 party convention. Because of PAS's determination to prove that it does not discriminate against women, party leaders relented and ruled that all women Central Committee members would be allowed to sit on the stage during meetings. Below the surface lies the larger question of whether PAS is willing to reassess its own deeply entrenched prejudice against a female public and political presence.

But in 2004, the party relented to allow women to contest in the 11th general election – 35 years since it last fielded its first woman candidate, who had won in 1969. If not for the politics of *Reformasi* and the prominent role that liberal feminists played in this phenomenon, and a challenge offered by UMNO, such a turnaround in PAS's principles on women would not have occurred. Of the ten women candidates fielded, two won – Rohani Ibrahim at the state level and Kalthom Othman at parliamentary level. But PAS's refusal to allow women to hold leadership positions in the party remains its stock character even after these results. It was only after much pressure from the media and its rival party UMNO that the PAS-controlled government of Kelantan appointed a woman to its state cabinet – as just a vice-chairperson of the Women, Youth and Sports portfolio.[20]

The other area inviting some dissent between the men and women of PAS has been over the issue of *Hudud* laws. As a whole, PAS women did not openly express disagreement with the enactment of such legislation for Terengganu when it was proposed. However, when the offence of rape was categorized in the same category as adultery in an early draft of the Bill, some PAS women were prepared to oppose this. Under this provision four male witnesses were required to verify a woman's claim that she was raped. There was no recourse to circumstantial evidence. If the survivor became pregnant, this could be turned against her as proof of fornication. Furthermore, if none of her allegations could be substantiated she would be charged for giving false evidence, and liable to 80 lashes of the whip. The outpouring of criticism from a broad spectrum of women's organizations forced the male drafters of the bill to back down and re-classify rape within another set of offences that allows for circumstantial evidence to be accepted as basis of proof.

Islamic feminists

A Malay-Muslim NGO that is in contrast to all the groups described so far is Sisters in Islam, formed in 1993 as a reaction to the escalating climate of Islamic intolerance and closed-mindedness of Islam's spokespersons. This was especially so in terms of reconciling Islam with the tenets of gender equality, human rights and democracy. Zainah Anwar, a founder-member, described the reason for coming together as being initially spurred by the group's 'deep concerns over the injustice women suffered under the implementation of *Syariah* law' (2001: 228). In trying to challenge this sense of injustice the group decided to return to the original source of Islam, which is the Qur'an:

> This questioning and above all, the conviction that Allah could never be unjust, eventually led us to go back to the primary source of the religion, the Qur'an. We felt the urgent need to read the Qu'ran for ourselves and to find out if the text actually supports the oppression and ill-treatment of women.
>
> (Zainah, 2001: 228)

In identifying the three strands of Islam, Zainah situated the cause promoted by Sisters in Islam within a 'precarious middle ground' (2001: 231). The first most open strand of Islam acknowledges that women are entitled to equal rights, such as rights to property, to contract a marriage and to be rid of scourges such as female infanticide. The extreme strand of Islam is the obscurantist strand, where the dominant belief is for the total segregation of women and men, to the extent of confining women to the home and denying schooling to girls. Hence, the middle ground that Sisters in Islam professes is based on legitimacy involving the critical re-examination and reinterpretation of Islamic texts so that an Islamic tradition advocating women's rights, human rights, democracy and modernity can be invoked (Zainah, 2001: 231).

The first realization is that the process of interpretation and codification of laws has all along been dominated by male jurists and scholars. This has led to the prevalence of a male-biased premise and conception of questions relating to women. The standard argument – and one clung to by communitarian Islamic groups in Malaysia – is that males and females are different. It follows that their roles can only be complementary rather than equal. It is at best a befuddled world-view according to Zainah when groups can think that 'women can work outside the home, but only with the permission of their husbands; women can be doctors but they must not touch male patients; women can be heads of departments in charge of men, but they cannot be in charge at home for they must remain obedient to their husbands' (2001: 231).

Sisters in Islam has played an important role in projecting a 'democratic' Islam when challenging the numerous laws that impinge upon the status of women. Among the more controversial laws that the group has challenged are the *Hudud* enactments adopted by the PAS-led Kelantan government in 1993 and the Terengganu government in 2002. Sisters in Islam was emboldened by high-level government support for their campaign to encourage monogamy among Muslim males, and also from the *Menteri Besar* (Chief Minister) of Selangor, Mohd Khir Toyo, over the proposed amendment to marriage laws to make it difficult for men to take on additional wives. The Minister for Women and Family Development, Shahrizat Abdul Jalil, endorsed the group's call to allow women to become judges of the *Syariah* court. These activities have received much support from the press, which has publicized most of the letters and memoranda issued by the group.

As Sisters in Islam also implicitly receives the backing of the country's highest leadership, they are relatively well protected from the wrath of Islam's extremist factions. Women from PAS, ABIM and JIM were initially more reticent about showing open support for Sisters in Islam but of late have shown some willingness to enter into dialogue with them. Opposition groups and some sections of the civil society show ambivalence towards Sisters in Islam because of the group's apparent close ties with the present establishment. Many see the government – which is 'liberal' when it comes to Islam – as having a poor record of observing genuine democratic and human rights practice in its treatment of political dissidents. Nonetheless, Sisters in Islam has consistently espoused the norms of equality and democracy and have been critical of repressive laws such as the Internal Security Act 1960 (ISA), although their 'patrons' have not endorsed such values.

But this may not be unique to Malaysia. Authoritarian regimes in places such as Peru and Iran are not necessarily averse to progressive women's rights and have even cultivated women's support by granting gender equality laws and institutional support for their mobility, albeit while disregarding political rights (Kazemi, 2000; Blondet, 2002). An alliance with progressive feminist groups provides benefits for an authoritarian regime. It prevents more damage to its battered political legitimacy and disarms a full-scale attack by its detractors.

Responses to gender reforms

The use of women's issues, either in support of liberal equality or in establishing Islamic strictures, has proved effective in propping up the credibility of governments as and when the situation demands it. For example, during the 1980s and early 1990s, the government used the Islamic discourse heavily to counter civil society groups which challenged some of its more anti-democratic policies.[21] The support for the state was then built on the back of an Islamic-Malay consensus which depended on the state for its Islamization agenda. In 1994, there was foot-dragging on the part of the state to pass the Domestic Violence Bill initiated by the feminist lobby. At the behest of an Islamic counter-lobby, conditional clauses were inserted to accommodate Islamic religious rights before the bill was tabled in parliament.[22] This of course had the effect of watering down the full intention of the legislation as conceived by feminist groups.

Even when the bill was passed, women representatives of Islamic bodies expressed their disagreement over the legality of the law because it was seen to supersede Islamic family law. In 1994, women members of ABIM voiced concern over the law because it did not differentiate the legal jurisdiction of Muslim women from that of non-Muslim women (Rahmah, 1996). Their point was that issues affecting Muslim women and their status within the family could not be governed by a civil act, as only *Syariah* family law has such jurisdiction (Zaitoon, 1996). They argued that *Syariah* has provisions to deal with the issue of spousal violence. The choice of language was also a source of contention, with the term 'family violence' preferred over 'domestic violence' and 'violence against women'. The connotation 'family' would seemingly cover all members of the household rather than focussing attention on unequal gender relations between women and men, if the term 'domestic violence' is used.

In the early 1990s, certain sections of the Islamic lobby and the state were mutually supportive of each other and their stance against implementation of the Domestic Violence Act reflected this alliance. But by the late 1990s, the state made an about-turn. During the phase of *Reformasi* there was much opposition from Islamic groups towards the Mahathir government. The state then readily used the notion of 'women's empowerment' to counter the challenge of Islamists. In the post-*Reformasi* period, the 'woman question' was used to challenge Islamic policies that were unfair to women. This was also done to appease the more liberal groups so that they would be supportive of the regime. For example, the challenge mounted by the federal government against the Terengganu government's enactment of the *Hudud* laws was wholly crafted on using the issue of justice and equality for women, in order to stall implementation.

As a reaction, PAS was forced to deal with the issue of women's electoral representation in its promotion of Islamic democracy. It was afraid of losing the support of liberals, which was needed to raise party credibility. By then, PAS was almost confident of capturing power at federal level, hence its realization of the importance of accommodating a more plural constituency. It was because of this change in political balance that the Mahathir government had to paint an 'anti-women' picture of PAS, while conjuring up the idea that UMNO was different. If truth be told, the state has not felt seriously threatened by women's demands over the years. Demands for it to discard its authoritarian policies and anti-democratic stances would have been far harder for it to consider.

Despite feminism's cross-cutting ethnic, class and religious implication and appeal, there has still not been enough of a bridge to bring middle-class Islamic women and feminist groups together. Islamic women are themselves split over many issues. Issues suggesting that women may be victimized by polygyny practices, restrictive dress codes or unequal punishments (as in *Hudud* laws) have not been taken up for reform.

This could be because the divine source, the Qu'ran, is silent on the question of rape, thus allowing for more flexible interpretation of the offence. In contrast, wife-beating is literally spelled out in the Qu'ran and often times interpreted as being condoned by divine revelations. Similarly, edicts on the issue of the headscarf, polygamy for men and unequal gender-based punishments under Hudud laws are adopted literally to become law and interpreted to be mandatory for Muslims to obey.

Although feminist groups (including multiethnic women's organizations) were the ones who strongly protested against the original rape provisions of the *Hudud* laws, some PAS women welcomed the basis for the objection. They even joined the sea of protest surrounding the issue, but would not go all the way to support the feminist protestors on every issue which involved discrimination against women. For example, they did not register any disquiet against the discriminatory requirement of only allowing male Muslim witnesses to testify in the Islamic court for offences under the *Hudud* laws.

There was little support as well for a campaign against polygamy. The campaign, launched in 2003 by Sisters in Islam and 11 women's organizations under the coalition of 'Women's Rights in Islam', called on men to strictly observe a monogamous marriage and to shun the right to polygyny as advocated by Islam.[23] Prominent Islamic women's organizations such as Wanita JIM, Helwa ABIM and the PAS Dewan Muslimat were all opposed to the idea of the campaign. Wanita JIM even issued a statement to condemn it, citing the role of polygyny as a solution to childless marriages. There was also fear that a campaign to denounce polygyny as a male right would cast aspersions over the integrity of Islam.[24] But the state was supportive, as symbolically portrayed by the then Deputy Prime Minister's wife, Endon Mahmood, in launching the campaign.

On what issues do Islamic women's groups unite? The raising of issues involving VAW and rape or physical harm will usually result in such acts being roundly condemned. Among some PAS women there has even been a willingness to oppose the provisions on rape as initially specified in the *Hudud* laws in Terengganu. This could be because liberal feminist groups have elevated the issue of VAW into a mainstream concern. During the 1980s and 1990s, only a few women's groups were involved in the campaigns against rape and violent crimes against women. By 2000, most women's wings of the BN component parties had made VAW a priority of their political agenda. In spite of the indifference of most Islamic women's groups, a new discourse and consciousness on violent crimes against women has been germinated.

Tensions and contradictions in political Islam

This section discusses some of the tensions and contradictions of political Islam and what effects these have had on women. If we look at the historical trend of political Islam's ascendance, we can see signs of its own undoing. From the time of its inception around the mid-1970s, the resurgent Islamic movement began shifting from a radical counter-voice of Malay youths to the last bastion of cultural conservatism in today's system. There remain pockets of confounding practices that seek to retain the extremely unequal gender relations within society. For example, the re-born Darul Arqam (House of Arqam) in the form of the Rufaqa Corporation has persistently tried to inform its members that polygamy is not only condoned by Islam but is a highly noble and desirable duty that should be practised by men for various reasons. Polygamy, according to members of the Rufaqa Corporation, was a means to enlarge and propagate the Islamic *umma*, acting as a great exponential multiplier of the Islamic population if it were practised by every generation down the line.[25] Women themselves are made to be the spokespersons of this practice.

Islamic and patriarchal forces that are determined to mitigate the march of feminist politics are still relentless, although their current tone is more defensive than self-righteous. Feminism is still considered an avenue which pits women against men, and women are still seen to be biologically and emotionally weaker than men (Abdul Rahim Abdul Rashid, 1998). PAS politicians continue to harp on the idea that women are not allowed by religious injunctions to hold public office as heads of state and in the judiciary. Then Terengganu *Menteri Besar*, Abdul Hadi Awang, said menstruation cycles and pregnancies would affect women's ability to cope with stress and pressure of work in critical professions.[26] Islamic literature on the issue of women's leadership abounds, peppered with authoritative verses from the Qu'ran and *Hadith* (Sayings of the Prophet), driving home the point that women by nature and God's command are not allowed to hold high public office.[27]

But even within PAS the contestation between openness and preservation of status quo goes on. For example, while some accommodation had been made to allow women to contest posts, the election of the leader of the Dewan Muslimat, Fatimah Zainab Ibrahim, reflected the persistence of Old Guard politics. Fatimah is the wife of the leader of the party's conservative Majlis Ulama (Council of Religious Scholars). At the time of her election in 2001 this signalled a reinstatement of 'backwardness' for women in the party.[28] But the latest election of the women's wing office bearers in 2003 showed that the more liberal and open faction of the women's groups has recaptured the leadership. Religious teacher and former Kelantan senator Kalthom Othman received the support of party progressives such as Lo' Lo' and Azizah Khatib. All this shows that a contest is still raging within the party, with women actually expressing a sharper appetite for reform than men.[29] Kalthom also won the Pasir Puteh parliamentary seat in the 2004 general election.

A continuing tension within the Islamic movement has always been the contradictory and ambivalent understanding of Islam's position on women. This has actually been capitalized upon by both orthodox forces and liberals to strengthen their authoritative voice. From one perspective, the fact that women cannot agree to take up a common 'pro-woman' stance may reflect the successful invocation of the Islamic literalist tradition by religious authorities and scholars. But these differences can also be viewed as denoting the vibrancy of a plural intellectual and cultural tradition allowing room for transformation. Social circumstances and imagination are mutable features of human existence and 'the participatory revolution now sweeping the Muslim world has, for example, provoked fierce debates over questions of Islam's social meaning and by whose authority it is defined' (Hefner, 2000: 10).

Muslim women in the more communitarian-oriented movements did prove that they could readily enter into an alliance with liberal feminists during the period of *Reformasi* mobilization (Tan and Ng, 2003: 113). The 'political opportunity structure' (Ray and Korteweg, 1999) or window of opportunity provided by *Reformasi* engendered the formation of new networks and alliances. A more multicultural approach to the understanding of political Islam and its implications for women was recently initiated by a secular, non-Islamic NGO such as the Women's Development Collective. In 2002, it organized a regional meeting themed 'Islam, Politics and Women: What Identities? Whose Interests? A Multicultural Dialogue'.[30] Such new modes of challenges proved threatening to both the old ruling alignment as well as to the religious orthodoxy. But the period of *Reformasi* was short-lived and the destabilization of authority became a fleeting phenomenon. We have yet to see the overturning of old politics and practices by a united women's movement comprising liberals as well as feminists from all religious faiths.

Nevertheless, PAS's new strategy of prominently profiling its women leaders and the establishment of Puteri Umno to enhance the credibility of patrimonial and male-centric political parties have been significant developments. It shows that there is pressure to reform the role of women within Malay-Muslim organizations that were hitherto only appendages of a larger patriarchy-centric system. There is pressure to revise the role of women, from one of passive supporters to one of active defenders, even reformers, of their organizations. This could be due to the breakdown of the consensual

Malay voice as the basis for perpetuating a Malay-dominant ruling system. During the pre-*Reformasi* political phase the consensual Malay voice had been taken for granted and always assured. Gender was practically a non-issue. Today, it is not easy for PAS to reconcile issues of group rights when there is a pervasive clamour for gender equality. Questions as to what should take precedence – individual freedom or group-compliance rights – will remain a contentious choice for members. Even as they are convinced about wanting to reclaim a communal identity they will also have to deal with the question of individual rights (Deveaux, 2000; Phillips, 2001).

Finally we can also see emerging contradictions and tensions in relation to political Islam's role in defining the Malay-ethnic identity. The implications on gender are not immediately apparent. However, a crack in any authoritative structure may also spell the undermining of an entrenched patriarchal order, with which political Islam is associated. Recently, the intellectual and social legitimacy of Malay-Islamic hegemony, predicated around the 'symbolic capital' of a divine and unquestionable Islam, has become more vulnerable to new challenges.

The terror attacks of September 11, 2001 in the United States caused the Malaysian government to act almost immediately to distance itself from a strident Islam. For example, in 2001 the government quickly detained many Muslim activists without trial under the ISA for alleged links with militant groups. In 2002, the government announced that it would cut off financial allocation and subsidies for privately run Islamic schools, a move that could prevent a parallel Islamic education system from flourishing. Islamic schooling has been the backbone of the *Dakwah* movement in which women played leading roles, especially as pre-school teachers and instructors. Another key policy – to replace the national language (Malay) with English in teaching two subjects in primary schools – has deflated the sense of a supreme Malay-Islamic national identity. This silent catharsis has weakened the foundations of Malay dominance in the political system. Perhaps this will also overturn the unequal gender politics within Islam.

Conclusion

Several structural factors combined with opportunities for Muslim women to assert their role as political agents of their movements have made it economically and politically impossible to contain their mobility. It cannot be discounted, for example, that the experience of Malaysia's economic and political transformation has undermined the conception of women being primarily suited to the domestic and private realm. Trends in economic development have resulted in the greater relative proportion of Muslim women in the workforce. The size of university enrolment among women in tertiary educational institutions has also exceeded that of men.[31]

This chapter examined how the participation of Malay-Muslim women in key organizations has been crucial in balancing the discourse between conservatism and liberalism. Malay-Muslim women participate in a diverse range of movements, from the pragmatist to the communitarian-oriented to one that is essentially liberal-feminist in character. If not for the diversity of such ideological and practical pursuits it would have been more difficult to counter the hegemonic power of a male-centric political Islam.

It was the experience and consequence of *Reformasi* which indirectly (though not insignificantly) stimulated the questioning and re-questioning of political Islam. At a time when the ruling regime was being threatened by opposition forces the women's movement was given prominence to act as the Achilles heel of political Islam's ascendance. To a large extent, the women's movement was successful in tempering the rise of political Islam in its patriarchal intention. However, there were other mediating factors too. A strong regime bent on not giving up its identity and purpose as a developmentalist state had actually given the liberal women's movement a boost. Given this, it is not certain if Malay-Muslim women's organizations can ever function as an autonomous entity or be a revolutionizing force. With the exception of Sisters in Islam, they all fall within the ambit of being a directed movement (Molyneux, 1998: 229). Yet, even an organization like the Sisters in Islam must depend on the strong backing of a secular-developmentalist state for its effectiveness in pushing for a new social consciousness. To say that feminist organizations were merely pawns in the agenda of the authoritarian-developmental state in its containment of oppositional forces would be unfair to those behind the movements. But to say that feminist movements had been successful in their engagement with the state would also be an exaggeration. Nevertheless, any form of a liberalizing Islam would benefit feminism.

Thus far the discussions and analysis have focused on how feminism and the women's movement have taken up the issues of VAW and political Islam, and how the state has responded to this situation. As we move to the next chapter we will see that other concerns have also been important in the shaping of Malaysian feminism. Capitalism has been an important driver of the Malaysian economy and therefore has had a profound impact on women's lives. Despite this, the women's movement has not adequately dealt with the issues of women's employment, specifically the concerns of women workers. Chapter 6 examines why the rights of women workers are inadequately addressed and highlights new challenges that have surfaced in the context of globalization.

6 Muted struggles

Challenges of women workers

> The manual dexterity of the oriental female is famous the world over. Her hands are small and she works fast with extreme care. Who, therefore, could be better qualified by nature and inheritance to contribute to the efficiency of a bench-assembly production line than the oriental girl? No need for a Zero defects program here! By nature, they 'quality control' themselves.[1]

This oft-quoted offer of the dexterous Oriental female to capitalist production from an investment brochure of the Malaysian government in the 1970s clearly defines the context in which Malaysian women workers are regarded – as mere objects to attract foreign investment who can be easily moulded by the dictates of industry. Although today this position has changed to some extent, the perception of Malaysian women workers as malleable and secondary labour remains. The policy of export-oriented industrialization fuelled by foreign direct investment continues to be the order of the day, leading to the influx of women workers into the manufacturing sector.

However, despite their immense contribution to the country's economic development the concerns of women workers are relatively invisible, compared with the various gender issues voiced by the women's movement. The inability of women industrial workers to organize is as much due to the impediments created by the state as to the various mechanisms of control and compliance set up by capital, and which divide and fragment the multi-ethnic working-class in Malaysia.

We argue that instead of being a protector of labour rights, the state is actually a mediator of capital within the prerogatives of neo-liberal economic globalization. Through the years, it has enacted a battery of laws to incapacitate and prevent workers from organizing. Ethnic divisions have permeated the working-class resulting in women workers perceiving themselves as belonging to their respective ethnic communities rather than to a unified social class. It is difficult for labour groups to organize them; in addition, only a sprinkling of NGOs actually take up the issue of labour rights. Hence, the voices of women workers are largely unheard.

Capital and state collude to contain and 'empower' workers at the same time, with capital utilizing a variety of management strategies to ensure the flexibilization of labour in the new labour regime under the era of globalization. Furthermore the opening up of the country to migrant workers has lent a new dimension that has further fragmented the labour movement. It has added another layer to the labour hierarchy which is already predicated upon divisiveness along an ethnic, class, national and a 'us' versus 'them' identity; today, migrant workers make up the new underclass.

This chapter attempts to uncover the reasons why the struggles of women workers have been generally neglected by both state and society, despite the prevalence of many pressing issues – from wages, health and safety and lack of unionization to demands for training, better maternity benefits and child-care facilities. It will also address current issues linked to globalization, the 'knowledge' (or k-) economy and female migrant workers, which raise concerns for the future of work for women in Malaysia.

The first section examines the impact of the country's development policies on the socio-economic conditions of women workers. Following this is a discussion of the barriers against organizing women workers, with a focus on the electronics industry and the protracted struggle waged by the pioneer in-house union for electronics workers, which remains unresolved until today. The final section looks at the challenges ahead, particularly those encountered by migrant and trafficked women in Malaysia and the region.

From industrialization to the k-economy

Since the 1980s the acceleration of neo-liberal globalization, particularly economic liberalization, has transformed the pattern of production and employment for women in Southeast Asia. Ghosh (1999) has identified three phases of this period of economic globalization:

- the phase of integration based on trade and foreign direct investment associated with rapidly increasing exports;
- the phase of financial integration; and
- the phase of crisis and adjustment, which is also associated with further liberalization.

In line with these development stages, the Malaysian economy grew by leaps and bounds from the 1980s right through the mid-1990s. Indeed, in an era of unparalleled growth in the Asia-Pacific region, Malaysia stood out as a success story with an average growth rate of 8.5 per cent per annum, making it one of the world's fastest growing economies. Focusing on export-oriented industrialization as the path towards development, the Sixth Malaysia Plan noted that:

This new approach to industrialization will emphasise the development of export-oriented, high value-added, high technology industries ...

the objective of the industrial policy is to move towards capital-intensive and technologically sophisticated industries producing better quality and competitive products that are integrated with the markets of the developed countries ... and in the long run, industrial development will emphasise greater automation and other labour-saving production processes to reduce labour utilization.

(Government of Malaysia, 1991: 137–9)

Ten years after this major policy pronouncement, the government had to alter its development course, particularly in the wake of the regional financial crisis in 1997, which saw the economy plummeting to almost zero growth in the late 1990s and for the first time in 20 years, the emergence of a labour surplus economy. While the economy has since reportedly made a turnaround, it has certainly not matched the pre-crisis growth rate. As a result, the Third Outline Perspective Plan (2001–10) determined that a knowledge-based economy, made urgent by the increasing pace of globalization and liberalization, would be the saviour of the economic impasse, as it 'will provide the platform to sustain a rapid rate of economic growth and enhance international competitiveness' (Government of Malaysia, 2001a: 119). Accordingly, the k-economy Master Plan was released in September 2002, defining a knowledge-based economy as one where knowledge, creativity and innovation play an increasing and important role in generating and sustaining growth.

What has been the impact of these policies on women? The shift towards export-led industrialization as a key development strategy has undoubtedly brought a wave of women workers into the labour force, dubbed the 'feminization' of labour. Industrialization in Malaysia (and in many developing nations) has been as much women-led as export-led. The labour force participation rate of women increased from 37 per cent in 1970 to 43.5 per cent in 1995 and 44.5 per cent in 2000 as documented in the Eighth Malaysia Plan (Government of Malaysia, 2001b). Today, about 85 per cent of women workers are in the manufacturing and services sector, with the majority located in urban areas. In manufacturing, they make up the bulk of production operators in the electronics and textiles and garments industries – jobs that are generally labour-intensive and low skilled. Indeed the so-called success of the Malaysian economy, where the electrical and electronics industries have consistently been the major export earners, has been built on the back of low-waged women labour. From just four companies with 577 employees in 1970, the electronics sector expanded to 850 companies with 321,700 workers in 1998. The sector now employs 27 per cent of the total manufacturing workforce, the majority of who are women.

With the modernization of the economy, women are slowly inching their way up to higher-paying occupations,[2] but the majority are still in unskilled or semi-skilled jobs with few prospects for upward mobility. What are their key concerns, particularly in this era of unbridled global competition and the shift towards the k-economy? Will there be gain or only more pain for women workers?

Women and work: gains and pains

Subordinate position

Although more women are earning an income, they are basically located in low-skilled jobs, in labour-intensive operations and in clerical and secretarial positions, rather than in the ranks of chief executive officers, managers or supervisors. For example in the manufacturing sector in 1993, only 15.8 per cent of the managerial and professional category comprised women, compared to 65.9 per cent and 57.9 per cent in the clerical and production categories (Aminah, 1999: 16). Similarly in the public sector, women are severely under-represented in top management positions; the majority serve as supportive or lower-level staff such as clerks, teachers, nurses and manual workers.

Women also earn less than men for the same type of job in some sectors in the private sector. Latest available figures recorded in 1992 reveal that the average monthly income of women factory operators was RM267 compared to RM493 for men operators. Gender disparity in wages was also seen in the hotel industry where women managers and assistant managers earned RM100 and RM300 less than their respective male counterparts. And to add insult to injury, although women are the main cooks at the household level, women chief cooks earned RM500 less than male chief cooks in the services sector (Ludher, 2001: 96).

Recent production trends arising from economic globalization are especially worrying for women workers. Catchwords such as labour flexibility, outsourcing and subcontracting are becoming the norm in managing production as firms compete in the global marketplace. With economic restructuring and an accelerated response to the 1997 financial crisis, firms are combining formal factory work with informal, sub-contracting and home-based work. Labour flexibility is increasingly being practised where:

- the fixed core of workers is reduced while non-essential work is outsourced to other firms;
- workers might be retrenched or offered 'voluntary separation schemes' (VSS) and then rehired but on lower wages and with less employment security;
- waged workers are replaced with unpaid family workers, mainly women;
- temporary, contract and/or casual workers are hired, increasingly by external agents or sub-contracted companies and paid on a daily basis.

Through the mechanism of flexibilization, workers have been made vulnerable and easily exploited due to the uncertainty of tenure. This has ensured benefits for owners of capital who are able to cut costs tremendously. In her study of women Chinese home-based sub-contractors in the garment industry, Ludher (2001: 337–8) pointed out that:

> Home-based sub-contractors offer tremendous advantages to the garment industry to ensure its competitiveness and flexibility. They offer chameleon-like adaptability to the industry to respond to the seasonal nature with its changing style and fashion. They offer their skills gained from experiences without the industry having to invest to train them. By being casual, the home sub-contractors are paid on piece-rate basis. They provide the industry with numerical and capacity flexibility. By working from home, they remain isolated, atomised and unorganized and are thus, politically weak. They receive no social or medical benefits and protective measures neither for themselves nor their family members. ... The home-based sub-contractors become prey to the exploitative and extractive nature of the garment industry.

In recent years bank workers, many of them women, have been going through similar turbulence as a result of the green light given in mid-2001 by Bank Negara (the Central Bank) for the banking industry to outsource certain functions. The banking sector's union seems unable to counter this move, as it is caught up in internal squabbling over leadership. Perhaps predicting the lean years ahead, a news report at the end of 2001 had this to say:

> Four out of 10 workers in the banking sector are facing the New Year with trepidation. They are facing the prospect of losing their jobs as banks turn to outsourcing non-core operations to third parties. Most of the staff affected are those providing backroom services and in the income range of RM1,000 to RM2,500.[3]

In one prominent domestic bank, three departments – the call centres, the cheque clearing and the payment processing departments – are being outsourced to subsidiary companies. Most of these new companies do not enable union protection and offer less lucrative jobs, as a result of which workers are experiencing high levels of anxiety. A female clerk who has been working for 15 years lamented that 'no one seems to care'. In addition, banks are simultaneously capitalizing on such deregulatory and cost-cutting measures by hiring contract and temporary staff. The same news report recorded the complaint of a bank worker in a foreign bank, which re-hired 30–50 per cent of the staff in his department as temporary or contract workers:

> One day they offer VSS to the staff and the next day they offer jobs to contract staff. It seems more like the banks are looking for cheap labour.[4]

Health and safety problems

With increasing computerization at the workplace, women workers suffer a whole range of health and safety problems associated with use of visual display units (VDUs). This is also because women are not only disproportionately represented at the clerical and production levels, but many also work longer hours on the keyboard compared to male employees. In a 1991–3 study of over 1,140 employees in the services sector, 70–80 per cent of women workers at the semi-skilled and lower-skill levels (clerks, telephone operators, VDU operators) suffered 'real' or 'extreme' problems in relation to their eyes and musculoskeletal system (Cardosa and Wan Fauziah, 1994: 72–3). This situation has not changed ten years down the road. A 2003 study of 200 workers conducted by the National Institute of Occupational Safety and Health reported that 77 per cent of women office workers suffered eye strain compared to 63 per cent of men, and 69 per cent of women office staff suffered excessive fatigue from using computers for long periods compared to 59 per cent of male workers.

Women workers in the electronics industry – a supposedly 'clean' industry – are not spared either. Because it is a chemical-intensive industry, women workers in the electronics sector suffer myriad health problems due to long-term exposure to chemical hazards. In addition, the nature of the labour processes and work organization requires a high level of discipline leading to heightened stress among the workers, especially those on the production floor who have to meet ever increasing productivity quotas. They share their pains in their own voices (Chee and Subramaniam, 1994):[5]

Rani: I suffer from bad headaches, eye tearing and eye pain. There are two kinds of solder – one has too much of fumes. The solder fumes are so bad, they come straight into my eyes.

Sal: The compound that we handle is dangerous. On the container itself it is written that you should not breathe it in. When you touch it, it causes itch and rashes. In the mold room the environment is hot and dusty. It is supposed to be a clean room but it's so dirty . . . One woman died of lung cancer in that department. Then we heard that four workers who had gone back to their *kampung* [village] also died.

Mani: Now they are checking to see how fast I can work. I can only do 3,000 a day, but when the technical engineer stands there to watch me, I can do so much more, maybe 1,000 more. Now our target has been increased from 10,000 to 16,000. It takes six to seven minutes to do [one process] but now I am told to do it in two minutes.

Sexual harassment at work

Sexual harassment in the workplace has become a serious problem too, with adverse consequences for women workers especially now that their numbers have increased in the labour force. Sexual harassment is defined as unwanted and unwelcome sexual conduct which often leads to a hostile and intimidating work environment. Research conducted from 2000 to 2001 by the All Women's Action Society (AWAM) and the Women's Development Collective (WDC) found that 35 per cent of the 1,483 respondents from six pioneer companies had experienced one or more forms of sexual harassment in their workplace.[6] A significantly higher proportion of female than male respondents indicated that they had experienced such harassment which ranged from dirty jokes (verbal) to visual and physical harassment. As a result of such harassment, many of the victims felt that their personal security was being threatened. Those interviewed reported feelings of fear, confusion, shock and anger. Often these feelings extended into their work environment – they could not concentrate on their work, in particular when the harassers were their superiors (Ng et al., 2003).

Women who are sexually harassed are afraid to complain for various reasons. Sometimes they endure verbal harassment which is often perceived to be part of the work culture. As conveyed by a woman officer:

> If I report to the management about the wolf-whistles and the dirty pictures in e-mails, I think management won't take action. They might blame us instead. Later the whole station would know and I'd feel embarrassed and I'll have to go on transfer. Better to report to the police than to the office if it is serious.
>
> (Ng et al., 2003: 99)

This statement is revealing because victims of sexual harassment often feel guilty and blame themselves for the harassment. They are also afraid that they will be put on 'trial' for kicking up a fuss and will be the ones ultimately punished, rather than the perpetrator. Again, even if they complain, many of them are afraid that the complaints procedure in the company will not protect them and instead there will be retaliation. At the end of the day, they are forced to quit their jobs, which is a loss to the company. In spite of all these barriers, complaints have been lodged, particularly when victims were physically harassed.

Although the Malaysian government has adopted a Code of Practice with the laudable intention of eradicating sexual harassment in the workplace, this does not have the legal force to oblige all companies to adopt sexual harassment policies. As a result, sexual harassment, with all its detrimental consequences, continues unabated.

Low level of unionization

The establishment of unions is critical in representing the interests of workers. However, the rate of unionization in Malaysia is abysmal. The latest available figures from 2000 disclose that out of a workforce of about 10 million, only 734,037 workers are unionized. This represents a mere seven per cent of the total, revealing the weakness of the trade union movement in claiming to be the genuine voice of labour. Furthermore, although women comprise 36.2 per cent (265,722) of total trade union membership, less than one per cent of women are represented at the leadership level, suggesting a patriarchal hierarchy in the trade union movement. It has been pointed out that there is lack of support from the male-dominated trade union leadership to train women leaders (Rohana, 1988).

As summed up in an interview with an activist involved in organizing women workers:

> Women's productive and reproductive issues are so intertwined. These include childcare support, health, sexual harassment, and upward mobility in the workplace. The sad thing here is that these are not considered workers' issues at all even by the trade unions … These unions tend to focus only on bread-and-butter issues and of course within that there's no place for women's issues.
>
> (Cited in Cabrera-Balleza, 1999: 27)

Malaysian unions are indeed more focused on bread-and-butter issues than workers' democratic rights, and will participate actively in collective bargaining agreements for their share of the company's economic cake. Even the notion of setting up unions is limited to workers who are allowed by their companies to organize. Gender issues are a low priority; if at all considered, the tendency is for gender to be subsumed under economic demands or to be influenced by male-dominated ideological constructs of the role of women. Research in a major telecommunications company showed that the union leaders still viewed women primarily as homemakers; as such, training activities for the female members revolved around home economics and health-related classes. There were only four women out of a total of 64 executive committee members in the union (Ng, 1999: 163).

It is difficult for women to be active in union activities because the bulk of women workers are found in free trade zones (FTZ), where multinational companies discourage outright the formation of unions. Trade union leadership, even in women-majority workforces, is dominated by men; most women therefore find the atmosphere for their participation far from conducive. They also face practical problems, including not being able to find household help to enable them to participate more fully in activities. Those who are active sometimes have to deal with resistance from their husbands, who demand that they prioritize their duties and responsibilities at home. This reinforces the patriarchal ideology of women's role in reproductive labour.

One of the major reasons for the low participation rate of women union members is the position of the state towards the unionization of workers in the FTZ. Although there have been attempts to organize electronics unions under a national banner, the government has consistently rejected such applications, grudgingly allowing instead the formation of in-house unions. The nature of state–labour relations is discussed in greater detail in the next section.

The k-economy: closing the gender digital divide?

It is also not clear if the k-economy will bring better prospects for Malaysian labour and women workers. It has been noted by the United Nations that the growing power of the Internet risks widening the digital divide between the world's haves and have-nots, between men and women, young and old, the literate and illiterate, urban and rural dwellers and between those who can and cannot speak English – 80 per cent of all web sites being in English (UNDP, 2001).

The k-economy will need knowledge workers who have access to the wonders of Information and Communication Technologies (ICTs) and who can be flexible as well; that is, workers who are autonomous, empowered to make decisions without supervision, multi-skilled and able to apply their initiative and creativity (Turner, 2002). The development of such 'cultural industries', defined in terms of the content and innovativeness of their work, is a critical element in the growth of the k-economy.[7] In the Malaysian context those who can be k-workers are obviously in those occupations listed as 'professional, managerial and technical', or those who have tertiary skills – about 11 per cent of the workforce. As seen, these top echelon occupations are male-dominated.

Nonetheless women are making a foray into this new technological field. A survey of 10 key software companies found that 30 per cent of their IT professionals were women. In terms of occupational categories, women formed 21 per cent of managerial, 28 per cent of executive and 59 per cent of non-executive staff, while only five per cent were in the technical section. However, there was just one woman chief executive officer. While there seem to be new opportunities for high-flying women to successfully integrate into the k-economy, the majority are still at the non-executive level – as clerks, data entry operators, secretaries and computer operators (Ng, 2001: 114).

Hence the migration towards a deregulated k-economy, whether in the services or manufacturing industries, will tend to produce two classes of workers. Polarization will be based on skills and mediated by gender. The first group will be those who are multi-skilled with secure employment and excellent remuneration. Most of these newcomers will be men, although a significant minority will be women, particularly in the ICT arena. The second group – clerical, operator and production workers, predominantly women – will see their employment status being threatened in various ways. The introduction of ICTs will make their tasks redundant with retrenchment being the option of companies. Jobs which require new technology knowledge-type skills will be given to graduates fresh from such training as the current batch will be either too old to be trained or would not have educational qualifications, having entered the labour force after nine or 11 years of schooling. At the same time, with ICTs, firms can now use such technologies to outsource their information processing operations either to other firms within the country or across national borders, where facilities and labour are cheaper.

Realizing the potential of educated women in the k-economy, the government intends to amend the Employment Act 1955 'to include new and flexible working arrangements such as teleworking, part-time work and job sharing to enable women to integrate career with household duties' (Eighth Malaysia Plan, 2001: 567). Teleworking which is a specific mode of distant work through the use of ICTs is often touted as the future of work in the information age. But here again, women are again framed by the patriarchal state in their 'feminine' role as 'homemakers'. At the end of the day, women will again be burdened by both domestic labour and working for a living. Female teleworkers who are married recount stories of having to work from the kitchen or late at night after completing their household chores (Ng, 2001: 123).

Organizing labour: opportunities and threats

The track record of the labour movement in Malaysia is rather dismal both in the scope of its organizing efforts and in its ability to fight for the rights of workers. This state of affairs can largely be attributed to the anti-labour stance of both the state and capital, as seen in the promulgation of anti-labour laws and in union busting measures. This section examines the series of amendments passed in relation to the labour laws, particularly since the 1980s, in which 'authoritarian and anti-labour policies were brought in quick succession' (Shamsul, 1992 cited in Turner, 2003: 23). However, the trade union movement was also afflicted by internal divisions and different power groupings, which did not help in consolidating an already emasculated movement.[8] Women's committees within these trade unions were not spared either in the factional and ideological struggles within the larger labour movement(s). Such problems as well as the weakness of women workers' NGOs and their inability to forge effective links with women workers will be the subject of discussion in the following section.

Labour amendments in the 1980s were already ensconced in earlier legislation which aimed to curtail the strong workers' movement during colonial times. Hence, in 1959 when the government passed the Trade Union Ordinance, restrictions had already been enforced by the British colonial state. Trade union federations of a general character (where membership is open to all workers in any occupation) were outlawed; in effect unions could only be formed for workers in similar trades, occupations or industries.

In 1965, the Essential Regulations were introduced in response to growing labour militancy in the early to mid-1960s as well as to the Confrontation with Indonesia, thereby providing the justification for compulsory arbitration.

Basically this limited the right to strike in a wide range of 'essential services', as well as prohibited strikes and proscribed industrial action among government employees. It also empowered the Ministry of Labour to 'intervene or conciliate in any dispute, and to compulsorily refer any unsettled dispute for binding arbitration even though the parties were unwilling or had not sought the Ministry's intervention' (Anantaraman, 1997: 6). Any industrial action by a union had to be endorsed by a secret ballot of two-thirds of its members affected by any strike action. In addition the Registrar of Trade Unions (RTU) was given sweeping discretionary powers to de-register or refuse to register a trade union.

In 1971 the Trade Unions (Amendments) Act further shrank the bargaining power of labour by inserting the 'management prerogative' clause. It prohibited trade unions from raising any bargaining demands on the promotion, internal transfer, recruitment, retrenchment, dismissal or reinstatement of an employee, including the assignment or allocation of duties or specific tasks to him/her. Indeed, these changes in the late 1960s and early 1970s reflected the changing investment scenario where the state was bent on maintaining industrial peace at all costs so as to attract foreign investors as part of its industrialization strategy. Thus by 1971 the right to collective bargaining was circumscribed and the freedom to take industrial action severely limited (Anantaraman, 1997).

Over and above these restrictions, the state threw another punch in 1980 when amendments were made to the Trades Unions Ordinance 1959 to further inhibit the rights of workers and sharply increase the RTU's powers. These amendments came on the heels of the historic Malaysian Airlines dispute of 1978–9 which saw several active unionists being detained under the Internal Security Act 1960. Under the amendments, union recognition or non-recognition by the RTU can no longer be disputed; unions that want to go on strike have to submit to the Registrar the results of the secret ballot calling for a strike; the Registrar will then, within seven days, rule whether or not the call to strike is legal. Only those directly involved can take part in the strike action. The Registrar is empowered to suspend any union for up to six months and to remove any executive member of the trade union leadership (Jomo and Todd, 1994).

In the wake of these labour-organizing restrictions, unions, particularly the Malaysian Trades Union Congress (MTUC) and the Electrical Industry Workers Union (EIWU), faced an uphill battle in trying to unionize the growing number of electronics workers. The collusion of the state and capital, especially the anti-union stance of American multinationals, proved to be the major source of obstruction.

Unionizing electronics workers: control and resistance

In addition to the above, two other factors hampered electronic workers from organizing. Firstly, the Malaysian government had promised industrial peace and harmony, guaranteeing smooth production operations to multinational capital in the FTZs set up in the 1970s. Secondly, the RTU's discretionary power to recognize the formation of new unions was fully utilized to ensure 'industrial harmony' and that there would be no undue disruptions. Thus in 1974 when the EIWU started to organize electronics workers, the RTU objected by arguing that its scope was limited to 'electrical' workers involved in producing finished goods and not 'electronics' workers producing electronics components. Subsequently, in 1978, when the MTUC submitted an application to form the National Union of Electronics Workers, the RTU kept the application in cold storage for a record 21 years before it issued an explicit rejection. While the pressure not to accord recognition came from multinationals in the FTZ area, especially American firms which had openly threatened to relocate if the government allowed electronics workers to organize, the situation was also consistent with the anti-union stance of the state through the years (Grace, 1990; Jomo and Todd, 1994).

However, in an apparent turnabout, in September 1988, the Minister of Labour, Lee Kim Sai, suddenly announced that the electronics workers could form their own trade union. The MTUC then submitted its application to get the union registered. But this process was turned into a charade when three weeks later, on 18 October 1988, the minister was forced to retract his statement in the face of protests from American firms; he then said only in-house or company-based unions would be allowed. As noted by Jomo and Todd (1994: 154), in allowing only in-house rather than national level unions, 'the capitulation of the Malaysian government to foreign capital was clear'.

The next section is a case study which illustrates efforts by workers in the predominantly women-dominated multinational electronics company to organize. This is a legal landmark case. It is interesting to note that the struggle was spearheaded and led by male leaders who had previously worked in community-based NGOs. Women formed the bulk of committee members in the struggle and were unrelenting in their demands. This battle is still being fought.

From RCA to ChipPAC: attempts to bust a union

Given that in-house unions are a recognized entity in Malaysia, workers in RCA Sdn Bhd – the locally incorporated arm of RCA Corporation USA and established in 1973 in the Ulu Kelang FTZ – decided to form such a union in late 1988.[9] Thus began the unbelievable saga of intimidations that hounded the only in-house union in an American multinational electronics company which changed its name five times – from RCA to GE to Harris to Intersil to Chip Pac – in a space of 12 years.

The RCA Workers Union (RCAWU) was registered on 31 January 1989. Following this, the company embarked on a series of actions to bust the nascent union – its officers and members were victimized, harassed and intimidated almost on a daily basis. Six months later when the union received a majority membership from the workers, it submitted its claim for recognition to the company management. However the company refused to recognize the union and as a result, on 18 July 1989, the matter was referred to the Industrial Relations Department.

Along the way the company was acquired by GE Corporation, also an American multinational company. However, no notice of the change to the informal name of GE-RCA was given to the Registrar of Companies. On 8 August 1989, the plant was sold to another American multinational, Harris Corporation, which then changed the company's name to Harris Solid-State (M) Sdn Bhd. The workers, however, were not notified of this change in name. The Director-General of Trade Unions (DGTU) ruled that RCAWU could no longer represent its members and ordered it to change its name to HSSM Workers Union, which it did; on 2 January 1990, the DGTU accepted the amendment and change of name. The company was given 14 days to recognize the union.

On the eve of the deadline for recognition, the management gave transfer letters to the workers to join another company called Harris Advanced Technology Sdn Bhd (HAT) – although it was actually the same company in the same location. Nonetheless, the Minister of Labour accorded recognition to the HSSM union in April 1990, but retrospective to 23 June 1989. A week later, although the company accorded recognition to the union as required under the law, it isolated 24 workers, including the entire Executive Council, in a deserted building with no work to do. It even advertised in the newspapers in August 1990 to fill their positions! In the meantime, the union commenced rather uneasy Collective Agreement (CA) negotiations with the management.

Five months later, on 22 September 1990, the company terminated the services of those who remained of the isolated workers on the ground that HSSM had 'ceased operation'.[10] The sacked workers picketed continuously for 21 days with the support of other workers until the case was referred to the Industrial Court on 12 October 1990 for arbitration. After protracted litigation over six years, the Court of Appeal in a landmark judgment ordered the reinstatement of all 21 workers on 1 October 1996 to HAT with no loss of seniority, benefits and wages.

Within these periods of intense drama, various tactics were used by the company to split the workers and to intimidate them into withdrawing from the union. This included using the political, ethnic and religious cards. For example, in the early years of establishing the union:

> . . . they set up an UMNO [United Malays National Organization, the dominant political party] branch to crush the unions in 1990. They said that UMNO would look after the welfare of the workers, not the Union as the chief was the number two man in the KL UMNO. He was the Human Resources Manager, he set up the Muslim Committee. They

hired him, he's a hired gun to bring in Malay chauvinism and bring in UMNO.

(Quoted in Bhopal and Rowley, n.d.: 16)

The management also tried to divide the members by saying that the Indian union president was manipulating the Malays, even though Malays make up the country's leaders. Gender and ethnicity were brought into the fray when the Indian union president was accused of sexually harassing a Malay female employee. Stirring religious sentiments, the management organized 20 two-hour lectures by an *Ustaz* (Islamic religious teacher) who consistently made anti-union comments as well as hinted openly that the union leaders were under police surveillance. In the same breath, the religious teacher praised the company and warned the workers about the difficulty of finding other jobs, all with the intention of creating fear and anxiety among them. As late as 1996, a poison-pen letter was circulated saying that the workers were supporting a Christian-based and Christian-influenced union.[11]

In January 1997, three months after the reinstatement of the 21 workers, the union changed its name to Harris Advanced Technology Workers Union (HATWU) and was accorded recognition by the DGTU. Again the company resisted the union and applied to the High Court of Kuala Lumpur for an order of *certiorari* to quash the decision of the DGTU. The Court granted this application on 29 April 1998, following which the union filed an appeal to the Court of Appeals in May 1998 against the High Court decision. The hearing date has yet to be fixed.

In the meantime, HATWU revived the CA submitted in 1990 but the company refused to negotiate stating that the union was void and non-existent. The union fought back and in May 1999 staged several pickets demanding the resumption of negotiations. Management gave in and met the union in June 1999 only to pronounce that it would assume the CA negotiation when HATWU was registered as a new union. In the midst of this, the company announced that it was going to be sold. Indeed, part of its manufacturing operations had already been hived off while other parts were moved to China and Thailand in the economic meltdown that followed the 1997 financial crisis.

In September 1999 the company changed its name to Intersil Technology Sdn Bhd. Eight months later the company announced that it had been sold to ChipPAC, and that its new name was ChipPAC Malaysia Sdn Bhd. The changing investment climate and instability of the electronics industry was reflected in the reduction of the company's labour force; the worker strength was reduced by half – from 4,200 in 1999 down to 1,800 workers in 2002 – and most of those who left were either retrenched or had received VSS offers for voluntarily resignation and stipulated compensation packages. Intake of new workers is now done on a contract and casualized basis; in fact because the new workers are brought in by a sub-contracted company and are paid on a daily basis, the main company does not bear any responsibility for the new workers, the majority of whom are women.

Lessons learnt

Culpability of the state

First, it is clear that in the era of neo-liberal globalization, the state, instead of protecting its citizens, has shifted its position to being a mediator and protector of capital. It does this in several ways by:

- denying the rights of labour to freely organize;
- systematically curtailing their scope and parameters to mobilize;
- detaining so-called militant labour leaders; and
- delaying the legal process of negotiation and arbitration.

In the case of the electronics union, the state only gave in to the workers' demands because of international pressure and a threat of withdrawal of privileges accorded under the American Generalized System of Preferences. However, at the last minute, it had to appease US capital which in Malaysia was virulently anti-union, and thus only agreed to the formation of in-house unions.

The state does not only rely on repressive legislation to keep labour movements in check. During the 1997 regional financial crisis, companies were required to report any retrenchment, lay-off, VSS or salary reduction plans to the Labour Department so that it could monitor these activities and assist in re-deploying affected workers. Although this move appeared motivated by concern for workers, it also had the desired effect of preventing strikes arising out of worker discontent.

Divide-and-rule strategy

The second observation is the arrogance of US multinational companies and their disrespect of national sovereignty, as evidenced by disregard and non-recognition of decisions made by Malaysian labour authorities. By viewing labour as mere objects in their pursuit of profit maximization, all kinds of tactics were used to both intimidate workers and 'win' them over. These ranged from a divide-and-rule strategy through the use of ethnicity, gender, culture and religion, to mollifying workers with company outings, handouts and 'empowerment' training programmes.

In interviews (Ng and Maznah, 1997: 198) with workers in a major US electronics factory before the 1997 financial crisis, a woman worker commented:

> The management tells us that we have an open policy so why do we need to form a union? Why do you need to pay a subscription to others to

settle your problems? We have an open-door policy. What you want we will give. The management brainwashed the workers against forming a union.

The comments of another worker from the same company appear to confirm that this brainwashing has yielded results:

There is freedom of speech. Now there is empowerment. We have a 'speak out' programme where we can air our problems to the personnel department. A paper with four columns is given and all you have to do is to tick one of the four ways you would like to settle your problems. The workers felt they do not need a union as whatever they asked for they always got. Even the GM [General Manager], when he meets workers, would greet them first before any one of the workers would think of greeting him.

In addition to practising apparent transparency of management, the factories also organize recreational and social activities to create the atmosphere that the workers are all part of one big family working towards the company vision. Such an environment creates difficulties for labour organizing. As observed by a former labour activist:

Management is very smart and organizes activities to take the minds of women workers away from their issues. They organize free aerobics exercises, sports activities and family days. So they [the workers] feel that management cares for them. Unions are not important. Anyway they are scared as management also warns them not to talk about unions. In fact this is done as soon as they are interviewed for their first jobs. And money is important for the workers so they have a lot to lose if they get fired.[12]

Even during the crisis, workers generally accepted the strategies used by their companies. This was also because the electronics industry was not hit as hard as the financial services sector. Indeed because of globalized production, multinational companies were able to re-structure using their shared global resources to reallocate production options and coordinate production shifts in a balanced way.

The nature and scale of restructuring during periods of economic crises vary according to individual factories. While some downsize or close down operations, others shuffle workers across the production floor until such a time that demand rises. The human resources director at one factory suggested two reasons for such organizational change rather than resorting to retrenchment: firstly, to preserve the company's public image; and secondly, to avoid the cost of having to train new workers once demand levels pick up (Maznah et al., 2001). Rather than retrench workers, some larger factories prefer to continue employing them at a loss, or even ask workers to use up their annual leave. Schemes such as the VSS are popular with employees, especially women. In many instances the scheme is over-subscribed by those who want to opt out and benefit from the pay-off. These schemes actually function to regulate labour by allowing management to 'get rid' of those no longer needed and at the same time avoid labour unrest.

Workers interviewed said that their greatest concern during the 1997 financial crisis revolved around wages. The industry-wide scaling down of overtime work was cited as a particular loss. For newly employed production operators, overtime work meant an extra RM500–600 each month on top of a basic wage of RM300–400.

However, poor working conditions or unsatisfactory benefits were not a major concern among workers. This seemed so in factories that managed to continue the practice of offering bonuses, profit-sharing schemes, medical and life insurance, or skills-upgrading opportunities during the lean period. This focus on worker welfare and security was part and parcel of the new management style that accompanied the switch to high value-added produc-tion over the last ten years. Production of this nature requires workers' skills to be enhanced and this in turn calls for long-term investment on the part of the companies.[13] As it is also necessary to circumvent the union's role in addressing workers' grievances, employers feel that it would be in their interest to view workers as 'partners' rather than adversaries.

Consequently, management has actively endeavoured to increase the commitment and loyalty of workers by providing 'perks' and portraying itself as being interested in empowering workers and democratizing factory-floor processes in aid of mutual profitability. In some instances, a paternalistic work culture was successfully cultivated with workers learning to regard themselves and their employers as being part of one big 'family'. Used craftily, the line between control and compliance is rather thin, if not amorphous.

As boasted by a manager in the Bayan Lepas Export Processing Zone in Penang in the aftermath of the regional financial crisis:

> Workers have not formed a union because the company takes care of their welfare very well. For example, besides their good wages and perks, the company provides a cyber cafe at the factory, good chairs at the cafe-teria which also has a two-million *ringgit* view [of the sea].[14]

Patriarchal ideology

There is also the patriarchal view of both state agents and owners of capital that women workers are a secondary and docile labour. The idea is to continue keeping them in a subordinate position in order to maintain prof-itability. As argued by Grace (1990: 19):

Women are to engage in wage labour primarily as a reserve army of labour – that is drawn upon when absolutely necessary because of capital's preference for female labour power and/or during times of labour shortage. The government therefore plays an active part in ensuring that women in Malaysia continue to be subordinated as a gender.

This view was proved wrong by militant labour action from 1985 to 1986 when thousands of women workers from the Mostek and Atlas factories in the Penang FTZ organized a 32-day picket and sit-in. However, the Penang government did not treat the workers seriously and apparently made impractical suggestions to the retrenched workers to be self-reliant and become freelance journalists or open up small electrical businesses.[15] The persistence of local ideologies about 'female suitability or docility' and the result of flexible labour strategies, such as the current use of casual and contract labour, will continue to reinforce the climate for trouble-free or union-free industrialization and to forestall the organization of workers around collective or global interests.

Ethnic divisions

The persistence of ethnic identification has weakened class unity and diminished the role of labour bodies like the MTUC. Many a time, workers ask ethnic-based political parties to redress their labour woes rather than seek recourse through an ethnic-blind trade union. Labour grievances are often channelled through UMNO if workers are Malay or the Malaysian Indian Congress if workers are Indian, rather than through the trade unions. As in instances involving the Harris unionization struggle, religious authorities are invited to deliver talks to workers to instil a sense of company loyalty, often arguing that religion does not condone workers to go on strike or be anti-management.

NGO organizing of women workers

Incipient mobilization: young workers project in Penang[16]

In the late 1970s when export-led industrialization came to Penang, a group of concerned activists and academics started a project to provide services and organize workers in the Bayan Lepas FTZ. The project had the unstated aim of raising the consciousness of workers. The Young Workers' Community Education Project (YWCEP) was first sponsored by the Federation of Family Planning Association, Malaysia and the Penang Family Planning Association and was conceived to fit the larger rubric of the Family Life Education programme.[17] International experts and consultants played some role in the early conception and implementation of the project. The stated aim was to reach out to young people so that they could be socialized early into responsible parenthood. A community development approach was used, eliciting the participation of all members of the community rather than just women workers.

At the time of implementation, the Bayan Lepas FTZ had just been created and accommodated many multinational companies. The recruitment of women workers was done with rapid speed, entailing the dislocation of rural women from familiar locales. The majority of the young women were therefore living independently away from home for the first time. Most had to rent premises situated in several Malay villages dotted around the industrial zone. Almost overnight these villages were inundated with young women of marriageable age. A social and cultural displacement of sorts started to occur. Many households either built extra rooms or created spaces within houses to accommodate the tenants, as there was extra income to be gained from rentals. On the flip side of this newfound gain was discontentment among a large population of male Malay youths, as the new employment opportunities were reserved for females. The inundation of a sudden and large population of young and nubile women into the community also led to incidents of sexual harassment.

The project thus evolved to take on the issues which were specific to women workers' interests and welfare. Those who worked on the project also tried to instil feminist and labour consciousness among the workers. At the same time service-oriented tasks were built into the immediate and short-term agenda of the project. Perhaps because managerial industrial relations tools had not yet become so sophisticated and fine-tuned, the project took up the slack by providing social services to workers who were adjusting to a new working environment. Thus, in the early days of its inception the project was even seen as a buffer against the infiltration of unionism. Although the fear of organized labour was strong among employers and management, the real issues of concern to workers were more mundane and benign than the need to unionize. According to Chan Lean Heng, who worked as one of the full-time coordinators when the project was first established, the major concern of the majority of the women workers was to earn more money, to get married and be able to leave the factory job soon (1991: 24).

Furthermore, Chan observed that,

> ... for most of the women workers, an unfair wage was never a perceived issue at the beginning. This was so because from a situation of non-wage to some wage was viewed positively. Thus the loud cries of economic exploitation, though true from objective analysis, were not of immediate prime significance to the women workers. In fact they were too cautious about making a wrong move to deprive them of that wage, no matter how little that might be. The selling points of unions then were rather irrelevant to the women workers' immediate concerns.
>
> (1991: 22)

The subsequent phases of the project finally led to the setting up of a Workers' Centre dubbed *Rumah Kita* (Our House). From 1983–7, due to the lack of funding, the project continued to be a platform for the development of skills, labour consciousness, collective work and leadership formation, while providing a drop-in service centre. However, the centre was not formally registered, which was a stumbling block in efforts to deal with authorities or in projecting a representative voice of the workers. In 1987, the project was terminated due to harassment from the authorities (especially the Special Branch of the police force) which strained the physical and psychological energies of those involved.[18] Hence while there is general acknowledgment that workers themselves may not be inclined towards union activities, direct coercion exercised by the repressive apparatuses of the state (in league with capital) often becomes an additional reason for workers to shun any activity that could go against the grain of profit accumulation.

> The system of control is so well regulated that company-run hostels are effectively extensions of the shop floor outside the factory. Tactics range from direct persistent intimidation/harassment to implementing no-union avoidance schemes. Collaboration between employers and state agencies is very efficient. Employers do not hesitate to refer what is [*sic*] normally industrial relations matters on the shop floor to the police to generate more intimidation, fear and embarrassment.
>
> (Chan, 1991: 23)

But there were many small gains too and the early experience of industrialization did produce workers who succeeded in asserting their rights, for example, standing up against arbitrary warning letters to demands at the workplace like getting the management to alter bus routes, to collective action at the place of residence to frighten off sexually perverse exhibitionists (Chan, 1991: 27).

But the greatest visible contribution of the Workers' Educational Project (as it was eventually called) towards spawning labour consciousness was in mobilizing and supporting workers in their public protests against mass retrenchment and induced voluntary resignation during the 1985–6 Mostek and Atlas protests discussed earlier. This was a period during which multinational companies went through a restructuring phase in the wake of a global recession. However, 1987 (the year the Workers' Centre was shut down) was a culminating moment after which the twin effects of economic recovery and pragmatic acquiescence of labour to state and capital moved in tandem to seemingly douse the labour movement.

Today, 20 years later, circumstances have not fundamentally changed with regard to the problems involved in organizing women workers. The sprinkling of women workers' NGOs, mainly led by middle-class women, have not been too successful in mobilizing women workers. Sahabat Wanita

(Friends of Women),[19] a small urban-based NGO, which aims to organize women workers, has been unable to formulate a clear-cut strategy to reach out to them and has not linked up with unions in any effective way. For example, one of the strategies was to run kindergarten classes as entry points to reach out to women workers, many of whom were staying in 'squatter' communities. Another was the establishment of a short-lived hotline service on occupational health and safety concerns. However, these did not materialize as successful organizing of the workers.[20] Police intimidation and mass arrests during the 1987 *Operasi Lalang* made the women workers associated with Sahabat Wanita fearful of further repression, forcing them to 'lie low' for a period of time.

Although there were attempts to establish a Labour Commission under the now defunct National Women's Coalition initiated in the early 1990s, there was not much support among women's organizations for such left-leaning politics.[21] Instead they are more focused on issues of violence against women (VAW) and have not utilized this platform to mobilize women workers, nor have they ventured beyond wider and more critical VAW concerns such as structural and/or state violence which impact decidedly on labour. While Sahabat Wanita had some links with women's organizations such as the Women's Development Collective[22] in terms of conducting training on occupational health and safety, these workshops were on an ad hoc basis, such that health and safety issues have not been an effective rallying point for organizing women workers. Links between the MTUC-Women's Section and women's groups, for example in the sexual harassment campaign, have similarly been intermittent in nature.

As explained by the then president of Sahabat Wanita, Irene Xavier:

> I think the issue of women workers is a very difficult one because in the labour movement the women are marginalised or their issues are not raised. In the women's movement their issues are not raised either or they are not given prominence. Women workers get the short deal in these two big movements. It's actually a very difficult struggle.
>
> (Cited in Cabrera-Balleza, 1999)

Emerging issues: migrant workers and sex workers

Two new challenges now demand the attention of those in the Malaysian labour and women's movements who have, thus far, been kept busy organizing themselves to ensure that their traditional interests are upheld, and that actions by employers and the state do not continue to erode their rights.

Migrant workers

Since the colonial period, migrant labour has played an important role in the expansion of the economy. Chinese and Indian immigrants, for example, were crucial in the tin-mining and rubber planting industries respectively. Within these communities, women contributed via functions that were assigned to them. Chinese women in the mining industry were mostly relegated to being *dulang* washers (to pan for tin) while Indian women plantation workers were initially weeders before being allowed to perform rubber-tapping duties.[23] Chinese migrant women also served as domestic workers in the homes of affluent Chinese members of society. Significantly, at least up to the 1930s, they were also a key to providing sexual services to Chinese men, working in brothels and, later, in 'entertainment' outlets such as dance halls and cabarets (Tan, 2003).

Until today, Malaysia continues to rely heavily on migrant labour even though official and public discourses are largely unwilling to acknowledge this. In fact, if one were to succumb to the dominant discourse, one would believe that these workers are a nuisance and the source of numerous social ills (Healy, 2000). The truth of the matter is that – like those who came as migrant labour and have since settled permanently here – these workers, particularly those who are low-skilled, perform crucial tasks that suffer from chronic labour shortages because locals are reluctant to take up such work.

This need for labour explains why, during the economic boom, the country recorded the presence of an estimated 1.7 million migrant workers.[24] By 2002, this figure had decreased in tandem with the economic slowdown but there were still at least 770,000 documented migrant workers[25] employed in various sectors including plantations, construction, services and manufacturing. Within this foreign workforce, women are well represented – a result which parallels a global trend of increasingly feminized migration (Sattherthwaite, 2003) – although they are concentrated chiefly in the domestic service and 'entertainment' industries.

While there may be many reasons why these migrant workers are drawn to our shores, at minimum their presence is mutually beneficial to themselves[26] and local industries. Unfortunately, the tendency has been to 'forget', or perhaps more accurately, hide, how Malaysia benefits from their input. What is worse is the way the under-valuation of their contributions has been used to justify their stigmatization and abuse. Like male migrant workers, females operate under poor working conditions – they are paid low wages, forced to work long hours and perform various forms of degrading work.

By being confined to their employers' homes, however, female domestic workers are made vulnerable to additional layers of discrimination, and often have little of no recourse to justice. Instead, they suffer abuse in silence or rely on external assistance to escape unsatisfactory conditions. Frequently they do not get time off, are denied access to family and friends, and are deprived of food.[27] The law has also failed to protect them against unscrupulous agencies, and sometimes they are at the mercy of unsympathetic police and immigration officers as well.[28] This situation is particularly true of Indonesian domestic workers who, unlike their Filipina counterparts, are not protected by a strong Memorandum of Understanding between the governments of Indonesia and Malaysia.[29] Although there has been some progress in this regard recently, such as the latest attempts to introduce identity cards for foreign workers – as they are frequently harassed to produce identification – the litmus test will be whether or not Malaysia ratifies and enforces the UN Convention on the Protection of the Rights of All Migrant Workers and Members of their Families. If it does, it would put its money where its mouth is.

The workers have few avenues to organize in order to defend their rights. This situation is exacerbated by the fact that the local labour movement, instead of extending solidarity to migrant workers, views them either suspiciously or with contempt. This is because it sees migrant workers as a main obstacle to its efforts to boost wages, since the lower wages offered to migrant workers also serve to depress overall wage levels in the market. As such it has been left to church groups and/or local embassies to extend a helping hand to migrant workers.[30]

Similarly, not many women's groups, progressive or otherwise, have taken up the cause of female migrant labour. The two that have – Tenaganita and Women's Aid Organisation (WAO) – usually come up against enormous hindrances ranging from an unsympathetic society that has imbibed all kinds of negative stereotypes about migrant workers to bureaucratic red-tape. Tenaganita's efforts to highlight the alleged ill-treatment and death of migrant workers in immigration detention centres in Malaysia earned its director a jail term of 12 months for publishing 'false news'.[31] WAO has seen its shelter being raided by overzealous immigration officials determined to discover undocumented migrant workers, and it has been falsely accused as an NGO with Christian proselytizing intentions.[32]

The lack of support shown by women's groups as a whole to female migrant domestic workers can perhaps be attributed to the fact that the predominantly middle-class women's movement has not reconciled the role it also plays in denying these workers their rights. Put differently, since many in women's groups are dependent on migrant domestic labour, there may be a conflict of interest in fighting for domestic workers to be better remunerated, for example.[33]

Sex workers

Possibly the category of workers that has been most neglected by the local labour and women's movements is that involving prostitution. Sex workers are not only scorned but they also work under dangerous and exploitative conditions.

As it stands local women in the sex sector are already poorly protected, with police harassment and raids of brothels being a common occurrence. In the age of HIV/AIDS, they are unprotected from this pandemic unless they are aware of the repercussions and are, at the same time, able to convince their clients to practise safe sex. Most of these women are perceived to have chosen to be in this industry because it is lucrative and brings wages that are much higher than what they may earn in other sectors, particularly if they are low skilled. The fact that many of these women also lack alternatives or support to leave the industry is often ignored.

While current laws do little to protect local sex workers, the plight of foreign women in prostitution is infinitely worse. Apart from suffering similar problems as their local counterparts, a number of women are victims of trafficking syndicates as news reports indicate.[34]

Many are duped into coming here; upon arrival, their chances of escape are slim because syndicate operators keep their passports and other personal documents and threaten them with police action. It is not uncommon too for the syndicates to take all the money earned by these women.[35] The public perception of foreign sex workers is, however, very different to this reality. For example, in trying to account for the lack of regulation of the sex sector by the Selangor government, the *Menteri Besar* (Chief Minister) blamed these women for choosing to put themselves in this situation so that they could make quick money for a night's work! Likewise, another national leader instructed Malaysian women to 'put on more lipstick and try not to put on weight' to dissuade their husbands from frequenting sex workers.[36]

Part of the difficulty that female sex workers face arises out of the illicit nature of their trade. On the one hand, it is somewhat accepted by many in the male-dominated society that there is a demand for such services.[37] On the other hand, instead of being recognized for this contribution as well as for the economic role they play in society,[38] they are forced to feel that what they are doing is morally incorrect and that their existence should thus be kept under wraps.[39] This situation of wanting to ignore those working in the sex industry is a contradiction that society and the state face. Indeed the state is unwilling to 'get rid' of what is perceived as an immoral occupation, yet it is also unwilling to openly accept that the industry is burgeoning,[40] and all because it does not want to be seen as legitimizing such 'immorality'. Consequently, rather than regulate this sector and ensure that female sex workers are protected from abuse and exploitation, the state chooses to close an eye to such happenings.

Some women's groups have started to take up the issue of sex workers' rights, which is a lot more than labour organizations have done. However, compared with organizations like Pink Triangle, an NGO that deals with HIV/AIDS and sexuality issues and ran a successful programme for sex workers in the mid- to late 1990s, they still have a long way to go. Certainly, as with many other issues around women's sexuality, sex work remains a thorny concern for women activists, and one which most would prefer to avoid than openly confront and debate.[41] Until such time that they do so, the women in this sector are forced to suffer the repercussions of entrenched prejudice and exploitation.

Conclusion

The potential of women workers to fight for their rights has been stifled by the combination of capital exploitation and labour flexibilization, state repression, ethnic divisions, middle-class hegemony over the women's movement and a weakened labour movement. Several attempts to inject women workers' issues into the overall concern of the women's movement have not been successfully sustained. In addition, management manipulation of human relations tactics have become more sophisticated through the appropriation of concepts such as 'empowerment' to inject a sense of pride, loyalty and belonging among workers. Management has gone to great lengths to cushion workers from the influence of trade unionism, by substituting their own version of workers' associational interests, through the formation of in-house unions and social activities organized under the company rubric. While 'traditional' labour issues remain unresolved, new challenges have emerged in the form of concerns that migrant workers and sex workers face. However, none of these have been adequately taken up by the state or civil society.

The gaps in social organizing and concrete social experiences reveal the inability of the women's movement in dealing with many contentious issues in society. Labour concerns that range from women in formal employment to those engaging in work within the informal sector have also overwhelmed the capacity of the movement to organize and affect change in this area. Yet another tricky issue is sexuality – a subject that will be explored in the following chapter. As an issue that is at the core of gender politics, sexuality has been insufficiently dealt with, as well as at the same time being considerably misunderstood by both women and men within the social movement circle.

7 Querying the forbidden discourse

Sexuality, power and dominance in Malaysia

The subject of sexuality[1] occupies an increasingly contentious domain in Malaysia today. In spite of being a very intimate aspect of every individual's being – and therefore one which she or he should be in control of – many Malaysians find themselves faced with a constant barrage of mixed and confused messages. Whether these are direct or indirect, they act to define the limits of acceptable sexuality. Much of this relies on 'normalizing' certain forms of sexuality (e.g. sexual behaviours or sexual preferences) over others, such that anyone who appears to choose sexual expressions that are not sanctioned is demonized and persecuted. In this equation, male and female sexuality are both regulated but there is also a gender-biased element at play and women have, by far, been at the end of greater regulation.

The state has played an active role in setting the limits of acceptable sexuality in Malaysia. Through the nation's political and religious leaders, and control of the media, it has been able to exploit this domain for political gain. It is important to note, however, that while the state may not always consciously set out to regulate the sexuality of its citizens, it does have the option to do so. And, when convenient, controls are exercised selectively.

Instead of leaping into the fray and trying to influence the discourse on sexuality that is being shaped, local women's groups along with civil liberties' organizations have, to a large extent, shied away from such issues. Their aversion reflects a larger societal problem, one where social taboos successfully silence public speech on the matter. More importantly, many issues that fall under this subject – prostitution, abortion, transvestism, homosexuality – are far too 'deviant' and are seen to come at too high a price for women's groups that want greater legitimacy in society. Hence it has taken a much longer time for sexuality rights to be put on the agenda of the Malaysian women's movement.

This chapter traces the origins and development of what has come to be considered today as 'acceptable' and 'unacceptable' forms of sexuality. It analyses the reasons for the imposition of these 'norms' and the impact of such defining mechanisms, showing how women, much more than men, suffer disproportionately from various forms of regulation. It examines the response (or lack of it) from women's and civil liberties' groups, and argues why they should be more proactive, rather than leaving conservative forces – including the state – to continue dominating this discourse. The chapter begins by narrating an episode which reflects the current challenges confronting women's groups which want to take on issues of sexuality in the country.

Guarding moralities: the V***** *Monologues*

In February 2002, theatre-goers in the Klang Valley experienced the wrath of Dewan Bandaraya Kuala Lumpur (DBKL – Kuala Lumpur City Hall), which dictated that the play *The Vagina Monologues* by Eve Ensler was unfit for public consumption and, accordingly, banned it.[2] This move came after the performance had shown to packed houses and its producers had sought a new permit to extend the run. Having received a letter of complaint from a religious body in Kedah, based not on a viewing of the play but, rather, a newspaper report on it, the DBKL reacted by rejecting the application.

When this decision was made public, the media went to town on the matter. The response was mixed. The English-language press was largely sympathetic to the fate of the play and raised issues of freedom of expression in their reports. The Malay press, on the other hand, overwhelmingly took a conservative position and supported the DBKL move. Either way, there was a fair amount of coverage and the more publicity the episode received the more determined DBKL became in assuming the role of a public moral watchdog.

This was the unfortunate situation in which the All Women's Action Society (AWAM) found itself when attempting to stage a different production of the same play later that year. Months earlier, the organization had conceived of the idea to stage *The Vagina Monologues* as a fund-raising charity premiere to coincide with International Women's Day. The play was chosen because of the way it highlighted the different dimensions of violence against women (VAW), not least in how the phenomenon relies on male control of female sexuality.

Unbeknown to AWAM then, commercial rights had been granted to a local arts outfit to stage another production of *The Vagina Monologues*. More importantly, AWAM had not counted on the controversy that erupted. By the time things came to a head, it was left in the unenviable position of deciding whether to abandon months of organizing or to proceed as planned. Its eventual decision to proceed was met with DBKL's stony silence. Finally, with only less than a week before the play was to be staged, AWAM was informed that its application for a permit had been rejected.

It appealed against the decision, hoping that the authorities would be able to distinguish between the two productions. The organization explained how its interest in *The Vagina Monologues* was related to its work on raising awareness and educating people about VAW issues. AWAM said it was not interested in sensationalizing the play, and pointed out the role of some sections of the media in fuelling such misconceptions.

DBKL subsequently relented but only to the extent of granting AWAM's appeal if the latter met with certain conditions, among which was the removal of words such as 'vagina' and 'lesbian' from the performance. This would have completely changed the meaning of the play and caused its messages about VAW and sexual violence to be lost. Left with such an alternative, AWAM withdrew its application to stage the play.[3]

Defining the boundaries of (acceptable) sexuality[4]

That episode pinpointed a number of disconcerting issues, not least the severely restricted space to question sexuality in Malaysia. It also revealed the difficulties civil society faces when trying to challenge these restrictions. Such a situation is a product of several factors including the strong silence that surrounds this issue, the dominance of narrow positions that are taken on it and the way society views women.

Embarrassed silence

Unquestionably, sexuality is seen as a taboo subject in Malaysia, something to avoid discussing in public. Seldom is it spoken about openly or constructively. Instead there is a lot of discomfort and euphemisms have to be utilized to raise such issues. So, for example, rather than referring to genitals as genitals (e.g. vagina, penis), phrases such as 'down there' or 'private parts' are invoked instead. Likewise, pubescent teenage girls do not call menstruation 'periods' but their 'visitor', 'best friend' or 'red flag'. And frequently the only time when references to sexuality are made in public is in the context of a 'dirty' joke.

Part of the problem has been caused by an absence of conducive and non-judgemental environments in which these issues can be spoken about. Instead, few people have been brought up to believe that it is all right to freely discuss anything to do with their bodies or sexuality. It does not help that, for the most part, sex education programmes in local schools fail to go beyond descriptions of body parts. Neither do they encourage students to feel comfortable when raising questions related to sex. When there are worthy attempts to educate the youth about their sexuality, these are either subject to censorship or banned outright. Take, for instance, the popular local television series *3R*.[5] In August 2003, an episode of the show – which amongst other things featured interviews that portrayed two lesbians in a positive light – was banned for supposedly promoting homosexuality. Reasons forwarded by the Censorship Board included how the show went 'against Islamic principles, the Constitution, the tenets of the *Rukunegara*, the government's policy of inculcating good morals and Malaysian cultural values'.[6]

Another reason for the problem of silence lies in how cultural and religious sensitivities have made it embarrassing or undesirable for these issues to be raised. Comments like 'It's not part of our culture' or 'Our religion does not permit such things' are often forwarded as excuses to resist change. In an age where HIV/AIDS has been internationally recognized as a scourge that needs urgent addressing, the speed with which efforts are made to bring about such change through a more informed populace has been excruciatingly slow.[7] Much of the foot-dragging around the move to revise the present sex-education curriculum can be attributed to a fear of offending perceived cultural and religious dictates.[8]

Narrow or skewed meanings

While silence is one problem, there is also the situation of what happens when sexuality is actually discussed, especially through public channels like the media. More often than not, discussions take place within limited bounds. Sexuality is narrowly defined as, or equated with, heterosexuality. There is little or no recognition of the fact that human sexuality is expressed in many ways apart from this. If other orientations like homosexuality, bisexuality or transsexuality are mentioned, they are presented as degraded forms – at best inferior, at worst, unnatural and perverted.[9] This is especially true of local portrayals, thus explaining the difficulty many may have in recalling the last time they read about or saw on our television screens positive coverage of a non-heterosexual experience in Malaysia.

Indeed, the authorities appear to be very concerned about the kinds of sexualities that are displayed through our media. However, their vigilance is selective and/or politically calculated.

The Chinese media, for instance, appear to be given greater leeway to be more sympathetic and objective in their portrayal of sexually marginalized communities. Hence they have demonstrated greater propensity to provide information on this subject in a less judgemental manner. This does not mean that the Chinese media are free of biases but, rather, in comparison to the Malay media, they take a less hostile stand on sexuality issues. The Malay press on the other hand is notoriously conservative, giving much room to their readers to indulge in gay-bashing.[10] Such double standards were evident when a local television station was able to take two contradictory positions *viz* sexuality within a short period during June–July 2003.[11] First, it showed to its Chinese audience a fairly positive portrayal of the lives of six Chinese male and female homosexuals; it then followed with two denigrating programmes on Malay *lelaki lembut* ('effeminate men') and *wanita keras* ('butch women') for its Malay viewers.

One possible explanation for this distinction is the importance placed by the leaders of the ruling Malay party, UMNO, on ensuring continued support by its Malay constituency. This means being stricter in controlling what this populace sees, hears and understands. At the same time, in having to promote itself as more morally upright next to its political foes PAS, they also have to promote a public face of intolerance towards subjects like sexually marginalized groups who are easy to demonize.

It is thus worth noting the efforts to shape what Malaysians understand as acceptable forms and expressions of sexuality for in this lies a connection to a larger goal of gaining political mileage. Anti-homosexual or homophobic stances appear to be successful issues in political campaigns for office. For example, despite having banned gays, transvestites and effeminate men from appearing on local television, the then Minister of Information Mohamed Rahmat only publicized this decision as a campaign stance a year later in the run-up to the 1994 general election[12] (Jayaseelan, n.d.: 7). Similarly in August 2003, seemingly out of the blue but in the midst of heavy speculation of a general election being called, the then Deputy Minister of Information Zainuddin Maidin issued a warning to an English-language daily for allegedly being too positive in its coverage of gays and lesbians.[13] Whether or not this was a coincidence, these actions have had the effect of projecting the state as guardians of morality. And while earning brownie points from the conservative public, it also has the effect of preventing many more from coming out in support of sexuality rights.

Gender as a factor

Another factor that affects how sexuality is treated in Malaysia is gender. Even though both men and women are subject to increasing rules as to what counts as proper sexual behaviour,[14] the latter is prone to a wider range of controls over the way they look, behave, dress, talk or choose to lead their lives. Women bear the brunt of sexual regulation because it is both a result of and a means to reinforce their subordinate status in society.

Several well-publicized incidents put this point in perspective. The first involved three young Malay women arrested by religious officers on a charge of indecently exposing their bodies during a beauty pageant.[15] The second saw two Chinese women being refused permission to take their driving test because they were deemed to be indecently dressed.[16] Third was the uproar that ensued after popular Malaysian artiste Ning Baizura appeared in a sexy pose on the front cover of a local magazine, and revealed that her fantasy was to have sex with five men at the same time.[17]

In some situations, even being suitably clothed or saying the 'right' thing is not the point. Instead it boils down to how one's choices are perceived. Such was the experience of local band member Azlina Aziz. Along with other Malay women in the restaurant where she was performing a gig, Azlina found herself charged under Section 10 of the Selangor *Syariah* (Islamic) laws for acts 'insulting or lowering the dignity of Islam'. Since she was 'totally covered' and performing traditional Malay songs at the time, she deduced that her only 'crime' was being present in a place that sold alcohol. Some weeks after the harrowing experience, she was told that the charges had been dropped. By then, however, the intended effect had set in – the experience caused Azlina (and probably all those in her shoes) to become more cautious. She vowed that she would cover her arms and shoulders with a shawl in all her subsequent performances.[18]

Because women are very often expected to express their sexuality only within specific boundaries, namely heterosexual marriage and in the service of procreation, it is easier for their conduct to be defined as unacceptable when they do not adhere to such dictated social norms. Spinsters, bisexual women, lesbians and celibate women, if known, all face some degree of hostility or ridicule, albeit to differing degrees, because they contravene social notions of acceptable sexual roles and behaviour for women. Heterosexual women who challenge social prescriptions – to be sexually submissive rather than active and in control of their own sexuality – face hostility too. Hence the widespread censure of Ning when she made the public revelation of her sexual fantasies. Similarly, women who work in the sex sector are stigmatized, ironically, while their services are in demand.

Not so 'natural' after all: evolution of (acceptable) sexuality

The dominant discourse on female sexuality in Malaysia insists that being 'female' is the same as being 'feminine'. Particular characteristics of femininity are essentialized and promoted as qualities that all 'good' women should naturally possess. However, precisely because there is no fixed way for women (and men) to be so, efforts have to be constantly made to reinforce particular interpretations of femininity (and masculinity) as natural and thus not open to change. Hence various codes of appearance and behaviour are formulated and imposed by families, peers, religion, culture, the media and government apparatuses, and through approval or punishment these eventually get naturalized as ways of being a woman.

This also makes it possible to label women who do not conform to conventionally defined forms of female behaviour as unnatural or deviant, and in turn, it becomes a method of keeping women 'in line'. Likewise, for various reasons including political and religious ones, those in positions of power often reinforce dominant definitions of sexuality so that people will believe that any form of sexuality different to this is unacceptable.

This section demonstrates how what has been 'normalized' in the discourse on sexuality in Asian society today is not as naturally occurring as we have been led to believe. Ideas and definitions of socially acceptable forms of sexuality have been created and maintained, frequently on the bodies of women and sexually marginalized communities. The following examples drawn from two different periods in the nation's history – one from colonial times and the other from less than ten years ago – illustrate this point.

The Women and Girls Protection Ordinance/Act[19]

We are given the impression that protectionist legislation for women and girls is necessarily good, and designed with their interests in mind. For a very long time, the Women and Girls Protection Act was touted as one such law. Yet protecting women and girls from abuse by traffickers, brothel-keepers and pimps was never the main intention of those who proposed this legislation in late nineteenth-century Malaya. Of greater concern to lawmakers then was to ensure that men in the colony had easy access to disease-free heterosexual sex. This explains why the very first law dealing with prostitution in this country was not the Women and Girls Protection Ordinance (WGPO) but the Contagious Diseases Ordinance (CDO).[20]

As its name suggests, the CDO was about keeping in check sexually transmitted diseases. This was to be done, however, by regulating women and girls in prostitution. Under this law, they were forced to undergo periodical medical examinations to make sure that they were not infected with venereal disease. Male clients were not subjected to the same treatment even though it was known that they could just as easily infect the women they slept with. The testimony of one Reverend W. G. Shellabear at the time makes the reason for this practice of double-standards clear: 'The man cannot be touched because he refuses to be touched; the woman we touch because she is in our power' (cited in Tan, 2003: 22).

The CDO operated for some 20 years before being replaced by the WGPO.[21] This change, however, had more to do with the conservative Purity Campaign in Britain which objected to what it saw as the UK government's licensing and sanctioning of immorality. In fact, advocates of the campaign were fighting to abolish a number of practices which they deemed immoral. In their mind, prostitution along with masturbation, schoolboy sex, incest, pornography, nude bathing, homosexuality and the age of consent for girls to have sex all had to be regulated.

On paper the Women and Girls Protection Ordinance was explicit in its desire to end the offensive aspects of the sex trade. In reality official measures to protect female prostitutes remained grossly ineffective. For one, although port inspections were recognized as important to sift out women and girls who had been trafficked, persistent understaffing seriously compromised results. It was reported that even with inspections taking place, kidnappers and procurers were still able to bypass this system and smuggle women and girls into the colony for sex work.

The law also provided for young women and girls to be 'rescued' from brothels, regardless of whether or not they wanted to leave. There could have been reasons why they may have chosen to stay put, but their opinions were never sought. Instead it was assumed that it was in their best interests to be 'rescued'. The way that homes designated as 'refuges' were run was equally contentious. The practice of punishing 'inmates' with solitary confinement when they flouted house rules or perhaps questioned the authority of those in charge gave these homes a reputation of being authoritarian and repressive. Any woman or girl brave enough to escape faced harsh penalties if caught.

Understanding the 'truth' about women's unruly bodies

To understand how a flawed piece of legislation could make its way into the system, it is worth tracing the real reasons for its introduction. What was behind the 'truths' that were being made about prostitution and sexual practices in the colony?

At this point, it is necessary to remember that the CDO and the WGPO were both introduced specifically in the name of protecting Chinese prostitutes. Although these laws were eventually used to regulate all prostitutes, the main emphasis was on the Chinese. It was they who mostly landed up in the homes designated as 'refuges'.

In the first place, the colonial government had argued that prostitution was inevitable because there was an unbalanced sex ratio among the Chinese. The assumption was that men had a right to satisfy their sexual desires and since most did not come to Malaya with their wives, services of women and girls in prostitution were necessary. The government, in turn, believed that it had to intervene to ensure that those in this trade were not exploited.

Exactly how 'inevitable' was prostitution? It was a known fact that the government only encouraged male Chinese immigrants in the early days of colonial expansion because they did not want a permanent labour force that would increase operational costs. Furthermore, if the unbalanced sex ratio was indeed unavoidable, how does one explain the same government managing to curb the emigration of Chinese men later in the 1930s? Not only were the authorities able to do this, but also they succeeded in bringing over more female migrants.

Another common excuse for the existence of prostitution was the 'low standard of morals' of the Chinese. The men were said to have 'loose morals' and untrained to restrain their desires because they lacked the 'moral influences' of the West. Many Chinese males who landed in Malaya certainly sought the services of prostitutes but their actions were attributed to two reasons. Most were young and, being away from home for the first time, they were responding to their newfound freedom. Furthermore, given their harsh lives on the colony, they were seeking solace and comfort from these women. Prostitutes thus played an important role in placating the backbone of colonial economic expansion.

A lesser-known reason as to why the authorities wanted prostitution to continue had to do with the colonial state's desire to suppress male homosexual activity among the Chinese labour population. Evidence in official records indicates that sexual relations between Chinese men were not uncommon, and that the British were aware and concerned about this development. Recorded cases of sodomy in *cooly bangsals* (labourers' barracks) and reports of 'intelligent Chinamen' descending to forms of 'unnatural vice' rather than visit brothels reveal that homosexual relations among Chinese men was not unusual and that these cut across class-lines. The British response, however – as reflected in the sentencing of a Chinese man to nine years of 'rigorous imprisonment' on three counts of 'unnatural offence' – shows the determination of the colonial state in deterring male homosexual activity. Prostitution was projected as a way out of this situation (Tan, 2003: 12).

Clearly, then, the true motivation for enacting protectionist legislation like the WGPO was questionable. Many colonial policy-makers were known to regard these women and girls in the lowest esteem, often calling them 'ignorant', 'idiotic' or 'stupid'. They treated all prostitutes as incapable of knowing what was in their best interests even though evidence showed otherwise. For example, the British were fond of saying that these women did not know how to care for themselves. Yet it is known that there were prostitutes who, on their own, sought medical assistance and protection from the police magistrate when needed. Perhaps most telling is the lack of support shown by the colonial authorities when a group of prostitutes formed a union so that those who wanted to leave brothels could do so.

If such condescending and paternalistic attitudes informed the law, it is no wonder that the kinds of 'protection' offered to women and girls ended up being flawed. Hence, what was meant to be a means of protection for female prostitutes failed miserably: it did not stop them from being ravaged by sexually transmitted diseases nor did it stop the abuse by traffickers and brothel-keepers. Despite this, because the colonial government *needed* prostitution to continue in the colony, the authorities had to justify its existence. This necessitated constant reinforcements of the 'truth' that this phenomenon was inevitable, and that the consequences of allowing this 'necessary evil' had to be curtailed. This came at a cost to female prostitutes because in the end it was their bodies that were policed, all in the name of 'protection'.

Worse, however, was the subsequent stigmatization of women and girls in the sex industry. At the same time that the colonial government extended protection to them, it also promoted a distinction between 'good' and 'bad' women. Often the sexuality of prostitutes was portrayed as dangerous and debilitating and hence in need of control. Similarly, those who had been 'rescued' were said to require rehabilitation because it was assumed that their involvement in prostitution had turned them into 'immoral' and 'deviant' beings.

The stigmatization of women in prostitution continues to exist in present times since not only did Malaysians inherit the system of laws introduced by the British, but also policy-makers today have insisted on preserving the same attitudes towards women and girls. Thus, even though the Women and Girls Protection Act (that succeeded the WGPO in 1973) has since been replaced by the Child Act 2001, the ideology of punishing deviant female sexuality continues to be embodied in the new law.

Understanding the history of this legislation makes it clearer how a law that claims to be in women's interests has come to be used to penalize certain groups – namely those who do not conform to acceptable female behavioural norms – instead of protecting them from male perpetrators.

Nowhere is this point better illustrated than in the infamous allegations involving a former Chief Minister of Malacca who allegedly committed statutory rape on a 15-year-old girl. Despite revealing the existence of 'strong suspicions', the Attorney-General eventually dropped charges against the politician due to 'insufficient evidence'. The girl on the other hand, portrayed in the media as promiscuous and rebellious, was sent to a rehabilitation centre under the Women and Girls Protection Act.[22]

The discourse on 'Asian values'[23]

As the next example shows, what we understand today as acceptable forms of sexual practice and identities have been directed and shaped rather than being naturally occurring phenomena.

Out of the mid-1990s emerged a state-generated discourse on values in Malaysia.[24] This was largely posited in terms of Eastern (Asian) versus Western values. In its crudest form, this discourse painted all Asian values as good and superior, and all Western ones as bad. It posited that contemporary Western societies had seen a breakdown in social relations and institutions such as marriage and the family because materialistic, selfish and greedy desires of individuals had been placed above the needs of their communities. This, the then Prime Minister of Malaysia Dr Mahathir Mohamad said, was why the West was 'riddled with single-parent families which foster incest, with homosexuality, with cohabitation, with unrestrained avarice, with disrespect for others and, of course, with rejection of religious teachings and values.'[25]

The image of the morally bankrupt West, contrasted against that of a harmonious and morally upright East, was used to warn all Malaysians of the dangers associated with jeopardizing the social order. By emphasizing the need to inculcate values that prioritize harmony, consensus, community and the family, Malaysian leaders – like others in the region, such as the former Prime Minister of Singapore, Lee Kuan Yew, who also invoke the Asian values rhetoric – have been able to justify their authoritarianism as *the* Asian brand of democracy.

At minimum, it is debatable whether values can be Asian or Western. Surely values do not have a cultural identity? More importantly, not all 'white' culture is rejected by this discourse – indeed, various facets of capitalism including materialist and consumerist lifestyles are promoted and exulted.[26] The Asian values rhetoric is only employed when greater social regulation is desired and certain differences among a country's people need to be rejected, all in the name of achieving a common national or collective 'good'.

Where women are concerned, the Asian values discourse has been used to promote a very strict prescription of female behaviour and roles in Malaysia. It casts them as symbols of nationalism and honour, indispensable to the preservation of the harmonious traditional family unit, which, as noted, is represented as crucial for the nation's well-being. Thus, even when women are allowed – and in most instances, encouraged – to go out of their homes to work in the public sphere whenever the need arises, they are also expected to give up their jobs and prioritize the interests of their family. If they do not, the disintegration of the family unit is blamed on their assertiveness in the public sphere and their neglect of domestic roles.

By linking women's morality to the maintenance of social order, the Asian values discourse, like other fundamentalist discourses, makes it possible to justify calls to 'protect' women from perceived threats (say, of Westernization). This has paved the way for greater controls to be imposed on women's bodies as demonstrated by the case of the three beauty-pageant contestants and the other examples cited earlier. Indeed, the period of the mid-1990s stands out as a time when controlling the morality of young women was almost a national obsession. In particular, leaders and their media mouthpieces saw it fit to launch an assault on groups of young women derogatorily dubbed *boh sia* ('loose' young women). Their 'crime'? Hanging out in public places and engaging in casual sex with men who pick them up. While these young women were rounded up and curfews were imposed on them – through the Women and Girls Protection Act that was meant to protect them – their male 'clients' went unpunished.[27]

At the same time, in contrast to previous discourses that concentrated on the construction of the 'women-as-mothers' ideology, advocates of Asian values went one step further, rejecting not only sexual relations outside marriage but also denouncing homosexuality and lesbianism. Thus, during the height of this debate in the mid-1990s, Mahathir was quoted as saying on numerous occasions that homosexuality contravened Asian values and culture:

> We want a family unit to remain, that is, having a husband and a wife and their children … not a man being married to another man or a woman and a woman, or single parenthood. We do not accept such means of unlimited freedom.
>
> (Mahathir quoted in *The Star*, 11 September 1994)

Today such pronouncements against 'single parenthood' – or more specifically those who are divorced or widowed single mothers – have no place in our society.[28] The then Ministry of Women and Family Development itself has recognized this fact and extended various forms of support to single mothers associations and the like. Yet at the time the above statement was made nobody publicly challenged it because single parenthood was juxtaposed against the nuclear family unit, and blamed for the latter's demise.

This example raises the important point that what is posed as socially acceptable can and does change over time depending on the circumstances (for example, culture and historical situation). A century ago, it was considered unnatural for most women to go to work. Those who wanted to keep women in the domestic sphere used this accusation successfully since the fear of being labelled 'abnormal' effectively influenced women to stick with the status quo. Similarly, homosexuality, bisexuality or transsexuality may be seen as 'unnatural' by society today, but this does not mean that it has always been so in the past, or will always be so in the future.[29] And the fact that multiple forms of sexual relationships have existed throughout history also shows that society must come to terms with this, rather than employ various denial and oppressive tactics against its recognition.

Through the discourse on Asian values, pronouncements against homosexuality have had the intended effect of creating an 'us' versus 'them' syndrome whereby the former (i.e. heterosexuality) is glorified and the latter (i.e. homosexuality) is marginalized. This was the strategy that was utilized to discredit the former Deputy Prime Minister, Anwar Ibrahim, and contribute to his eventual incarceration.[30] Few then publicly questioned why homosexuals were dragged into what obviously was a power struggle between Mahathir and Anwar, his former protégé. Such a discourse also gave room to PASRAH, an avowedly anti-homosexual organization, to form in the midst of this debacle and announce its intentions to eradicate all homosexuals without fearing any consequences – even when its actions were unlawful (Tan, 1999a: 21).[31]

Restraining female desire: the case of Azizah and Rohana

The impact of the Asian values discourse on women's sexuality is aptly illustrated in the following case study.

At the end of 1996, Malaysia's national dailies embarked on a series of articles featuring Azizah and Rohana, two women who got married with the former impersonating a man.[32] Both this story and the media's treatment of Azizah is best understood as being part and parcel of how women and their bodies are regarded in the discourse on Asian values that is promoted by state and religious leaders in the country.

When the story broke, the press set it apart by hailing it as the first incident of its kind in Malaysian history. The offender, the 21-year-old Azizah, was said to have committed a grave and heinous crime by marrying another woman. The reports focused on how she managed to pull off this feat and concentrated on the number of people she had fooled along the way, including her bride and the *kadi* (religious judge) who conducted the marriage ceremony. She was eventually charged with impersonation and the possession of a false identity card, but only because there was no specific Malaysian law that penalized lesbianism.[33]

Despite her subsequent conviction, the media continued its coverage. After portraying it as a dramatic account of a woman who 'shook the nation', they moved to paint a picture of Azizah as a woman who had gone 'wrong', and of Rohana as the helpless victim. The press turned to demonstrating the effects of rehabilitation on Azizah, who by then had already been in prison for a month – 'Azizah returns to womanhood' was the headline of one account. This claimed that her prison sentence had succeeded in returning her to 'normality' and pointed to her admission of regret over her erroneous ways as evidence of this. Stories of her past were also told to show that she was a 'genuine' woman who had gone astray due to the lack of familial support and guidance.

The way in which Azizah was treated has to be understood in terms of where women like her fit into the standards of acceptable female sexuality that are imposed and reinforced by the discourse on Asian values. Already in most families and communities, a woman essentially has no status unless she is married and has children. Accordingly, she needs to display certain qualities that will fetch a husband. She has to be obedient, demure, chaste and a virgin. The media coverage of Azizah's case suggests that she not only contravened these norms but, worse, had trespassed into the forbidden territory of heterosexual male privilege. Stated differently, dressing up and behaving like a man may be tolerated in some situations. However, the minute a woman tries to get married and is seen as wanting to claim the privileges associated with her new status, that is as a husband, she is seen as rebelling against gender stereotypes and hence must be punished.

Because femininity and heterosexuality are portrayed as innate features of women, all other forms of behaviour that do not conform to this are seen as 'deviant' and temporary. This explains why the media concentrated on 'normalizing' Azizah after she had been imprisoned, even to the extent of getting her to explicitly say that she did not rule out marriage again, but that next time it would be to a man. The underlying message was that sexual transgression was a disease and women can be or, rather, must be 'saved' with proper guidance and family support. In this way, those who insist on going against the standard 'ideal' womanhood are then cast as truly evil and unnatural, and as sources of societal disorder and decay. These are the women who 'deserve' condemnation and persecution.

Since the Asian values discourse is gendered, its treatment of men and women who do not stick within sexual norms is also different. Around the same time as Azizah's case, there was another incident involving two men who wanted to get married as well. The way the accused, Fauzi, a 15-year-old male, was depicted by the press was very similar to the way Azizah had been treated. Both cases were highlighted because the accused had transgressed sexual boundaries. Despite the parallels, there were some notable differences, not least being the duration of media coverage on this case (five days for Fauzi as opposed to three months for Azizah), and how the verdict in this case was never made known. Till today, readers remain in the dark as to whether or not Fauzi ever suffered the same fate as Azizah and was imprisoned for his actions.

The point here is not that male 'deviants' are necessarily treated better than their female counterparts. Raids in spots frequented by male transvestites will attest to this.[34] Rather, the purpose in highlighting the differences between the two cases is to show that even though male 'deviants' also face discrimination, this has more to do with the greater opportunities that they have had to lead public and visible lives. Women on the other hand have been largely invisible and in cases like Azizah's, where a woman cross-dresser gets public recognition, immediate measures are taken to curb her 'deviant' behaviour because it directly challenges the reproduction of the 'ideal' woman.

While the Azizah-and-Rohana episode gave lesbian relationships unprece-dented visibility in this country, it also had the effect of precipitating or hastening the process of more legal restrictions on women who violate the norms of sexual and gender relations. Thus, where previously 'bad' women were equated only to the promiscuous types (e.g. those who have sex outside marriage or are involved in prostitution), today there are *Syariah* criminal enactments against women who have sexual relations with other women. Both the Johor and Federal Territories' administrations, for instance, crimi-nalize *musahaqah*[35] by imposing a fine of up to RM5,000, six strokes of the *rotan* (cane), or a jail sentence of up to three years, or any combination of these penalties upon conviction.

Ironically, the PAS-led government of Kelantan tried to criminalize the same act of *musahaqah* under the *Hudud* (Islamic criminal) provisions as early as 1993 but this move failed when the Barisan Nasional-led (BN – National Front) Federal government opposed the implementation of the *Hudud*.[36] In matters of discriminating against women on the basis of their sexuality, there is really little to distinguish between those in BN and in Parti Islam Se Malaysia (PAS – Islamic Party of Malaysia). If and when they espouse the democracy and human rights rhetoric, it is always done selec-tively and will not include sexual rights and freedoms.

Taking a stand: response of the women's and civil liberties' movement

Sexuality has long been regarded a thorny matter by the Malaysian civil liberties movement. For much of the movement's history, there has been a deafening silence on this subject. On a rare occasion in 1993, a human rights organization Suara Rakyat Malaysia (SUARAM - Malaysian People's Voice) bravely tried to include a provision on the right to sexual orientation in the 'Malaysian NGO Charter on Human Rights' that it was then putting together. When the point was brought up during the consultation, half the meeting – oblivious to the contradictions in their stand – adopted the same arguments used by the state to silence those who are not heterosexual. Among other points, they claimed that gay and lesbian rights were not human rights, neither were these a Malaysian concern, and that the inclusion of such a provision would be detrimental to the entire human rights struggle in the country (Jayaseelan, n.d.: 7).

Among women's groups, too, there has been no shortage of those who support the state's efforts at stamping out homosexuality. In the early 1990s, when police raided a gay bar in Kuala Lumpur – allegedly as part of a routine anti-crime operation – and detained over 250 male patrons, the largest umbrella body of women's groups, the National Council of Women's Organisations, publicly supported this action. Its president claimed that such clubs were a breeding ground for AIDS and promoted practices that contravened the nation's religious values and principles. When Pink Triangle, an organization dealing with HIV/AIDS and sexuality, questioned the consequences that the raids, harassment and negative media reports had on HIV/AIDS prevention, neither the Ministry of Health nor any of the NGOs that ran such programmes responded (Jayaseelan, n.d.: 9).

It is not that women's groups have totally ignored sexuality issues in the past. After all, many of those who seek to counter VAW have worked on the premise that it is a woman's right to control her own sexuality. Similarly, others have looked at sexuality in relation to women's health (e.g. HIV/AIDS and sexually transmitted infections). A large majority of these groups, however, have stopped short of extending their understanding of sexuality into the sphere of a woman's right to determine her sexual preference, identity, behaviour or practices, especially when these fall outside the normalized heterosexual framework.

This may account for the lack of progress made on the issue of prostitution which the Joint Action Group against Violence Against Women (JAG-VAW) raised in 1985. Unlike the other issues highlighted at the same time (i.e. rape, domestic violence, sexual harassment and the negative portrayal of women in the media), the position of the majority of women's groups on prostitution has remained largely ambivalent and stagnant. The lack of a more holistic understanding also partly explains why, when the Azizah-and-Rohana case transpired, there was hardly any response from women's groups – even among those who identified themselves as feminists and/or were advocates of women's human rights – to denounce the persecution of Azizah.

Women's agenda for change, chapter 11

Fortunately, over the years, some quarters within the women's movement have started to take a holistic approach in dealing with sexuality. One of the biggest gains for the movement and sexuality rights advocates has been the inclusion of a chapter on sexuality in a document called the 'Women's Agenda for Change' (WAC). This was a collectively drawn-up document that was endorsed by 76 NGOs across the country when it was launched.[37] Conceived in light of the 1999 general election to highlight the concerns of Malaysian women to all politicians, the WAC was an important document that had significant impact.

The Introduction to the document, however, hinted that the incorporation of the chapter on sexuality had not been a painless process. Specifically, it stated that in the initial draft presented to the 34 organizations which had attended a national consultation, only ten key issues were included. The paper on sexuality was added, pretty much at the eleventh hour, as an outcome of the consultation. Indeed, many of the same problems that plagued the women's movement and prevented it from taking a public stand on sexuality rights in the past resurfaced in the process of drawing up the WAC.

To explain: even though the situation is changing slowly today, there has traditionally been a gap between women's groups and sexual minorities (e.g. lesbians) in Malaysia. While some attempts had been made to address the issues of other marginalized women (e.g. indigenous, workers and urban settlers), the same cannot be said for women from sexually marginalized groups. By and large, for instance, the women's movement has ignored issues identified by lesbians as being of importance to them – discrimination on the basis of sexuality, fear of being 'discovered' and thrown out of their homes or jobs, or having nowhere to turn to for help.[38] The movement has not been inclusive about these concerns but, rather, neglected the importance of extending its understanding and analysis of women's oppression to the issue of sexuality rights. This contributed to a certain lack of conceptual clarity during the WAC process when the issue of sexuality arose and, subsequently, to the difficulties in finalizing a paper on the issue in the final document.

In addition, since women's groups themselves are a marginalized sector of civil society, some of those in the Organizing Committee were worried about what would happen if the group were to take a public stand on this issue. No doubt, past experience fuelled part of their anxiety.

In 1994, for example, in the early days of HIV/AIDS education, AWAM tried to teach younger women the benefits of safer sex through a cartoon-booklet called *Lina's Dilemma*. For this, they were attacked and accused of promoting promiscuity and free sex, and the publication was labelled culturally inappropriate. *Harian Metro*, a Malay tabloid that took them to task, plastered on its front page, the headline '*Risalah biadab*' ('Offensive booklet'), in reference to illustrations on how condoms were to be put on. Although never explicitly stated, the paper was most likely also protesting at how the booklet encouraged younger women to take control of their sexuality.

None of these concerns appeared to matter as much as the possibility that Muslim-based women's organizations supporting the WAC initiative might reject the entire document because of objections to the chapter on sexuality. As argued by one Organizing Committee member:

> I feel rather uneasy that whether or not a group endorses the whole agenda may hinge on the 11th paper [i.e. that on sexuality] . . . I [also] stand by my position to have some concern for polarization between Islamic and non-Islamic groups, and to try and avoid it if possible.[39]

Certainly, for many years secular-type women's organizations had been hoping that Muslim-based groups would become interested in and demonstrate their support for women's issues. Understood this way, it is clearer why there was much caution by some in the Organizing Committee about having a chapter on sexuality in the WAC.

Others, however, took the position that the paper was far too 'important to be just dropped off from the women's agenda if the Muslim groups express reservations on it'. Interestingly enough, this was a comment from a key Muslim feminist in Malaysia. She took the approach that there would never be the 'right time' to introduce something as controversial as sexuality rights in this country. The question was whether or not the women's movement was ready to face the criticism and come up with strategies to deflect them so that the rest of its agenda would not be buried under lesbian phobia. Rather than fearing the rejection of the paper and hence the WAC by other Muslim women, she argued that: 'Given the political climate and dire need for alliances and support from both the government and the opposition, we do have the upper hand in dealing with the issue from the perspective of rights, compassion and non-discrimination.'[40]

Eventually the outcome was a compromise and somewhat watered-down version of the group's stand on sexuality rights. Apart from the title of the chapter 'Women, Health and Sexuality' that had been framed to minimize attention on the sexuality aspects of its contents, arguments and words perceived as potentially objectionable (e.g. lesbianism), were kept to the minimum.[41] Despite this, the final chapter could still be regarded as an achievement insofar that it put the sexuality issue up front while, at the same time, keeping the WAC document palatable to all.

Unlike the attempt by several progressive women's groups to come up with a similar document called the 'Women's Manifesto'[42] almost ten years earlier – when even basic demands like the removal of the draconian Internal Security Act 1960 was unacceptable to most – the support for the WAC was overwhelming. This was due largely to the contrasting political situations in the country compared to before.[43] This notwithstanding, with the change in political climate, the women's movement could now speak of a common stand on sexuality rights, in particular, the right of all individuals to choose their own sexual orientation and practices, without regulation, harassment or discrimination by the state.

The V***** *Monologues* revisited and other emerging concerns

Whether or not women's groups that support sexuality rights can stand their ground is one thing as *The Vagina Monologues* episode showed. Another equally important question is whether or not they are able *and* willing to forward arguments based on sexuality rights to justify their stand. Thus even though AWAM was not able to persuade the DBKL authorities to allow them to put on a public production of the play, at least it did not shun questioning the authorities but instead tried to argue its case. This action was important on three counts.

Firstly, the DBKL stance reflected a societal view that it is shameful or offensive to talk about women's genitals or even mention words such as 'vagina'. In other words, even if the DBKL may have wanted to be accommodating, it was operating within a larger culture that does not accept initiatives to discuss or educate people about women's bodies and sexuality in an open and uninhibited way. Yet there is nothing shameful about such words, or about the parts of the body to which these refer. By insisting that the performance should have been allowed to run, AWAM sought to challenge this element of societal misconception which, in the long run, serves to perpetuate the widespread culture of shame and secrecy *viz* women's bodies. This in turn poses a serious obstacle to any effort to empower women and girls, for instance to help them protect themselves from sexual abuse, unwanted pregnancy or diseases such as HIV. If there is no space to talk openly about sexuality, they are unable to make informed decisions on these matters.

Admittedly, sometimes people talk about women's bodies and genitals in a lewd or demeaning way. However, there should be a distinction between this and attempts to educate and empower women by helping them to be more informed about their bodies and about issues such as sexual violence. Failure to do this leads authorities to ban responsible attempts to educate people about these subjects, the same way they ban irresponsible representations or sensationalist performances. A blanket rule is applied despite the huge differences which underlie the reasons for and manner of broaching a topic related to sexuality.

Secondly, *The Vagina Monologues* incident highlighted the importance of questioning the whole idea of cultural values. Often, the authorities condemn things or ideas that they do not like as culturally inappropriate or as going against Asian values. For instance, unless endorsed by the state, Malaysians have been told that they cannot hold political demonstrations because this goes against Asian values, even though the right to peaceful demonstrations is a fundamental human right. Are street demonstrations really against Asian values, or is this simply a convenient way of denying Malaysians their rights?

Also, as we have already seen, the Asian values discourse has been used to vilify certain sexually marginalized groups – homosexuals, transvestites, young single women who appear to be promiscuous, and the like – saying that these people are aberrations of society and not part of Asian culture. In fact, there is enough evidence to show that homosexual relations were not only common but also accepted in many parts of this region. Even in Malaysia, what is derogatorily referred to as the *pondan*[44] (the effeminate man) was traditionally a valued member of *kampung* (village) communities, respected, among other things, for the *mak andam*[45] role they played at weddings. In light of such evidence, it would be worth asking which exactly is alien – homosexuality or homophobia?

Sometimes then the charge of being culturally inappropriate is made to legitimize actions to silence certain groups or to prohibit certain behaviours.

But this can have damaging effects. Not too long ago, it was considered culturally unacceptable to talk openly about rape and domestic violence. As a result, survivors of rape and violence were often too ashamed to seek help and so had to suffer in silence. Even if talking openly about women's bodies and sexuality is culturally inappropriate, ideas of what is culturally appropriate must be re-examined and broadened because the reality calls for it. Factors such as the high numbers of women who are contracting HIV from their husbands and partners and the high incidence of violence against women mean that we cannot leave cultural norms unchallenged. In choosing to stand its ground, AWAM showed how narrow ideas of what is culturally appropriate should not be allowed to stand in our way of addressing these problems.

Looking at the larger picture, a key factor highlighted by the situation around *The Vagina Monologues* is how the understanding or views of sexuality are not derived in a vacuum. These ideas are formed in relation to the views expressed by parents, families, religious leaders, political leaders and so on. The access one has to information about sexuality also affects how the issue is understood. When a performance like *The Vagina Monologues* is banned, the authorities are denying Malaysians access to a particular perspective on sexuality. This is a perspective which is feminist, which is inclusive of the range of female sexualities, which condemns the colonization or abuse of women's bodies and sexuality as well as the systems or structures which allow this to happen, and which seeks to empower women.

In the past, organizations like AWAM may have left the state to freely exert its control over how sexuality can be understood. However, with the inroads that have been made in this sphere, such groups are better placed to resist this state hegemony today while promoting real tolerance or even acceptance of diversity. This cause is greatly assisted by the inconsistent positions taken by the state authorities, a situation that is now gradually being made use of by sexuality rights advocates.[46]

For instance, as much as the transsexual community has been condemned, there have been occasions where national leaders have been seen to be sympathetic. In 1986, the Minister of Welfare Services, Abu Hassan Omar, gave *mak nyah* (transsexuals) due recognition when he was invited to launch the formation of the Selangor and Wilayah Persekutuan Mak Nyah Association, the country's first such organization (*The Star*, 27 November 2002). Even the current Minister for Women, Family and Community Development, Shahrizat Abdul Jalil – who was quick to condemn the PAS-led governments of Terengganu and Kelantan for supposedly licensing husbands to sodomize their wives[47] – has been supportive despite her sometimes misguided intentions.[48] Another good sign of the slow but definite change was the recent announcement by the Human Rights Commission of Malaysia (SUHAKAM) in 2003. Following the submission of a petition signed by more than 130 individuals, one of its Commissioners publicly chastized the Malay media for its biased coverage of sexually marginalized groups.[49]

Conclusion

Sexuality is an intrinsic part of our lives. It is also increasingly a publicly contested area, but one that is dominated by conservative forces. Hence it is important for people with different agendas and perspectives on this subject to make themselves heard. Their failure to do so up to now has left those who promote a very narrow and conservative viewpoint to dominate and thereby encourage disrespect and hostility towards differences on the basis of sexuality. After many years of chipping away at the margins of the Malaysian women's movement, sexuality rights advocates – some of whom are part of this movement – have made a dent and started this process of widening the understanding of sexuality in this country. It is an understanding that promotes tolerance of diversity, not encourages discrimination and hatred against those who are different.

Nevertheless, because efforts like these are seen as challenging the range of controls that are exerted over women's bodies, many in positions of power are not only resistant to such change but also try to ensure that it does not take place. This they have tried to do by arguing that women need 'protection' to prevent them from becoming 'bad' or by labelling all socially unacceptable (but legitimate) forms of sexuality as 'deviant'. Both protectionist legislation for women and girls, as well as the discourse on Asian values, have been effectively utilized for these purposes.

Given this, women's groups and other civil society organizations will have to continuously assert the belief that every person has a right to control her/his own body before it can become a reality. Leaving this project aside will result in even greater restrictions placed on the bodies of all women, men, girls and boys regardless of sexual preference, behaviour or practice.

8 Conclusion

The women's movement and discourse on sexuality

Three major themes have run through this account of feminism and the women's movement in Malaysia. We see the movement as being:

1   an outcome of the developmentalist state and its economic project;
2   an entity organized to either counter or further the hegemonic perspective of restricted democracy;
3   a repository for the discourse on sexuality.

In this chapter, we recap the highlights and move on to postulate the future of feminism and challenges for the women's movement.

The developmentalist state and the women's movement

We dwelled extensively on the issue of gender disparity and dislocation as Malaysia entered modern nationhood, embarked on the course of industrialization and confronted the travails of globalization. In this respect, the position of women in the labour force raises particular issues.

While economic gains have allowed for women's public roles to be enhanced, this phenomenon has not led to political and cultural enrichment in consonance with women's economic mobility. Instead, the economic empowerment achieved by virtue of their increased participation in higher education and employment has made them more strategic as consumers than as political players. This resulting disjuncture, in combination with their continued political emasculation, has given rise to a form of feminism that is largely market-driven. Women are mainly seen as a growing niche market and a valuable political constituency in the face of the developmentalist state's challenges against its oppositional forces.

The state has also given women's rights much attention whenever it needs to mute the rise of forces such as political Islam. Nevertheless, even if recent events have propounded a widespread discourse on gender equality, the realm of culture and politics has continued to limit the full recognition of women as equals in the workplace and in their engagement of the state.

LIVERPOOL JOHN MOORES UNIVERSITY
LEARNING & INFORMATION SERVICES

It is evidence of how 'the upper echelons of political power have remained a remarkably resilient bastion of male exclusivity' (Molyneux, 1998: 223). This syndrome reflects the features of a developmentalist state which is sometimes seen to be projecting a 'hypermasculine' agenda, using women to propagate both its economic and political power (Ling, 2000: 180–1). Its economic power is derived by 'thrusting millions of women into the workforce' and its political power by projecting itself as a patriarch and protector of women who are kept in the role of guardians of family values, morals and culture (Alvarez, 1991: 60).

The waxing and waning of feminism in Malaysia has been similarly affected by the state's shifting prerogatives either for economic advantage or political gains. Even though the women's movement has consciously attempted to become an autonomous force in civil society it is still circumscribed in its purpose and achievements. It has to mediate competing forces, comprising government, political parties, religious lobbies and the representatives of capital to achieve its purpose. These conflicting interests have made it less than easy for the women's movement to successfully push for gender-based reforms. Nevertheless, there is a remarkable tendency for Malaysian feminism to take on several variants in order to be responsive to the requirements of the time. We noted the shifting and fluid notions of feminism in the context of a multicultural and multi-religious society like Malaysia.

Hence our own framework in understanding the evolution of feminism in Malaysia has identified the presence of four dominant feminisms – nationalist, social, political and market-driven. The latter two have especially resulted from the specific conditions of the developmental Malaysian state and its economic project. They also reflect how the synchronization of state authoritarianism and its political agenda to limit democracy and the domination of global capital has created tensions and contestations within society. Civil society and the women's movement have tried to create a more just and equitable space to realize people's autonomy. But in cases where resistance has faltered, social movements have succumbed to the power of the market and state. At one period political feminism did rise to resist hegemony, but the culmination of that period saw the emergence of feminism driven by the dictates of market and state.

We ourselves do not subscribe to any standard definition of what feminism really means within a truly universal or Malaysian context. Most of what is understood as feminism throughout our discourse is based on a liberal, humanistic – and even, it could be argued, a socialist – perspective of justice and equality. Opponents of this definition will be critical of this conception as it is often associated with 'Western' values, particularly the emphasis on personal choice and attaining of individual freedom. But throughout this book we have stuck to the notion of feminism as embodying women's needs, interests and rights that are of both practical and strategic value.

Molyneux (1985, 1998) has set a whole train of debate in motion with arguments for and against such a conceptual scheme. To put it simply, a practical interest denotes the fulfilment of women's basic needs (such as personal safety, food, water, shelter, etc.) that do not require the overhaul of the existing gender order. Unlike practical needs, anything along the lines of a strategic interest implies questioning and challenging the structures of gender inequality. In order to assert their rights and dignity within the Malaysian context, women will have to mobilize to assert both their practical and strategic needs. Hence, the concept of feminism used to describe the activities of women's groups in this country is an inclusive notion and covers a wide spectrum of women's mobilization.

We minimally subscribe to the notion that a feminist must be someone who believes in the objectives of gender justice, if not equality, and works either actively or covertly to change the *status quo*. Given such a framework, even women who work within the paradigms and strictures of religion but with the intention of informing justice for women are also rightly feminists. Although their inclination towards gender equality is often ambiguous, perhaps even barely up to scratch, they too have had a part in shaping the notion of a just society. Our discussion of Muslim women's groups which are pragmatic and communitarian has shown that they have been responsive to gender reforms initiated by liberal feminists, even though from the outset most of them do not posture themselves as feminists.

The women's movement and hegemony

Malaysia's experience with establishing a democracy has seen women exerting their agency in various ways. They can range from being the staunchest defenders of conservative and even misogynistic ideological systems to being the most vocal advocates of radical cultural and religious reforms. But as our discussions have pointed out, either form of participation can deliver only limited benefits for women. This is because women have not participated fully in strategic organizations and where they have, did not occupy important ranks in the leadership hierarchy.

Despite this, feminism as an ideology and belief system is not totally shunned. The multifaceted aspects of civil society as well as the multi-pronged strategy that the state employs to control or neutralize an adversarial civil society have actually given liberal feminism some leeway to exert influence. This is because the state appears to be relatively less threatened by the demands of the women's movement compared with those of opposition Islam, the labour movement and human rights advocacy.

Indeed, the state's use of the discourse on women's rights, in tandem with its own repressive actions, has been successful in staving off the challenge of an oppositionist political Islam. What resulted, though, is not liberal democracy but mere lip service to human and women's rights. The state has continued to employ undemocratic means to maintain its power and entrenched hegemony. Its claim that a limited form of democratic participation is better than full democracy is bolstered by arguments geared towards political, economic and social stability.

Such a need to gain legitimacy is related to the concept of hegemony.[1] As propounded by Gramsci, this implies that rule by physical repression normally associated with a dictatorship can actually be absent in a modern but authoritarian state. Yet, the state is able to amass support through moral and intellectual persuasion even without the use of instruments of coercion such as the police, the military or the power of the law. Control is instead implemented in an influential and convincing manner through use of, or with cooperation from, social and cultural institutions such as religious institutions, labour unions, civic associations, schools and the press. The state can succeed in exerting hegemony when the people are persuaded that it would be in their best interests to maintain the *status quo*. As hegemony is progressively secured, the state would even go to the extent of accommodating alternative and counter-hegemonic cultural forces, but for the purpose of 'neutralising, changing or actually incorporating them' (Entwistle, 1979: 12–13).

It has been argued that the Malaysian state has used both repressive and consensual strategies to win acceptance (Hilley, 2001: 22). It has functioned as a contradictory entity because it is selectively authoritarian and arbitrarily democratic at the same time. As a newly industrializing state, Malaysia has severely suppressed any challenge of its political and business interests – among its first actions, for example, has been to eliminate trade union activities within a growing class of industrial workers. It has also cracked down on any direct undermining of the 'canonical' conception of Malay dominance and its elite consociational basis of governance; in 1987, political scapegoating resulted in the mass arrest of large numbers of social activists. But the Malaysian state has been liberal in other matters, notably on women's issues that do not directly challenge many of its established tenets – the tenets of Malay, Islamic and capitalist hegemony.

Nevertheless, the women's movement had always felt compelled to be strategic in its exercise of political strength in order to make headway in matters of violence against women (VAW) and sexuality. Women activists have had to unhappily accommodate and compromise on certain issues so as to not totally lose out on their main goal. In confronting gendered violence and structural inequality, women's groups have depended quite substantially on the mechanism of the law for redress. But the legal and political campaign against VAW has been a lengthy one and the outcome of that bargain has delivered only partial gains to women.

What we have described in our account of the women's movement underscores the capacity of the state to neutralize women's rights. It has accommodated some demands by appropriating much of the rights rhetoric. In the case of the challenges that *Reformasi* brought about on the evolution of feminism and on its own authority, the state has been able to reinforce its legitimacy by appropriating the causes of both the women's and the political reform movement. Whether the state had 'neutralized', 'changed' or actually 'incorporated' the movements, the outcome has been one of persuasion, not coercion, of citizens to support it even as it denies their political rights.

Indeed, the state has been cognizant of exactly what to absorb in order to remain legitimate in the eyes of a growing number of the new middle and urban classes. For example, the issues and remedies connected to VAW have already been mainstreamed in a significant way. From 2003, the Ministry of Health started working with other ministries in its campaign to prevent domestic violence. Malaysia thus became the first country in the region to endorse the 56th World Health Assembly resolution that urged all its members to comply with the guidelines of the World Health Organization's World Report on Violence and Health. The government committed itself towards a national action plan for violence prevention and data collection.[2] Government budgetary allocation announced on 12 September 2003 also specifically singled out women as one of its more important beneficiaries. Although welfaristic in orientation, it does indicate that women are being considered an important political constituency.[3]

Seemingly retrogressive movement as embodied in political Islam has also brought about paradoxical developments within the system, allowing women in Malay-Muslim organizations to find basis for empowerment within these groups. In the process of negotiating with Islam they have been forced, consciously or unconsciously, to become more socially and politically prominent in society. However, this goal has been very much facilitated by the state's agenda to contain an oppositionist political Islam and the latter's intention to remain relevant. Advocates of political Islam have themselves become concerned about winning credibility for their perspectives and have therefore had to give in to pressures for liberalizing some aspects of the movement.[4] In the final analysis, the strategy to accept and support certain women's rights has been expediently used by both government and opposition Islam in reclaiming lost ground for legitimacy.

The women's movement and the discourse on sexuality

The third major theme explored in this book is the issue of sexuality, both as subject of VAW and as a focal element in the assertion of identity. People are generally not indifferent towards crimes which have a direct or indirect sexual implication, ranging from domestic violence to rape. However, the search by feminist groups for redress through the formulation and implementation of new laws has proved to be a protracted and complex process and one that has been influenced by discriminatory values.

Also explored is sexuality as a focal point of identity politics. For most of the last two decades, the women's movement in Malaysia has evaded the treatment of sexuality as a human rights issue. However, it has since become significant because civil society is now attempting to deal with the issue in a more prominent way. Although still a marginal shift, the women's movement has attempted to go beyond a heterosexual discourse (and hegemony) to one that is able to contain the discursive and practical concerns of sexuality in all its plural, non-binarial aspects, and work towards the recognition of difference.

What accounts for the nature of the current discourse and action around sexuality? Sexuality is one area easily subsumed under the gaze and control of the authoritarian state because of the latter's capacity to regulate almost everything. In Malaysia with the rise of religiosity, morality has become the purview of not only personal but public scrutiny and control. Power over the discourse and practice of sexuality is both a coercive and non-coercive means to elicit submission. People are extremely defenceless when put to shame. This can cut many ways, either to be used over powerful dissidents or to pacify further a powerless underclass.

In coercive ways a state like Malaysia has used anachronistic laws on sexual practices such as sodomy to character assassinate a political leader, as in the case of the former deputy premier Anwar Ibrahim in 1998. In non-coercive ways, morality norms can be readily invoked to conjure up the superiority of 'Asian values' and thereby win public legitimation. National leaders like former Singapore premier Lee Kuan Yew and the former Malaysian premier Mahathir Mohamad tried to negate Western-led pressure for more democracy and human rights in Asia by playing the morality card. They argued against the universality of human rights by claiming that the extension of human rights to homosexual relationships, as promoted by Western advocates, is simply immoral and 'not Asian'.[5]

In this book, several case-studies have been cited to show how state-directed discourse and its hold over sexuality have been utilized for social control. The reality is that unfettered public discourse on sexuality may threaten the legitimacy of a strong state. For example, when women or homosexuals are allowed to openly assert their sexuality beyond the circumscribed limit, the state's authority over such discourse would be weakened. Not only would this chip away at the formidability of the state, but it would ultimately force the state to surrender the use of sexuality as a tool of coercion and compliance.

The slippery slope of eliciting recognition for sexuality rights has had mixed results. This issue can be, and has been, used for the political survival of those in power. Under Mahathir, sexuality was deployed as a shaming device against his opponent, Anwar. However, the establishment does not consistently exert itself in a clear-cut manner in dealing with such matters. In the case of Puteri UMNO leader Azalina Othman Said, allegations about her sexuality have been brushed aside and have not been allowed to get in the way of UMNO's own agenda of wooing younger women into the party. Azalina was appointed Minister of Youth and Sports in March 2004 after having won uncontested in her maiden election outing, reflecting a meteoric political rise in her case. This has shown that sexuality need not be deemed an issue whenever leadership, dynamism and ability to deliver are the main considerations. Hence sexuality is only a tool used by political powers if they feel the situation warrants this. But at the end of it all, the state will not risk its tenuous legitimacy by providing a legal avenue for the recognition of sexual differences.

Opportunities and obstacles for the future of Malaysian feminism

Our account would be incomplete without an analysis and some postulations on what the future holds for feminism in Malaysia. For this, we focus on emerging factors that will have an influential role in directing and fashioning feminism and the women's movement.

Politics of funding

The question of funding for women's NGOs in Malaysia[6] is an important area of discussion because of the way in which it has contributed to the shaping of feminism – whether service-oriented, advocacy-based, education-directed or transformative in nature. Looking back, funding became an important concern for women's groups from the late 1980s. Prior to this, they had functioned primarily on the energies of volunteers, which was indicative of the kind of activism then. Coinciding with the rise of the global women's movement and the United Nations (UN)-endorsed women's decade and world conferences, substantive and readily available funds came through European development aid agencies to improve the status of women in Malaysia. This reached a peak in the mid-1990s which led to the establishment and/or strengthening of women's organizations interested in public education, advocacy and the provision of services for women in crisis.

Having become used to this financial support, many of these groups were confronted with difficult times when the politics of funding changed towards the end of the 1990s, on grounds that Malaysia had fallen out of the 'developing nations' economic category.[7] Indeed, even though some money continues to be made available through diplomatic missions based in the country, the heyday of bloc foreign funding appears to have come to an end for women's NGOs. More importantly, any remaining funding is now mainly directed to those willing to run projects that fit into the agenda of donors. Although the previous situation was similar to this, there had been a happy meeting of agendas – what women's groups wanted to achieve had matched the criteria for funding. With the change in donor priorities, this is no longer guaranteed.

In light of this, women's groups have had to turn to other sources for financial support. The two main avenues are the government and members of the public. In the first instance, financial assistance has increasingly been made available through the Women's Ministry. Since its establishment in 2001, the ministry has disbursed tens of thousands of *ringgit* to the entire spectrum of women's organizations, including those that are more independent.

Women's groups are also relying more on members of the public and corporate bodies to support their work financially. However, this has serious implications relating to their autonomy, direction and nature of activities.

The ability of women's groups to tap into sources of funding now depends on whether they fit the criteria set by prospective donors. In the case of the ministry, proposals for projects that give the government a high profile are more likely to be approved than those that intend to provide counselling or refuge services. Similarly, the ministry has shown a greater preference for commissioning NGOs to conduct training courses on gender-mainstreaming, rather than providing funds for lobbying and advocacy work. When appealing to the public for funds, women's bodies are confronted with a different situation – groups that offer services and appear more 'benevolent' are better placed to raise money, compared with those who express intentions to challenge the *status quo*.

Yet it must be pointed out that the so-called 'government' funds are derived from public monies. This poses the question as to why certain groups are given privileged access when it is the right of all sectors of civil society to utilize such funds. Worse, at the same time that the government does not want to fund certain activities such as the provision of services, it nonetheless obliges NGOs to raise money independently to take on this responsibility. Not only does the state wash its hands of basic welfare services, but it also ensures that this burden falls on civil society groups.[8]

Another dilemma that women's groups face in relation to utilizing government funds is that this can be, and has been, perceived as allowing themselves to be 'bought over' by the state. Varying degrees of criticism are being levelled that women's issues are 'soft' and easily co-opted by the state to its benefit. A further risk of accepting government money is that this is perceived to lend credibility to the authoritarian Malaysian state.

Balancing financial needs and an organization's own agenda thus must be carefully carried out. If there is no satisfactory compromise, it may be necessary to remain open to the idea of returning to the days when there was less contention as to whether it was money or commitment that propelled activism – or a time when obtaining funds was hardly a consideration in organizing activities.

Needs versus rights

In addition to advocacy campaigns, women's groups have long focused their attention on the practical needs of women by providing various services to those in crisis. Their dispensation of tangible services such as access to shelters, face-to-face counselling, telephone hotlines, legal aid, and education and skills training seemed to be an effective way to establish confidence in their credibility. But such services were also much needed because the state either did not provide these or, if it did, the women were viewed as mere welfare cases. Women's groups thus consciously took an approach which stressed that women have a right not to be violated under any circumstances and that they should be provided options to be empowered to make their own decisions.

It is only within the last ten years that the global women's movement has actively promoted the notion that 'women's rights are human rights'.[9] Discrimination against women is a fundamental denial of women's human rights. Accordingly, the gender- and rights-based approach has established norms of conduct for people in relation to the state and to one another. Molyneux and Razavi (2002: 12) have urged the women's movement to use the language of rights as 'rights confer agency and enable women in particular to articulate strong claims for equality'.

It is thus important that the women's movement shift from a needs-based to a rights-based approach by asserting that women's rights are human rights and by insisting that civil society groups incorporate women's rights as part of their constitutive struggle and agenda. Furthermore, rights-based development puts the onus back on the state to ensure that every human being can claim and enjoy these minimum civil, cultural, economic, political and social entitlements. This means that citizens have a duty to contribute to society as well as have a right to demand accountability from the state.

In this context, it is critical that the women's movement begins to claim such entitlements from the Malaysian government. This is particularly since the latter has ratified – and thus obliged to fulfil the conditions of – the Convention on the Elimination of all Forms of Discrimination against Women (CEDAW), as well as the Convention on the Rights of the Child, which includes the girl child. Additionally, one of the challenges in the globalized era is to move forward from being a localized needs provider to becoming a national and global human rights advocate through systematic networking and lobbying at the international level. In this regard, utilizing the UN treaty body system, particularly CEDAW, could be one way forward.[10]

Market feminism

Women with consumption power

Although the 'woman question' has essentially remained as consistent as it was conceived in the early 1980s, a new and competitive discourse about women's rights has recently emerged to suit the ambit of economic liberalization and notions of *bourgeois* consumer 'freedoms'. Some have called this particular phase the era of 'commodity feminism' as even the discourses of feminism can be used to sell commodities for profit.[11] A study conducted by MasterCard International in its report entitled 'The Future of Malaysia's Consumer Market: Dynamic Transformation and Rising Affluence' found that the rate of single women above 40 is growing at 5.5 per cent a year, and that more of them will be heads of households and will grow to be the most significant spenders by 2013.[12] It is not surprising then that the market is now keener than ever to deal with this new group of potential consumers. In 2002, a big department store in Malaysia had already cashed in on the concept of empowering and providing services to women by setting up a Mothers' Club. There was no attempt to hide the commercial agenda behind this move, which was launched by the Minister for Women, Shahrizat Abdul Jalil. The Club, it seemed, would organize consumer-oriented activities such as teaching women how to improve themselves through make-up classes, fashion shows and sessions on home decoration.

The management of various shopping centres are now jumping on the bandwagon of 'women's rights' – ostensibly to promote an awareness of its importance. The International Women's Day (8 March) of 2004 was celebrated with the participation of the private sector.[13] One commercial company mobilized several NGOs working on women's rights to participate in a two-day mega carnival at the biggest shopping mall in the Klang Valley. Rather than coming right out to promote women's rights, however, the message was all about 'respect'. Similarly the notion of 'girl power' has been sold to young women to assert their individuality and autonomy through innovative and attention grabbing fashion, hairdo, cosmetics and the like. Insurance companies and credit card firms have also caught on by offering special insurance coverage, in the guise of empowerment and freedom to single women.

Localized trends which celebrate women's and girls' individuality seem to concur with the emergence of what is now labelled 'third-wave' feminism in the West. This is a form of feminism which is said to have 'no unifying cause' or 'collective political responsibility' but having activities mainly organized around 'sexuality and identity' (Purvis, 2004: 3).

In the last few years, novel outlets for women's economic empowerment have also been created. For example, there is now a group calling themselves 'Mothers-for-Mothers', which zeroes in on the needs and interests of women who work out of their homes.[14] With electronic modes of communication, it seeks to break the sense of isolation and lack of social connectedness among women who are confined to their homes. Access to communication tools has been harnessed to sustain women's empowerment not just as gainfully waged workers but as effective mothers and homemakers. As the founder for the group said:

> I can't live without technology now. It gives women freedom. We may stay at home to take care of family but our brains still function as well. Gone are the days when women who stay home are called housewives and are looked down on because society thought we had little to contribute to society.
>
> (Cited in Hermida, 2001)

The group has succeeded in producing a book, 'Working @ Home: A guidebook for working women and homemakers', a project sponsored not only by the Canadian and Australian High Commissions, but also corporate sponsors Nestle and myHRpal.com (Hooi, 2004). In line with this concept, female electronic homemakers were honoured by the Human Resources Minister, Fong Chan Onn, at a recent prize presentation for the 'Best Teleworking Moms' contest.[15] This market-driven type of liberation is a form of feminism that places its emphasis on fulfilling women's needs, rather than challenging the patriarchal order. In encouraging women to be economically active, it also tends to glorify women's ability to combine both work and family commitments. The question is how the women's rights movement will fare in such an individualized, depoliticized and market-driven environment.

Has the women's movement become 'demobilized' in this new climate of appropriation by not only the state but the market? Take the example of the Women's Aid Organisation (WAO), one of the most high-profile women's group in the country. Although it was established in the early 1980s its current activities and services have only recently been extensively promoted by prominent companies and corporations in fund-raising drives. Companies such as La Senza which sells women's lingerie and garments, the Body Shop which sells cosmetics and publishing houses which produce women's lifestyle magazines such as *Female* and *Glam* have all profiled WAO in their own product promotion. The juxtaposition of women as a growing consumer market and a contemporary theme of independence in all aspects (but more specifically an independent purchasing power) has worked well to create niche products that are geared for this market segment.

Another example is in the launching of a new radio station specially created for women listeners. The launch of a radio station for women, WFM 88.1, in early 2005, speaks volumes for the growing importance of women consumers for advertisers. It is of no surprise that the drivers behind this new enterprise were all men, hard-nosed business people who see feasible profit opportunities in this venture. They claim to be starting the first radio station in the country (if not the region) for women.[16] Still, commercialized radio stations may not be a total loss for feminist activists as they may be given opportunities to broadcast issues on domestic violence, sexual crimes and relationships in a more politicized way.

Here we have to question the role of global capitalism in pushing for some of the trappings of this new feminism, which is even adding a new face to political Islam. In Malaysia's earlier history, its Islamic resurgence phase had actually put a restraint on consumption. But now that that the restraining force has somewhat loosened, consumer sovereignty has been reasserted. With this, even Islamization has been 'marketized' to cater for this new development. The proliferation of industries in the areas of Islamic finance, *halal*[17] food and Muslim garments is one indication. In 2004 the Malaysian government gave its full support to the staging of a 'halal' trade exhibition – the MIHAS (Malaysia International *Halal* Showcase) Exhibition was held in Kuala Lumpur, with some 500 exhibitors participating. Even an Islamic fashion show was held as part of the event.[18] In December 2004, a group called the Malaysian Muslim Women Consultative Council of Malaysia (MMWCCM), in collaboration with the Islamic Development Bank, Universiti Teknologi Mara and a private company called Positive Grooming Sdn. Bhd., presented the first ever International Muslim Women's Textile and Apparel Conference. All of these activities have been initiated by the Islamic Dakwah Foundation (YADIM), which is the Islamic body controlled directly by Prime Minister Abdullah Ahmad Badawi. One may read this as the administration's move to modernize Islam by taking it away from the grip of traditional institutions which are still under the purview of more conservative elements in the country. The state *per se* had been quite successful in moderating or depoliticizing the radical elements of Islam. But even this role is now being 'shared' or even overtaken by the market.

Transcending market feminism

Despite the gains that market feminism may accrue towards recognizing women's rights, this new phenomenon must nevertheless be treated as both a force and a barrier to feminism's real agenda of bringing about gender equality. By nature, market mechanisms are selective and dictated by profit-motives. There are certain areas that will remain sensitive and even immune to business concerns. For example, the bill on sexual harassment at the work-place was not accepted as it is not supported by the majority of big business. Any interruption of the production process by investigations and public prosecutions or individual lawsuits will cost companies in dollars and cents – hence their reluctance to support this bill.

At the end of the day, the market is only interested in women as consumers with new spending power. It will continue to reinforce and repro-duce the notion of women as consumers of 'independent will'. The ideal women who are portrayed as aesthetically pleasing, well-groomed, success-fully balancing career and family are the ones who will be projected as the image which sells, rather than the thinking women.

Even though corporations may even fund programmes in support of the feminist agenda, they also expect something in return. In the process there will be compromises and accommodations even to the extent of giving in to neo-conservatism, where emphasis on family and motherhood can be reasserted.

Rather than looking at market involvement in women's issues as a new practice or social movement it may be more suitably viewed as an appropria-tion of a feminist culture – one that was so vigorously drawn out by political feminism. Nonetheless, the capture of the feminist essence or symbols by the market will inevitably constitute a force compelling enough to influence how the masses, the state and civil society will engage with gender politics.

But we do need to question the future of feminism beyond its appropria-tion by the state or the market. Is 'second-wave' feminism (or political feminism in the Malaysian context) being phased out to herald a 'third-wave' feminism? Instead of centring a uniform 'women's liberation' discourse the 'third-wave' may embrace a more diverse and 'polyvocal' feminism; instead of embracing identity politics as the key to liberation it may even seek freedom by resisting identity (Mann, 2005). All of these cultural shifts are identifiable today. The only thing is that we are still not seeing strong tendencies among a younger generation of Malaysian feminists to create political movements out of this 'third-wave', perhaps market-inspired sentiments.

Other issues

Feminism and men

Another recent development in the Malaysian women's movement is the involvement of men. Although various individuals have been sympathetic to the feminist cause in the past, it was not until mid-2002 that a group was formed to provide men with an avenue to examine and problematize their roles in patriarchal society. The formation of MAN.V (Man's Action Network Against Violence) was the brainchild of the All Women's Action Society (AWAM) and was conceived after a series of workshops, where the male participants concluded that they had to be part of the solution to solve the problem of gender violence. As a pioneering effort, the group has seen a slow but steady rise in membership, with those joining sharing a commitment to put an end to men's role in perpetuating VAW.[19]

A main strategy of MAN.V has been to speak out as men against VAW and, through this, encourage other male counterparts to do the same. In December 2003, MAN.V launched the Malaysian chapter of the global White Ribbon Campaign – an event to give visibility to male efforts such as MAN.V in addressing gender violence.[20] The campaign, which drew pledges from a host of local male personalities, was deemed a success, at least in terms of the positive publicity that ensued. AWAM sees this partnership with MAN.V as a way forward since it believes that men must take equal responsibility and work together with women to build an egalitarian and just society where the rights of women, men and children are upheld.

Another emerging concern that needs to be addressed is the 'crisis of masculinity' where men sense and experience a diminishing masculinity alongside women's assertion of their own economic and social autonomy, brought about by the influx of women into the labour market, as well as the visibility of the women's rights movement. This challenges patriarchy whether at home, in the community or in the workplace. The situation has been made worse in the era of labour flexibilization, where male jobs are becoming more insecure and unstable, thus depriving men of the traditional breadwinner's role in the family. To compound matters, while women have been transformed to be more aware of their rights, men have not followed suit, leading to the likely outcome of increased tension and violence at home and in society.

How exactly MAN.V will impact on the future of feminism is still too early to tell. While early signs are promising, the group will have to go beyond the basics of gender violence and look instead at the root causes as well as contributing factors (which include the 'crisis of masculinity') if it is to succeed in its mission. Nevertheless it has the hallmarks of being a form of feminism that challenges the current gender order.

Feminism and younger women

On the whole, Malaysian civil society groups, and particularly those which explicitly seek to challenge unequal power relations or raise human rights concerns, suffer from an inability to attract younger people into their fold. The women's movement is no different.[21] Like others, it is confronted by a society that is, by and large, apathetic, fearful of the repercussions of questioning authority, or too much caught up in day-to-day pursuits of the 'good life' – a better income, more material possessions and higher standards of living.

Women's groups suffer from an additional disadvantage due to the negative connotations associated with feminism and women's rights. The concept of feminism, in particular, has been much maligned and portrayed negatively by the media and national leaders alike as associated with being anti-men, radical and Western-influenced. Hence, even as the everyday woman agrees with the goals of feminism (e.g. the right of women to education, employment, health services), persuading her to publicly identify as a feminist is quite another matter.

Other factors influence the extent of younger women's participation in Malaysian NGOs. In many ways, women's groups, again, like other civil society groups, have not kept abreast of issues that are perceived as important to the youth.[22] Prioritizing the involvement of the younger generation calls for a qualitative shift in strategy from merely running programmes for younger people, such as those dealing with sexual assault and child sexual abuse, as conducted by groups like WCC and AWAM. Furthermore, even if there is recognition of the need to take up issues relating to youth, this has not been accompanied by action often because resources are already overstretched in meeting current commitments. This has been a long-standing predicament that, unless rectified, could lead to the women's movement being rendered irrelevant.

Among the few younger women who are able to look beyond an unattractive menu of activities to the larger goal of women's equality and social justice, the level of enthusiasm is sometimes doused by the lack of real spaces to express their opinions or initiate action. Clearly, women activists who have spent many years in the movement need to change the nature of their involvement so that their presence, which can sometimes be daunting if not dominating, does not stifle new ideas and ways of doing. Newcomers now often have to put up with pre-existing politicking and dynamics within and between organizations, which often leaves them between a rock and a hard place.

Fortunately, activism among younger women has not been quelled despite the deterrents mentioned. There is a small but not insignificant number who are concerned about social justice and human rights. Through them new initiatives are being formed and, while these may not take the shape of traditional women's groups,[23] they still need to be encouraged for it is diversity that also allows feminism and the women's movement to survive. More importantly, women's NGOs have to engage with this growing constituency, and efforts to bridge any 'older–younger' divide are thus paramount towards building the next generation of leadership.

Stirrings of 'third-wave' feminism seem to be apparent from the above rendition. There is definitely a need to address this gap between 'second wave' and 'third wave' feminists. Instead of seeing it as leading to an inter-generational conflict many have called for a cross-generational dialogue instead, where feminism can be seen as a 'process of becoming' rather than a consciousness fossilized in artificial time-frames (Purvis, 2004: 18).

After Mahathir: the start of a new era?

In October 2003, after a record-breaking 22-year term, Malaysia's fourth Prime Minister, Mahathir Mohamad, finally retired. This paved the way for a government under the leadership of Abdullah Ahmad Badawi. The backing for Pak Lah, as he is popularly known, was reinforced in the March 2004 general election when he led the ruling coalition Barisan Nasional (BN) to a resounding win. Although there were numerous reasons for the devastating collapse of the opposition vote – ranging from an uneven playing field to serious misconceptions of the opposition's popularity and the lack of any contentious political issues – the most important was probably that many Malaysians saw hope in the new leadership.

Abdullah has come across initially as being more affable, kind and approachable compared with his predecessor. By projecting himself as 'Mr Clean',[24] knowledgeable about Islam and, most importantly, as a trustworthy proponent of moderate and progressive Islam, he has generated renewed optimism among the populace. Whether or not their hopes are well placed will only be fully known in time.[25]

Where women's interests are concerned, early signs of what is in store are at best ambivalent. Even though he is also known to be sympathetic to their cause, Abdullah appears to have got off to a poor start. Given that women's groups have long demanded to see increased women's participation in polit-ical decision-making, his post-election strategies do not augur well. This is worsened by the fact that he had no qualms about the BN using women in its media campaign – projecting itself as a champion of women's rights – to attract female votes. Not only was there a dismally low percentage of women candidates nominated by BN component parties,[26] the percentage of women ministers in his restructured and expanded cabinet fell in comparison with that under Mahathir, although the number of women ministers in the cabinet remained the same at three. Currently there are 23 (10.5 per cent) female Members of Parliament out of a total of 219 parliamentarians compared with 20 females (10.3 per cent) out of 193 parliamentarians after the 1999 general election. This remains far below the UN call, endorsed by Women's Agenda for Change and the government, for a 30 per cent represen-tation of women in decision-making processes.

Admittedly Pak Lah did the right thing by expanding the Ministry of Women and Family Development to become the Ministry of Women, Family and Community Development,[27] and, along with it, provided the newly created post of Deputy Minister. However, exactly how effective the new Deputy, G. Palanivel, will be in promoting women's rights is seriously in question as he assumes the post with no track record.

Perhaps of greater concern is the lack of concrete plans to ensure much-needed gender-sensitivity among lawmakers, bureaucrats and the media. Nonetheless, indicative of his stated seriousness in dismantling gender inequality, Abdullah held a public meeting in May 2004 with women's groups – and a separate meeting later with the Joint Action Group against Violence Against Women (JAG-VAW) and National Council of Women's Organisations – to state his stand against sex crimes.[28] Later that month, on 25 May 2004, JAG-VAW initiated a meeting with Abdullah who agreed to look into the various memoranda put forward by JAG-VAW and the women's movement since the 1980s. The response has been laudable in that, since then, a key recommendation of JAG-VAW – the Cabinet Committee on Gender Equality – was established in August 2004. In presumably the first meeting of the Cabinet Committee chaired by Abdullah on 6 December 2004, it was announced that five existing shelters will be gazetted for abused women,[29] that the public sector achieve a quota of at least 30 per cent women in senior level positions, and that all ministries must set up 'gender focal points' to speed up the government's objective of ensuring gender equality at all levels.[30]

By way of a conclusion

The women's movement and democracy

Malaysia's progress towards a more genuine democracy still appears to be constricted. There continues to be a belief that multicultural stability can only be achieved with a strong-arm state in place. Even worse for women, the phasing out of the authoritarian state may not necessarily lead to the removal of a 'hypermasculinized' politics, of either government or opposi-tion. Although on balance, feminism has been a significant movement upon which the identity of the Malaysian state has been carved. But the presence of a feminist culture has not succeeded in changing the style of political leadership nor has it been capable of overturning maladies such as corruption and abuse of public power.

In fact, if one were to use the Gramscian notion of 'hegemony', the women's movement can be said to have contributed to the strengthening of state legitimacy and credibility. There was hardly any need to use oppressive state instruments to secure compliance when it came to state negotiations with the feminist force. While some aspects of the women's movement may counter mainstream patriarchal ideology, the appropriation and cultivation of the movement by the state (no matter if is inconsistently and sporadically done) has contributed to legitimize the workings of this authoritarian body.

Discernible trends in the West have led feminists to conclude that a 'second-wave' feminism is moving into a 'third-wave' variant. In developing countries, what is becoming more observable is that feminist movements have now been integrated by the state. Prominent feminists within movements may now be involved in 'gender policy assessment, project execution, and social service delivery', hence leading to the paradox wherein the capacity of feminist NGOs to advocate feminism may even be curtailed (Franceschet, 2003).

Given the above, a strong case can be made for the Malaysian women's movement not to be reliant on the state to realize its objectives. If anything, the time may be right to move efforts against VAW to another level by, for example, systematically going back to communities to build greater public consciousness, regain the movement's autonomy and continue to advocate feminism from the outside rather than from within.

We have argued that Malaysian women's NGOs are sometimes easily swayed by paternalistic influences because of their need to accommodate ideological differences and the conflicting demands of a multicultural entity. In fact, to survive the potential disuniting impact of multicultural politics, the price that women activists pay is to relent to the discourse of order and stability. This is in turn has hinged upon a male-centric, even heterosexual, world-view of women as secondary actors and men as primary players in the public and private spheres. As such, the issue of how much rights women should have remains a contentious one, with many even within the movement not always in favour of complete and unequivocal rights for women. If they see women's rights being achieved at the expense of community rights, they may even choose to support the latter.[31]

At another level, the regime favours the participation of women in formal or electoral politics with the backing of male patrons, rather than their participation in autonomous civil movements. Women participate in electoral politics not as autonomous agents but as the purveyor of partisan politics determined by male-elite leaders. Indeed present-day women politicians in government argue smugly that they are in no great need of large numbers of effective feminist supporters when it becomes necessary for them to articulate women's causes.[32]

Among many women politicians today, appropriating the messages, symbols and language or the broad narratives of successful feminist NGOs has become the quickest way to winning the confidence of the middle-class, urban constituency. The groundwork laid by feminist movements of the early 1980s – such as the aspiration for gender equality, for resisting patriarchal tyranny and for securing women's rights – have all become ostensibly acceptable in the everyday discourse of Malaysians, although there has been no far-reaching commitment from politicians to the delivery of these ideals.

Why the women's movement matters

Looked at from a larger perspective, the Malaysian women's movement has always been part and parcel of a transnational civil society for the creation of global democracy. On a national level, it provides a legitimate avenue for women to fight for their cultural, social, economic and political rights. It has added value to women's lives by making the development process more gender-sensitive, and prevented debilitating consequences to economic growth and human development.

Conceptually, feminism has paved the way for speaking to the intersecting concerns brought about by class, ethnic, religious, cultural and gender divides. In Malaysia, the women's movement has notably succeeded in providing peaceful networking opportunities for a multicultural population, while building effective structures for addressing fundamental issues in women's lives. The narratives of feminism have constructed, as well as reclaimed, institutions, policies, laws and social spaces for women's visibility and, even if it may have remained largely unsung as a grand political force, the feminist (r)evolution in Malaysia *does* matter for those who moved it and were moved by it.

Appendix A

Key members of the Joint Action Group against Violence Against Women (JAG-VAW)[1]

All Women's Action Society (AWAM)

This is an independent feminist organization committed to improving the lives of women in Malaysia. The impetus for its formation came from the 1985 Joint Action Group against Violence Against Women (JAG-VAW) event. Although it started organizing around this time, it was only accorded official registration in 1988. Its vision is to create a just and equitable society where women are treated with respect, and are free from all forms of violence and discrimination. Its programmes hence inform, connect and mobilize those interested in securing women's rights, bringing about gender equality, and supporting women in crisis.

Its activities can be divided into five categories:

- public education (e.g. exhibitions, information booths, talks, seminars, media statements, outreach programme);
- training (e.g. gender analysis, rape, sexual harassment, feminist counselling);
- lobbying and advocacy (e.g. amendments to laws relating to rape, enactment of the Domestic Violence Act, setting up of One-Stop Crisis Centres in major government hospitals, introduction of the Code of Practice on the Prevention and Eradication of Sexual Harassment in the Workplace);
- services (e.g. telephone and face-to-face counselling, legal information service);
- research (e.g. on rape, sexual harassment, media portrayal of women).

In 2002, the organization initiated the formation of MAN.V (Man's Action Network Against Violence) for men concerned over the recurring violence perpetrated against women and children.

Sabah Women Action Resource Group (SAWO)

This was formed in 1985 by a group of women and men concerned about the increasing trend of violence against women (VAW) and children in

Sabah and at the national level. Its work over the first five years started with a workshop and exhibition on VAW in early 1986 at the Kota Kinabalu Community Centre. This was followed by a sustained campaign to get the authorities to implement the resolutions of the workshop. Some of the activities during this time included mobilizing other women's groups in the state to conduct joint activities, talks to the public and in schools, training of volunteer counsellors; and the setting up and running of a crisis and counselling line.

From its experience and growth, SAWO realized the need to work on other areas as well in order to achieve its vision of an egalitarian society where women, children and the poor are treated equally. SAWO therefore also worked on consumer and environmental issues, and encouraged greater focus on the needs of women at all stages of development in Sabah. Its current goal is to push the state authorities to adopt and implement federal laws and policies, such as the National Policy on Women. At the same time it is building its own capacity and that of other women's groups through leadership training and awareness on gender and women's issues.

Sarawak Women for Women Society (SWWS)

SWWS was set up in 1985. The founding members of the society felt that a broad-based women's organization was needed as an alternative to other groups linked to political parties or which are based on religious or ethnic affiliation. Such groups have also tended to focus on promoting activities related to women's traditional roles (e.g. cooking, cake-making, floral arrangement).

The initial focus of SWWS was on awareness-raising of gender issues such as VAW, through workshops, seminars and public exhibitions. It has since established a centre staffed by a full-time worker. This took much effort because it was decided to maintain autonomy in fund-raising efforts. Currently, SWWS runs a crisis telephone service and a drop-in centre for women. Its membership has expanded to 80.

Sisters in Islam (SIS)

Sisters in Islam (SIS) was formed in 1988 and registered as an NGO in 1993 under the name SIS Forum (Malaysia) Bhd. (The name Sisters in Islam is retained as an authorship name.) The group was initiated by Muslim professional women based in Kuala Lumpur, whose careers ranged from journalism to law. The organization is committed to promoting the rights of Muslim women within the framework of Islam, that is based on the principles of equality, justice and freedom enjoined by the Qur'an.

In developing and promoting a framework of women's rights in Islam, it has proposed *Syariah* law reforms, and has been an active initiator of campaigns against the implementation of the *Hudud* (Islamic criminal laws).

Its activities include study sessions, public lectures, workshops and the issuance of press statements on various topical issues affecting Muslim women. The group has produced some 29 publications, including such titles as "Are Women and Men Equal Before Allah?" and *Freedom of Expression in Islam*. Publications have been produced in both English and the Malay language. Among the titles of its study sessions are "Hermeneutics as an Approach to Gender Studies in Islam and Dress and Modesty in Islam".

Women's Aid Organisation (WAO)

Through the financial support of a former Malaysian Minister of Finance, the Women's Aid Organisation (WAO) was started in 1982 to provide refuge, counselling services and child support to battered women. While this remains an important function of the group, WAO's scope and outlook have expanded over the years. Today, its mission is also to eliminate discrimination against women and to bring about equality between the sexes. Thus, apart from running a shelter for women in crisis, a childcare centre, and telephone and face-to-face counselling services, it seeks to empower women to make informed choices as well.

This it does through a public education programme (e.g. talks, workshops, media statements and articles), and advocating women's rights (e.g. policy and legal reform). WAO was part of the JAG-VAW initiative that campaigned for a Domestic Violence Act. Since the passage of legislation, it has been monitoring the effectiveness of implementation *viz* three agencies: the police, welfare services department and the courts. It has also taken up the issue of migrant domestic workers, especially in relation to those who have been abused by their employers. Along with AWAM, SIS, WCC and WDC, it has been a steadfast partner in the JAG-VAW entity.

Women's Centre for Change (WCC)

Known as the Women's Crisis Centre when formed in 1982 and as the Women's Centre for Change since 2003, the WCC is based in Penang. Its formation was mooted by women in Penang and the northern region, to assist women experiencing domestic violence and with no place to turn for help. An effort was made in its early founding stage to bring together diverse women's groups linked to welfare associations, universities and other voluntary NGOs to come together in the establishment of a first crisis centre in the island to provide counselling and shelter services for abused women. The WCC was registered as a non-profit voluntary society in 1985. The initial group of women who volunteered in its activities came from varied backgrounds – academia, law, family planning, consumer activism and homemaking.

When it was registered, WCC's main goals were to provide counselling, legal advice and temporary shelter for women and children facing domestic crisis and abuse. Over the years it has expanded its goals to include public education and consciousness-raising, especially among youths. Its role in law reform and women's rights advocacy has also become an important component of its work. The name change from Women's Crisis Centre to Women's Centre for Change reflects this shift in direction – from being strictly service-oriented to being proactive in advocacy. WCC has, however, continued to maintain a shelter and to provide free social and legal counselling for women. Its public education and training activities have been conducted with the co-operation and support of government bodies such as the education, welfare and women's development ministries. WCC initiated the ongoing campaign amongst women's groups for a bill against sexual harassment at the workplace.

Women's Development Collective (WDC)

WDC was formed in the early 1980s when a group of young women came together to discuss issues relating to women and feminism. This later sparked a process of working with individuals and groups on legal reforms, training programmes, public education and advocacy. Formally registered in 1988, the organization has since concentrated on research, education and training. Its programmes focus on gender and feminist analysis, paralegal training particularly for women workers, leadership and organizing.

One of its main activities is the Women Organizing Network (previously known as the Women in Development programme) which aims to work with women activists to build a progressive women's movement. As noted in its brochure, WDC is a collective of feminists committed to building a progressive women's movement in Malaysia. It envisions a democratic society based on political, economic and social justice. WDC has been a prime mover and served as secretariat of various campaigns related to women and democracy. These include the 'Women's Manifesto', the Women's Agenda for Change (WAC) and Women Monitoring Election Candidates (WOMEC). The organization is not the same as the Women's Development Centre, started in 2004 by a female politician from a Chinese political party in the ruling coalition government.

Appendix B

The Women's Agenda for Change[1]

Introduction

The 1990s saw the acceleration of women's groups lobbying for policy changes and action at the national and international level. In Malaysia, the Women's Manifesto was launched in 1990, prior to the general elections, to secure commitments from all political parties to improve the status of women in the key concerns of work, the law, violence against women, development, health, corruption and human rights. Towards the mid-1990s, women's groups all over the world were preparing for the UN Fourth World Conference on Women as well as the NGO Forum on Women in Beijing. Keeping pace with this development, several women's groups in Malaysia came up with the '11-point Agenda' which was presented to the Malaysian government to obtain its commitment to women.

On the part of the Malaysian government, the National Policy on Women was formulated in 1989 in consultation with the National Council of Women's Organisations (NCWO), Malaysia. This was a follow-up to the 1985 UN Third World Conference on Women in Nairobi, Kenya. However, it was only in 1997 that the Women's Affairs Department, under the Ministry of National Unity and Social Development, began to formulate a follow-up Action Plan for Woman in Development to translate policies into action. The Malaysian government's commitment to improving the status of women is stated in the chapters on 'Women and Development' in the Sixth (1991–5) and Seventh (1996–2000) Malaysia Plans. Its commitment was reaffirmed when it ratified the UN Convention on the Elimination of All Forms of Discrimination against Women (CEDAW) in 1995.

Today, as we enter the third millennium, we recognize that many of the key issues brought up throughout the 1990s have remained on paper. They have not been acted upon. Although women's groups successfully fought for the enactment of the Domestic Violence Act in 1994, many laws still discriminate against women. Moreover, as Malaysia enters the global economic race and opens its doors to increased economic liberalization, women's position could be adversely affected due to their subordinate status in society.

The recent political developments in Malaysia have added to the impetus and urgency to strengthen women's participation in the cultural, economic and political life of the nation. We deplore the manipulation of ethnicity and religion, as well as the use of fear and oppressive forces, to divide us. We wish to contribute towards the building of a just, democratic and peaceful society for ourselves and future generations.

Hence, the Women's Agenda for Change is a reflection of our commitment towards the achievement of gender equality and sustainable development for women and men in Malaysia. The aims of this initiative are to:

- draw attention to specific problems, issues and needs of women which should be recognised and addressed;
- raise awareness of women and men on the position of women in Malaysia;
- strengthen the political participation and voices of women in Malaysia so as to promote and achieve gender equality and to work for a just and democratic society; and
- strengthen a network of women's organizations and NGOs to work towards the advancement of the status of women in Malaysia.

On 9 and 10 January 1999, a National Workshop on the Women's Agenda for Change was jointly organized by the Women's Development Collective (WDC), Sisters in Islam, Persatuan Sahabat Wanita, Selangor (PSWS) and the All Women's Action Society (AWAM). The four organizations and individuals at the workshop identified ten key issues[2] of concern on the basis of their various experiences and positions in society. These issues were presented and discussed at the National Workshop. A total of 34 women's organizations and NGOs attended and provided their recommendations to the position papers. An eleventh paper on Women, Health and Sexuality was added to the Women's Agenda for Change.

Therefore, we present here the 11 major issues with which we are concerned with. These issues are not exhaustive and we urge you to add on your own concerns. This is your agenda. Use it to lobby:

- the government and institutions for their support in terms of policy measures and actions;
- the politicians so that they will incorporate the issues and recommendations into their election manifesto and, if elected, their constituency programmes; and
- the general public to raise their awareness on the issues and challenges facing women in Malaysia.

Malaysia is in the midst of change – push the women's agenda forward!

Appendix C

As Malaysians and as women – questions for our politicians and a manifesto for the 1990s

As Malaysians and as women,

- we recognize that we live in a country endowed with immense natural wealth;
- we are aware that through the efforts of all Malaysians great progress has been made in developing this natural wealth;
- we acknowledge that the present government has recently approved a National Policy on Women.

However,

- we deplore the fact that, more than 30 years after Merdeka, race and religion continue to divide us;
- we deplore the several amendments to the Constitution which have eroded many of our fundamental civil rights;
- we regret that women are still discriminated against in many aspects of our lives;
- we regret that the fruits of development have been inequitably distributed and the gap between rich and poor has widened.

As Malaysians and as women, we believe that people of diverse cultural backgrounds and faiths can live together in peace and mutual respect. We are convinced that we can build a just, peaceful and stable society for ourselves and our children. We assert that development must put people's welfare and a clean environment over and above all other goals. Finally, we insist that women be treated with respect and dignity, and as equal partners, both inside and outside the home.

As Malaysians and as women, we are aware that we can make a difference, but only if:

- we understand the vital issues of national life;
- we begin now to discuss these issues with all Malaysia;

- we secure firm commitments from all political parties to improve significantly the status of women in society;
- we make sure that in the forthcoming general elections our votes count.

This then is our declaration as Malaysians and as women. This is our Manifesto for the 1990s. These are our concerns.

Women and work

As women of Malaysia, we have contributed immensely to the development of the nation. Yet our contribution is not properly rewarded. A majority of us work at low-skilled, low-paying jobs. Our working conditions are poor, our opportunities for advancement limited.

In industry and estates, women workers – well represented in numbers – are particularly oppressed. Since the jobs we as women workers hold are mostly unskilled, we are easily replaced by machines. In industry and estates, there are few jobs we hold which are not hazardous to health, and there are few employers who provide child-care facilities.

And for those of our sisters labouring in the Free Trade Zones – a majority of the workforce – the basic right of unionization has long been denied. It has been 20 years since the Free Trade Zones were set up. *A whole generation of women has been denied this right!*

So we ask of our politicians:

- Will you and your party fight for a minimum living wage for all workers?
- Does your party advocate state/employer child-care support services?
- How will your party work towards the welfare and safety of workers, in particular women workers?
- Does your party support, and will it guarantee, the basic right of all workers, inside Free Trade Zones and outside, in industry and estates, to unionize?

Our legal standing

Today, laws still exist which discriminate against the women of Malaysia. This in spite of the constitutional guarantee that all, whether male or female, are equal under the law, and that all enjoy equal protection under the law. Time and time again, as Malaysians and as women we have called upon these unjust laws to be amended. But only a few have been amended – the Law Reform (Marriage and Divorce) Act 1976, the Islamic Family Law Enactments and the laws pertaining to rape.

These are some of the laws which *still* discriminate against the women of Malaysia:

- Article 8 (Equality) of the Federal Constitution
- The Guardianship of Infants Act 1961
- The Distribution Act 1958
- The Immigration Act 1959/1963
- The Workmen's Compensation Act 1952
- The Employment Act 1955 (revised 1981) and laws pertaining to citizenship, income tax and social security

So we ask of our politicians:

- What has your party done, now and in the past, to amend these laws?
- What will your party do to ensure that reforms to these laws will be implemented in letter and in spirit?
- How will your party ensure the uniformity of the Islamic Family Law Enactments?
- How, specifically, will your party monitor the implementation of the Islamic Family Law Enactments?

Violence against women

Wife beating. Sexual harassment. Rape. These are all acts of violence against women. Society indirectly condones such violence through institutions which promote derogatory attitudes towards women. One such institution is the mass media. On TV and in newspapers, advertisements portray women as *sex objects*. Little wonder that violence inflicted against women is not recognized for what it is – *violence*.

Little wonder, then, that little has been done by the powers-that-be to curb this violence. A Domestic Violence Act is still to be enacted. Shelters for survivors of violence are insufficient.

Sexual harassment on the job, the most hidden form of violence, is increasing. A 1987 survey by the Malaysian Trades Union Congress (Penang branch) disclosed that 80 per cent of women workers interviewed admitted to either having been sexually harassed while at work, or know of someone else who suffered the same fate. No channels exist to stop these harassments, much less to punish the culprits.

So we ask our politicians:

- What will your party do about advertisements in the mass media which portray women as sex objects, and to promote education to counter such degrading images of women?
- Will your party fight for an increase in funds to voluntary organizations to provide shelters and counseling for survivors of violence?
- Will your party support our campaign for the immediate enactment of the Domestic Violence Act?

- Does your party recognize that sexual harassment is an occupational hazard, that it causes mental and physical illness and can cost some women their jobs?

Development

Development should be people-centred. Development must be equitable and sustainable. It must ensure that the majority of the people own and have a say in the disposal of the country's resources. *However, this is not now the case.*

There is no minimum living wage for workers. Occupational health and workers' safety are not emphasized. Rural development programmes have largely ignored women's rights to land and other agricultural resources. Indiscriminate logging has deprived native groups of their homes and means of subsistence, and has jeopardized the eco-system.

So we ask of our politicians:

Is your party willing to commit to people-centred development by:

- Establishing a minimum living wage for all working people?
- Ensuring that occupational health and safety legislation is enforced so that our health is not sacrificed for profit?
- Stopping indiscriminate logging and championing the rights of native groups, such as the Penans, to their own land?
- Ensuring that rural women can participate equally in rural and land development, and have access to and control of land and other resources?

Health

As women, as workers and as bearers of children, we have special health needs: we suffer health problems related to pregnancy, childbirth, abortions and contraception.

Malaysia's health delivery system is undoubtedly among the best in the region. But there is still a wide disparity in health services and health status between urban and rural areas, as well as between Peninsular Malaysia and Sabah and Sarawak.

Also, the needs of special groups – the mentally ill, the handicapped, the elderly, the terminally ill – have received little attention, and even less funding.

Another deplorable trend is increased privatization. Privatization is contrary to the aim of 'Health for All'. For decent health care will then be available only to those who can afford it. Health care is the right of all, *not* a privilege.

So we ask our politicians:

- Will your party support the participation of women in the formulation of a national health policy which ensures the maintenance of the good health of women and men alike, and a policy which must include the following:
- an emphasis on preventive and promotive health care and the provision of basic amenities like clean water supply;
- an increase in maternal and child health and family planning services, and easy access to such services, especially in the rural areas;
- more equitable distribution of health care facilities between urban and rural areas, and between Peninsular Malaysia, Sabah and Sarawak;
- attention to the needs of the mentally ill, the handicapped, the elderly and the terminally ill, with emphasis on supportive services and rehabilitation.
- Will your party insist that the national health care system continue to be fully financed from the national budget?

Corruption

Long is the list of scandals in the last decade. BMF. The deposit-taking cooperatives. The North–South Highway. All are examples of corruption and how public funds are misused.

As Malaysians and as women, we say now to our politicians that *we oppose all forms of corruption*. We condemn the lack of accountability in high places and low, in all nooks and corners of government and society.

And so we ask our politicians:

- What is your party's stand towards corruption and public accountability?
- What will your party do to implement a system of public accountability?
- What actions has your party taken to stop corruption?
- What actions will your party take to uncover the whole truth behind the known scandals and expose the corruption in high places and low?

Democracy and human rights

The last few years have seen the passing of laws and amendments to existing laws that have further restricted our freedom. One example is the Internal Security Act which provides for detention without trial. Parliament, instead of being responsive and accountable to the people, has over the years become a rubber stamp for the ruling parties to legislate more power for themselves.

This concentration of power in the executive has been used to silence critics from all sectors – opposition parties, religious groups, social activists, etc. We want to say right now: *stop the narrowing of our democratic space!*

So, politicians, we ask you:

- Does your party have a vigorous human rights programme?
- Will your party take active steps to abolish the ISA which allows for detention without trial?
- What steps will your party take to restore the independence of the judiciary?

A women's manifesto for the 1990s

As Malaysians and as women, we demand that efforts be made to narrow the income gap. We demand our politicians to stop dividing us on the basis of race and religion.

We demand:

Women and work

Child-care support services to be set up in the public and private sectors.
The principle of equal pay for equal work, equal employment opportunities and equal access to promotion, education and training.
Electronics workers to be allowed to form a national union.
Our legal standing
Amendment of the following laws to ensure equal status and rights for women:
Article 8 (Equality) of the Federal Constitution
The Guardianship of Infants Act 1961
The Distribution Act 1958
The Immigration Act 1959/1963
The Workmen's Compensation Act 1952
The Employment Act 1955 (revised 1981)
The Income Tax Act
The Employees' Social Security Act 1969
Violence against women
Ending the mass media portrayal of women as sex objects.
Immediate enactment of the Domestic Violence Act.
Increased funding of voluntary organizations to provide shelters and counselling for survivors of violence.
Development
Development to be people-centred, sustainable and equitable.
Development to ensure that the majority of the people and local community own and control the country's resources and all economic and social activities.
A minimum living wage for working people to be ensured.
Laws to be enacted to safeguard the health and safety of all workers in both the formal and informal sectors.

Indiscriminate logging which is detrimental to the environment and which jeopardizes the livelihood of the native peoples to be ended.

Rural and land development programmes to ensure the equal participation of women and their access to and control of rural resources.

Health

A national health policy, formulated with the participation of women, to ensure the maintenance of the good health of women, and of all citizens, to include:

- Emphasis on preventive and promotive health care.
- Increase in maternal and child health and family planning services especially in the rural areas.
- More equitable distribution of health-care facilities between urban and rural areas, as well as Peninsular Malaysia and Sabah and Sarawak.
- More attention given to the needs of the mentally ill, handicapped, elderly and terminally ill, with emphasis on supportive services and rehabilitation.
- Increased allocation of funds to health.

The trend of increasing privatization in health care to be stopped, and health care to be made available to all who need it.

The national health care system to be fully financed form the national budget.

Corruption

A system of public accountability to be set up to ensure a proper system of checks and balances.

A Royal Commission of Enquiry to be set up to investigate major scandals and the reports to be made public.

Democracy and human rights

The Internal Security Act (ISA) which allows for detention without trial to be abolished.

The Independence of the Judiciary to be restored.

Women! Vote wisely! Let us make our votes count for a better Malaysia!

Note: This document should not be construed as supporting any political party.

Notes

Chapter 1

1   The concept of 'consociationalism' was first developed by Arend Lijphart (1969, 1977) to explain how ethnically diverse societies can be governed peacefully. The elements involved in the 'consociational' model of governance are: a grand coalition government, a mutual veto, high degree of autonomy for each group and public acquiescence to most compromises that are brokered by the elite behind closed doors (Milne and Mauzy, 1978: 352; Carroll and Carroll, 2000: 123; Saravanamuttu, 2002a: 11).
2   The term 'sexual molestation' was used then. However, since the 1970s such incidents have been termed as sexual harassment and publicly recognized as a form of discrimination against women (MacKinnon, 1979).
3   In the West, this period of visibly fighting for such rights in the nineteenth and early twentieth centuries is popularly called 'first-wave' feminism. The emergence of 'second-wave' feminism grew out of the consciousness-raising women's groups in the 1960s, particularly in the context of the civil rights and anti-Vietnam War movements in the United States. See Mies and Jayawardena (1981) for an elaboration of the liberal and socialist struggles in Europe in the eighteenth and nineteenth centuries.
4   Some of the discussions here are taken from Ng (1994).
5   For example, Vargas (1995: 75) identifies three distinct streams in the pluralistic women's movement in Peru – the feminist stream, the popular women's stream and that emerging from traditional public spaces.
6   Interview with Janice Duddy of the Association of Women's Rights in Development, *Resource Net*, 25 April 2003.
7   Malay-Muslim organizations refer to groups with a large if not predominant Malay-Muslim membership. However, the main agenda of such organizations may not necessarily be to further the cause of Islam. There are many political parties and welfare organizations in Malaysia with such membership composition that are devoted to achieving purposes other than the propagation of Islam *per se.*

Chapter 2

1   This information was given by F. R. Bhupalan in 1995. She has been active in the NCWO since its inception. By profession she was a school teacher and was also active in the WTU, which must have been one of the earliest associations with a multi-racial women's membership. To date there is a dearth of studies on this association.

2 The *pro-tem* committee of NCWO was initiated by the YWCA in 1960, with F. R. Bhupalan as chairperson, and had as its members Kamsiah Ibrahim, Ruby Lee, Rani Elizir, Lakshmi Navaratnam and legal adviser P. G. Lim. The composition of this committee reflected its multiethnic representation. (Interview with F. R Bhupalan, 12 May 1995.)

3 See Chapter 6 for details of women's involvement in the labour force.

4 In Malaysia, the identity of 'race' is virtually pre-determined. Being Malay also means being Muslim, according to the Federal Constitution. Further, Malays and other indigenous communities are conferred the status of *bumiputera*, literally, 'sons of the soil'. Under the aegis of the NEP, which was promulgated in 1972, *bumiputera* are entitled to special privileges or subsidies ranging from places in higher education to preferential credit access.

5 The NEP was replaced by the New Development Policy (NDP) in 1990. The NDP focuses on maximizing the growth potential of the economy. It is not coincidental that this policy was in tune with the global neo-liberal phase of free market emphasis. The NDP did not in practice replace the NEP since preferential social and economic policies continue to be put in place. Today, under the political mood of 'democratization' there has been more forceful questioning of the NDP, especially through calls for it to be dismantled or modified to shift development priorities away from ethnicity. Debate over this issue, which was once downplayed for fear of reprisal through the Sedition Act, is now being freely aired via the Internet. See, for example, P. Ramasamy, 'Diabolical game of the Malay hegemonic state', in www.malaysiakini.com (28 February 2001) and Nik Nazmi Nik Ahmad, 'Saying yes to non-racial affirmative action' in www.geocities.com/niknazmi/ (n.d).

6 A fuller discussion and analysis of this phenomenon is found in Chapter 6.

7 The concepts 'pragmatic acquiescence' and 'instrumental acceptance' are borrowed from Held (1997: 182).

8 See Chapter 3 for an elaboration of JAG-VAW. Appendix A also provides details of some of the key JAG-VAW members.

9 See Chapter 1 for an explanation of these models.

10 See Chapter 3 for a detailed discussion of VAW issues and Appendix A for a description of women's groups involved.

11 See Chapter 6 for a longer discussion about early attempts to organize industrial women workers in Penang.

12 A fascinating book written by Suriani Abdullah (1999), who herself was one of the foremost leaders of this regiment, says little of the role of women in the camps, but contains many pictures of Malay women soldiers dressed in their outfits and bearing weapons.

13 In 1992, the WCC and the WDC jointly organized and sponsored an international workshop entitled 'Women and Islam: towards a new approach'. Sisters in Islam also organized a workshop entitled, 'Islam, Women and the Nation State', in 1994. Both events were attended by Muslims and non-Muslims.

14 Chapter 5 takes this up as its focus of discussion and analysis.

15 See Chapter 1 for details of Anwar's sacking and the *Reformasi* movement.

16 For accounts of the 1999 Malaysian general election see Funston (2000) and Weiss (1999).

17 The WDC, the MTUC – Women's Section, AWAM, Sahabat Wanita, Wanita JIM, Sisters in Islam and the Selangor Chinese Assembly Hall – Women's Section as well as several key individuals.

18 Chapter 4 discusses the objectives and developments around the Women's Agenda for Change.

19 When the political crisis broke out, leaders of JIM played a key role in the formation of a new opposition party, Keadilan. The founders came from various

ethnic, religious, class and professional backgrounds. JIM itself was politicized almost overnight, providing the party with its grassroots base comprising its network of branches and membership spread throughout the country.

20 The candidate was Zaitun Kasim. See Chapter 4 for a discussion on the performance of women election candidates in 1999.

21 In a January 2002 by-election in Perlis, Puteri Umno was said to have played a crucial role in delivering the votes of young Malays. See Nash Rahman, 'Malay votes delivered victory to MCA, says UMNO leader', http://.malaysiakini.com (22 January 2002).

22 See an unattributed piece entitled, 'Muslimat Chief: We won't demand for posts', posted on http://thestar.com.my (3 June 2001).

23 See Chapter 5 for a further discussion of Puteri UMNO's inception.

24 Chapter 5 provides a discussion of the controversy and women's resistance against this law.

25 Some have called this particular phase the era of 'commodity feminism'. Even the discourses of feminism can be used to sell commodities for profit. See an unattributed editorial piece, 'Post-feminism, the market and the media', *Media and Gender Monitor,* Issue No. 14, September 2003, p. 4.

26 See Shaila Koshy, 'More women elected but will they speak up?', *The Star* (25 March 2004).

27 In 1988, the WCC devoted a special issue of its newsletter to the subject of feminism. The anonymous writer stressed that, 'Feminism goes to the sexist root of human oppression, a consequence of patriarchy which means male power, rule, and domination in values, in governance, in all institutions' (*Herizons,* Newsletter of the Women's Crisis Centre, September, 1988, p. 3).

28 See Chapter 3 for a critique of the women-led initiative for legal reform.

29 PAS, being the oldest and biggest party, was the leader within the BA coalition which grew out of the *Reformasi* movement. Although the other partners vociferously supported women's rights, their association with PAS – a party which did not even allow its own women members to stand in elections – cost them valuable support from liberals in society.

30 Just a few weeks before the date of the country's 11th general election was announced, the government arrested and charged a prominent businessman and a politician with corruption. A few weeks before this the Abdullah Ahmad Badawi government had announced the setting up of an independent commission to look into issues of policing, including investigating public complaints of abuse. This was quite a successful image of reforms which won the BN its support during the elections.

31 Halina Mohd Noor, 'Wanita ketuai hampir sejuta keluarga' (Women head almost a million households), *Utusan Malaysia* (25 May 2002).

32 In February 2004, the Atria Shopping Centre in Selango, together with the Youth and Sports Ministry, organized a three-day event to create awareness of 'Prevention of Violence against Women and Children'. Zuraidah Abdullah, the mother of a rape and murder victim Farah Deeba Rustam, was invited to give a speech at the launch of the campaign. See Azura Abas, 'Learn from me, says Deeba's mum', *New Sunday Times* (22 February 2004).

Chapter 3

1 Between January and May 2003, there was an average of four rape cases daily. See 'Rapes and murders on the increase', *The Star* (1 July 2003). It is widely believed that these figures, while not insignificant, are only the tip of the iceberg.

2 From January to June 2003, there were 116 incidences of reported incest. The number rose to 161 during the same period in 2004. See Rose Ismail, '95 per cent of incest cases go unreported', *New Straits Times* (10 October 2004).

3 Since it started in 1985, JAG-VAW has remained an ad hoc and non-formalized body. Its composition has varied depending on the issue involved, e.g. rape, domestic violence, sexual harassment. Thus, while some actors have remained constant in the various formations of JAG-VAW, others have entered and exited at different times. For details of key members of this entity, see Appendix A.

4 WAO was the first NGO set up directly in response to VAW. It was launched as a service and welfare centre for battered women in 1982 through financial assistance from a former Minister of Finance, Tan Siew Sin (Tan, 1999b: 52). See Appendix A for additional information.

5 These included the All Women's Action Society and Sabah Women Action Resource Group. Others like the Women's Development Collective, Women's Crisis Centre (now Women's Centre for Change) and Sarawak Women for Women Society were already in the process of being set up.

6 The AWL was instrumental in drawing up the memorandum on the laws relating to rape.

7 Her bloodied body was discovered with a 10-foot pole thrust up her vagina. See 'Cold rape and murder cases', *The Malay Mail* (6 July 2003).

8 *The Star* (24 May 1987).

9 They were Cecilia Ng, Chee Heng Leng and Lim Chin Chin, founding members of WDC and AWAM. The fourth, Irene Xavier, worked with a women workers' organization Sahabat Wanita (Friends of Women). All were charged with being Marxists who were mobilizing workers and women to overthrow the state.

10 The Anti-ISA Committee was led by the WDC, three of whose members had been detained, and two others whose husbands were also arrested.

11 Together with NCWO and the women's wings of ruling political parties, the AWL managed to push for the bill to be tabled. One strategy involved a whisper campaign in the corridors of parliament.

12 Prior to this, abortion was only permitted if the life of the mother was threatened (Fernandez, 1992: 115).

13 Non-consensual acts of anal sex, fellatio and cunnilingus, along with the insertion of objects such as bottles or hands into a woman's vagina or anus, were more often than not, regarded as 'secondary indecent assaults' and not as primary offences. As such they were penalized under the provision of the Penal Code dealing with 'outrages of modesty' (Section 354) that also carried a lighter sentence. In proposing that they be criminalized, women's groups had hoped to show how such acts were violent and constituted a form of rape.

14 Only when providing details of the alleged rape act is the trial held in chambers or *in camera*. However, this is probably done to avert the possibility that such information would be sensationalized or used by the media to titillate the sexual curiosity of the public. In other words it is done to preserve 'morality' rather than preserve the anonymity of the rape survivor against insensitive media reporting.

15 See *Women Alert*, May/June 1989.

16 Prior to this campaign, various education and awareness programmes on rape had taken place but on a small-scale basis. Research focusing on rape cases in Penang had also been conducted.

17 As explained, the 1989 amendments to the laws relating to rape made it illegal to bring up a victim's sexual past and character except in relation to the accused. The current proposal is seeking to extend this provision to include *any* sexual history a victim may have with the accused. This, women's groups believe, will give victims of date rape a better opportunity for a fair trial.

18 See 'Give rape victims financial assistance', *New Straits Times* (16 August 2004).

19 See 'Tough laws for incest', *The Star* (12 January 2003).
20 See 'Don't castrate or hang rapists', *The Sun* (17 October 2002).
21 For example, the Kuala Lumpur Bar Council Legal Aid Centre runs a Legal Information Clinic together with AWAM where chambering students provide free advice to women in crisis.
22 In fact, women's groups are not united on this. Some are still adamant that whipping is a necessary deterrent to prevent rape, and a justifiable punishment for this crime.
23 There have been cases of statutory rape reported not by the girls involved but their mothers who do not know how else to stop their daughters from seeing their boyfriends. This has led to innocent boys being sent to prison for no less than five years under the provisions of the Penal Code (JAG-VAW discussions, 21 October 2004).
24 If voluntarily committed, the punishment for such acts was a jail term of up to 20 years and, possibly, whipping (Section 377B). In the case of anal rape, i.e. non-consensual anal sex, offenders would be jailed a minimum of five years and not more than 20 years, and would also be liable to whipping (Section 377C). It is also worth noting that the act of cunnilingus can still be penalized under the law but as a less grave offence under Section 377D 'Outrages on decency' which prescribes imprisonment of not more than two years.
25 While it is true that this threat existed even under the pre-existing Section 377, which was a legacy of British colonial rule, the point here remains that the explicit naming of consensual anal and oral sex as crimes only happened after the reforms in 1989. This in turn has given rise to different problems such as limiting one's ability to argue that Section 377 can possibly be interpreted as not including such acts.
26 Nowhere is this clearer than in the episode where after the former Deputy Prime Minister Anwar Ibrahim was stripped of his post, a full-scale campaign was launched to justify this on the grounds that he had committed the crime of sodomy as stipulated under Section 377 of the law. See also Chapter 7 for further information.
27 The idea to hold this event stemmed from the public debate around the rape and murder of Canny Ong in June 2003. It was conceived to allow those who were upset by the incident to publicly express their feelings, while being an avenue for turning grief into constructive action. It was also meant to be a platform to revive the CAR initiative.
28 The organizers were not only subjected to a series of 'interviews' with the Special Branch of the police force, but also given the run-around in efforts to secure a police permit for this event. In the end, the rally was postponed from 20 July to 3 August 2003, and was only allowed in the reconstituted form of a 'gathering' in a much smaller and more private venue.
29 According to the organizers, they invited the minister and police representative so that members of the public could hear first hand what the state intended to do about this problem. Critics, however, argue that this was an unnecessary gesture since the state already has sufficient avenues to provide its points of view to the public. More importantly, they felt that the purpose of the rally should have been to protest against the state's ineffectual stance against rape. As such, inviting its representatives to participate in the rally was inappropriate. In any case, at the 'gathering' that finally took place, few were surprised when the minister, invited to say a few words, took full advantage of the opportunity and turned it into a political speech against the main opposition party, Parti Islam Se Malaysia (PAS).
30 See Chapter 4 for an in-depth account and critique of the women's movement's experience in engaging with the Malaysian state.
31 Statistics compiled by WAO in 2004 revealed that out of 700 domestic violence cases in Malaysia, 10 per cent involved marital or spousal rape. Cited in WAO (2004).

32 See *New Straits Times* (8 August 2004).

33 The groups involved in the JAG-VAW campaign for a DVA were AWAM – which also served as the secretariat – WAO, Sisters in Islam, NCWO, AWL and the Selangor Chinese Assembly Hall – Women's Section.

34 The then Deputy Minister in charge of Islamic Affairs, Abdul Hamid Othman, agreed with them that the passing of the Act would not be contrary to Islam. See 'Wife-beating soon a *Syariah* offence', *The Star* (10 March 1994).

35 A 1998 directive by the then Inspector-General of Police, Abdul Rahim Noor, partly mitigated this problem. In response to women's groups highlighting the shortcomings of the DVA in the press, he announced that the police would investigate all cases of domestic violence. However, only husbands who inflicted 'seizable' injuries upon their partners could be charged, leaving those who caused 'non-seizable' injuries to go unpunished.

36 As previously noted, the laws relating to rape did not consider marital rape an offence.

37 See 'Violence bill too soft', *The Sun* (29 April 1994).

38 It is believed that late as it was, the minister, Napsiah Omar, persevered in pushing the bill through that very night because it was the last day of sitting for that session. Had the bill not gone through then, she would have had to re-table it when the House reconvened two months later, a move she was uncertain would work to the bill's advantage.

39 This was a time when funding was not as accessible as it was in the 1990s. The majority of women's NGOs functioned through the energies of volunteers and had at most, one or two paid full-time staff.

40 See *Waves*, Newsletter of AWAM, 1993, p. 13.

41 The DVA was implemented on 1 June 1996 but only after Pusat Islam (Islamic Centre) had clarified that it would not conflict with *Syariah* laws and that this should not be used as an excuse to further delay the gazetting of the Act. For details, see WAO (2000).

42 Some of the information in this section is drawn from Ng et al. (2003).

43 See Chapter 6 for further details of the Code.

44 See, 'Most bosses yet to adopt code on sexual harassment', *New Straits Times* (21 March 2001).

45 Apart from WCC, the members of the JAG-VAW coalition against sexual harassment are WDC, AWAM, Sisters in Islam, WAO, MTUC – Women's Section, Sahabat Wanita and the Women's Candidacy Initiative.

46 See Chapter 6 for details of the research.

47 In contrast, another employer body, the Federation of Malaysian Manufacturers, was receptive to the idea.

48 According to a letter from the Ministry, the government was unable to pursue such a legislation for now since: (i) it wished to study the appropriateness of including the crime of sexual harassment in the Penal Code; (ii) it also wished to strengthen several other workplace-related legislation to ensure that they could cover sexual harassment cases; and (iii) it believed that more prevention, awareness-raising and rehabilitation programmes, as well as training for employers and employees, had to be carried out.

49 Women would be victimized since, to prove rape, they would have to rely on the evidence of four male witnesses. See Chapter 5 for a discussion of this support.

Chapter 4

1 The ministry was established on 17 January 2001 as the Ministry of Women's Affairs. A month later, on 15 February the minister in charge, Sharizat Abdul

Jalil, changed its name to the Ministry of Women and Family Development. Following the March 2004 general election, a cabinet reshuffle saw the name of this body change for a third time when it took on the portfolio of community and welfare issues of the former Ministry of National Unity and Social Development. It is currently known as the Ministry of Women, Family and Community Development.

2　On the other hand, there is also another position, influenced by postmodernism, which points out that the state as a network of power, in the final analysis can only produce subordinated and disciplined state subjects (Rai, 1996).

3　In the 1960s, female teachers took to the streets to demonstrate for equal pay as earned by their male counterparts.

4　See Chapter 2 for a discussion of this phase of social feminism.

5　There is more than sufficient literature on this theme and their revised versions of the nimble fingers of Asian women. See Lim (1978); Grossman (1979); Ng and Maznah (1997); Elson and Pearson and (1981).

6　See Chapter 6 for a discussion of the issues confronting women workers in the country.

7　Appendix C contains details of the 'Women's Manifesto'.

8　See Chapter 3 for details of the anti-rape campaign and *Operasi Lalang*.

9　See newsletter of SUARAM, *Suaram Komunikasi*, 1998.

10　By then HAWA had been moved from the Prime Minister's Department to the Ministry of National Unity and Social Development. The Minister then was Napsiah Omar, a former lecturer from Universiti Pertanian Malayisa (now Universiti Putra Malaysia) and already known for her concern for women's issues.

11　See 'Malaysia's political parties shift to courting women', *Wall Street Journal* (28 July 1999).

12　These included the NCWO, WAO and WCC.

13　Of course, globalization is not a new phenomenon, only that this phase of global capitalist development is marked by trade and financial liberalization as never accelerated before.

14　In recognition of the different socio-economic and political contexts of a particular country, state parties are allowed to place reservations when they ratify CEDAW. However, these reservations cannot be permanently placed, and must be progressively removed over time. On 6 February 1998, the Malaysian government withdrew its reservation in respect of Articles 2 (f), 9 (1), 16 (b), 16 (e) and 16 (h). Posted on: http://www.unhchr.ch/html/menu3/b/treaty9 _ asp.htm.

15　These were the WDC, AWAM, Sisters in Islam and Sahabat Wanita.

16　See Appendix B for details of the WAC document.

17　This is not to say that the whole range of autonomous women's groups supported the 1990 'Women's Manifesto', as explained earlier.

18　By the end of 1999 a total of 88 NGOs had endorsed the WAC document. The WAC Organizing Committee expanded to include Wanita JIM, Selangor Chinese Assembly Hall – Women's Section and BATA Union. The WAC Secretariat then was held by WDC. See Tan and Ng (2003).

19　By 2001, the 30-plus recommendations had been streamlined to six major demands – from legislative changes and women's increased political participation to the repeal of draconian laws in the country.

20　Wan Azizah Wan Ismail is the wife of Anwar Ibrahim. She became the President of the newly formed Keadilan and stood in Anwar's parliamentary constituency, winning by a thumping majority. See Loh and Saravanamuttu (2003) for details of the contestation and the entry of civil society in the 1999 general election.

21　See Chapter 5 for an elaboration of the dispute within BA.

22　As mentioned previously, the Ministry of National Unity and Social Development was disbanded following a cabinet reshuffle after the March 2004 general election.

23 We would like to thank Lee Shook Fong and Wathshlah Naidu from WAO as well as Manohara Subramaniam from AWAM for providing the relevant information on the role and participation of women's groups in these committees or task forces (Interviews conducted on 3 and 7 June 2003).

24 These NGOs were AWAM, WAO and WCC.

25 For example, the Minister officiated at the International Women's Day celebration organized by the Malaysian Trades Union Congress (MTUC) – Women's Section in March 2002. She then promptly announced the setting up of a TWG on women workers, to loud applause from the audience. However, a year on, the demands raised by the MTUC – Women's Section, such as extended maternity leave and a Sexual Harassment Act, had yet to be addressed.

26 See Appendix A for a description of the key groups in this entity.

27 See 'WDC to ensure candidates fulfil election pledges', *Malay Mail* (10 March 2004); 'WoMEC rally candidates to their cause', *New Straits Times* (12 March 2004); 'Wanita tagih janji belum terlaksana', *Berita Harian* (6 March 2004); 'Women, where is your voice', *New Straits Times* (25 March 2004); 'More women elected but will they speak up', *The Star* (25 March 2004).

28 The term 'femocrats' was used in the 1980s to denote those feminists, or those sympathetic to the women's cause, who had joined the government bureaucracy in order to advance women's position through policy formulation and implementation.

29 One year upon ratification of CEDAW, states are supposed to submit their initial reports to the CEDAW Committee, after which reports are due every four years. Although the Malaysian government ratified the convention in 1995, it only submitted its first report in 2004.

30 The impact of neo-liberal globalization on the lives of women workers is elaborated in Chapter 6.

Chapter 5

1 An earlier version of this chapter was published in the journal *Global Change, Peace and Security* (Maznah, 2004).

2 In Malaysia, Malays as an ethnic group form the majority (56 per cent) of the population. Constitutionally all Malays are defined as being Muslims although not all Muslims in the country have ethnic Malay roots.

3 Malay women (who are synonymously Muslims) played an active role in the Malay Women Teachers' Organisation whose aim was to encourage schooling for girls during the colonial era. A more contemporary organization among young Malay women is *Puteri Islam* (Islamic Princess), which models its function upon the Girl Guides Movement. A more state-oriented and older established organization of wives of Malay bureaucrats and elite is the *Lembaga Perempuan Islam Malaysia* (Islamic Women's Board of Malaysia). These are the examples of Malay-Muslim women's organizations that did not have the expressed aim of spreading or deepening the influence of Islam among members. They are Muslim organizations but are not necessarily Islamic organizations.

4 The term 'political Islam' is used here to distinguish it from the religion Islam in its cultural, social and spiritual sense. When Islam is politicized it is usually the capture of statehood and the total implementation of the *Syariah* legal system within the nation that will constitute the aims of the proponents. There are both moderates and radicals among the advocates all over the Muslim world, but 'all acknowledge the necessity of controlling political power' (Roy, 1999: 41). The Islamic resurgent movements in Malaysia were largely of the moderate variety, in the sense that they are 'partisans of re-Islamization from the bottom up

(preaching, establishing socio-cultural movements) while pressuring the leaders (in particular through political alliances) to promote Islamization from the top (introducing the *Syariah* into legislation)' (Roy, 1999: 41). In contrast, the radical branch of Islam would aspire to totally displace a secularist government either through militant or forced means.

5 See the analysis of Malaysia as an authoritarian-developmental state in Loh and Saravanamuttu (2003) and Loh (2002: 19–50). The studies argue that the developmental feature of the state gives rise to non-democratic politics that do not threaten the goals of capital accumulation.

6 *Syariah* denotes laws that have been formulated and codified based on *Quranic* precepts.

7 Under the affirmative action thrust of the NEP, almost all Malay students who obtained places in foreign institutions of higher learning were financed by government scholarships. Thus the contractual agreement for the scholarship tied them down to future jobs in various public sector agencies at the end of their studies.

8 Islamic fundamentalism is distinguished from Islam because this is associated with a particular feature of Islamic movements. As a general description, fundamentalist Islam is likened to the Western reference to fundamentalist Christians who 'protect an old and above all literal interpretation of the doctrine of their faith against attempts to reinterpret is as metaphorical, symbolic, social, functional or whatever' (Gellner, 1994: 16). But there is an added feature of fundamentalism in Islam. Besides its literalist character, it is also a revivalist movement, meaning that it is an Islam which has been re-understood in a different light, and is therefore very concerned about countering distortions by folk or customary practices, superstitions and the focus on mere rituals.

9 It actually went through several name changes. When it was initially formed it was simply known as *Ahli-Ahli Perempuan UMNO* (women members of UMNO). Then it adopted the better-known name of *Pergerakan Kaum Ibu* (Mothers' Movement). Later it became known as *Wanita* (Women) until it finally settled on *Pergerakan Wanita UMNO* (UMNO Women's Movement). See Wanita UMNO (1989: 51).

10 See Chapter 1 for details of this episode.

11 Many novels and films pitched at young women were produced during the period of Puteri UMNO's formation. One example was the much publicized film *Embun* (Dew), which was directed by Erma Fatimah, a well-known female film maker who was also a high-ranking pro-tem committee member in Puteri UMNO at that time. The film signified freshness and a new beginning, with a female protagonist as the ideal role model for young women. The message was simple, if not simplistic. She was portrayed as being brave and a fighter. She was a heroine though not necessarily in the mould of a self-sacrificing mother. In *Embun* the new Malay woman was unearthed.

12 Translation from *Berperanan untuk membantu UMNO di dalam semua pilihanraya dan meneruskan ketuanan Melayu di Malaysia*, see chapter on '*Visi dan Manifesto* (Vision and Manifesto)', Puteri UMNO (2001: 8).

13 This is of course controversial given that such a line is almost bordering on UMNO wanting to have an Islamic state. See '*Wawasan Wanita UMNO* (Wanita UMNO's Vision)', *Suara Wanita* (2001: 2).

14 See '*Dalil daripada Al-Quran dan As-Sunnah mengenai kelebihan berbuat kebajikan* (Justifications from the Al-Quran and As-Sunnah on the benefit of doing charity)', Puteri UMNO (2001: 9).

15 Keadilan today stands out as the only political party headed by a woman. Nevertheless, the leadership of Wan Azizah is often seen as token or temporary in that she is really standing in for her husband, Anwar Ibrahim.

16 Personal interview with two members of Puteri UMNO *pro-tem* committee at the headquarters in June 2002.

17 See *Memorandum Pelajaran 1974* (Memorandum on Education 1974), submitted by ABIM to the Minister of Education, 22 October 1974 (Md. Sidin, 1996: 27–32).

18 Among the 14-member committee, there are three medical doctors, two science officers, two engineers, two university lecturers, one pharmacist and one dentist. Their credentials are all prominently displayed in their brochure for promotion (Unit Perhubungan Raya Wanita JIM, n.d.).

19 See 'Sejarah Penubuhan (History of Formation)', *Mujahidah*, 2001, p. 8.

20 The position of vice-chairperson was specially created in the state cabinet to accommodate its sole woman's representative. UMNO pointed out that in PAS' campaign manifesto it had promised to appoint a woman to the cabinet to implement the State Policy on Women. This had put much pressure on PAS to put its money where its mouth is. While the male cabinet members were sworn in on 23 March 2004, the woman, Rohani Ibrahim was only appointed on 7 April 2004. See 'Kerajaan PAS lantik Rohani timbalan exco (PAS government appoints Rohani as vice-exco)', *Utusan Malaysia* (15 April 2004).

21 For a long time after independence and especially after Mahathir became Malaysia's fourth Prime Minister, there was erosion of democratic institutions. This ranged from the dominance of the Executive to the enactment of repressive legislation denying due process. See a collection of readings on these various issues in Loh and Khoo (2002).

22 A clause was inserted into the bill to practically excuse Muslim men from beating their wives if the latter refused sex. Sex, under any circumstances, is considered an unequivocal right of married Islamic men according to the prevailing religious authority then.

23 Among the organizations which endorsed the campaign were AWAM, Organisation of Police Wives and Families, National Association of Perkim Women, Women's Aid Organisation and Wanita Ikram.

24 See Nyza Ayob 'Kempen monogami menyimpang dari kewajaran – Wanita JIM' (Monogamy campaign a deviation from correctness), *Harakah Daily* (20 March 2003).

25 In 2003, a Polygamy Club was launched by the Rufuqa Corporation in Rawang, Selangor. The group produced a special issue magazine devoted to the subject of polygamy, touting the following justification – *Bayangkan seorang yang mempunyai 4 orang isteri dan berpuluh anak, manakala anak-anaknya juga turut berpoligami dan melahirkan ratusan cucu dan cicit, maka dalam masa 50 tahun akan muncul satu Bani baru.* This is translated to read: 'Imagine if one were to have 4 wives and hundreds of offspring, wherein all these children in turn will also practise polygamy and produce hundreds of grandchildren and great-grandchildren, in 50 years to come there will be a new tribe (Bani)' in *'Perancangan Yahudi di Sebalik Penolakan Poligami* (Jewish Plot Behind Rejection of Polygamy)', in magazine-formatted publication, *Rahsia Pembentukan Keluarga Supe*, compiled by Murshidah Mustaffa; n.d, p. 47.

26 For coverage and reactions on this issue see, 'Hadi gets flak over remarks on women', *The Star* (6 August 2003) and K. Suthakar, 'Hadi faults media for not giving "proper" coverage', *The Star* (7 August 2003).

27 One example is Haji Muhammad Nur Lubis (2000).

28 Upon the election of Fatimah Zainab Ibrahim as the new head of the *Dewan Muslimat*, an article in a Malay press quoted one of the delegates as remarking, 'Do not put too much hope that women in the party will be given a chance to be vocal in the era of Ustazah Fatimah's leadership. . . . Knowing Ustazah Fatimah we get the feeling that women's struggle in the party will be moved a few steps

backwards.' See Siti Mariam Md. Zain, 'Penentuan Arah Tuju Muslimat PAS (Determining the direction of PAS women)' in *Utusan Malaysia* (29 May 2002).

29 Of the 12 *Dewan Muslimat* committee members elected in September 2003, nine were professionals. The women within the party had strongly pushed for women's candidacy in the 2004 general election. See 'New leaders likely to mend rift in party's women's wing', *New Sunday Times* (14 September 2003).

30 This meeting was held in Kuala Lumpur in October 2002 and was jointly organized with DAWN, a regional Third World feminist network. It was attended by about 50 women activists from South Asia and Southeast Asia, representing different cultures and faiths.

31 Statistics from 1996 to 2000 show that, except at the primary school level, the enrolment of girls has exceeded that of boys. For example, at the pre-university level in 2000, the percentage of girls enrolled was 66.45 per cent compared to 33.55 per cent for boys. At the university level in the same year, 56.22 per cent of university students were girls. This is based on surveys conducted by researchers from Universiti Kebangsaan Malaysia. See Elizabeth John, 'Girls put boys to shame', *New Sunday Times Focus* (31 August 2003).

Chapter 6

1 Quote taken from brochure entitled, 'The Solid State for Electronics, An Invitation for Investment', issued by the Federal Industrial Development Authority of Malaysia, 1970–1, p. 12.

2 The proportion of women in the professional and technical category increased from 12.7 per cent in 1995 to 13.5 per cent in 2000, while those in the administrative and managerial group increased from 1.8 per cent to 2.2 per cent during the same period (Government of Malaysia, 2001b: 558).

3 See, 'Hard times for bank staff', *The Sun* (6 December 2001).

4 *Ibid.*

5 The following quotations are extracted from the chapter 'Speaking Out' by Chee and Subramanian (1994).

6 These were some of the 14 companies that had initially adopted the 1999 Code of Practice on the Prevention and Eradication of Sexual Harassment in the Workplace launched by the Ministry of Human Resources.

7 These occupations include innovative cultural production such as independent television producers, graphic designers, multimedia professionals and those providing Internet services (Walby, 2001).

8 A clear example is the long-standing dispute, since 2001, between two factions of the National Union of Bank Employees, each claiming to be the legitimate office-bearers. See 'Protracted leadership tussle leaves richest and best-managed trade union in disarray', *New Sunday Times* (17 August 2003).

9 The discussion on this struggle is extracted from the union documents. We would like to thank Bruno Pereira, one of the key founders of the union, for his assistance in sharing his materials and experiences with us.

10 Three of the workers had left the firm by then.

11 Interviews done in 1999 and 2003 (Bhopal and Rowley, n.d.).

12 Interview with Manohara (7 June 2003), who was a kindergarten teacher and later a labour organizer with Sahabat Wanita for about 10 years up to the early 1990s.

13 Although the skills of women workers have been upgraded, particularly in firms which have switched to adopting new technologies, there is no concomitant increase in their occupational status.

14 Interview in 1999 with the Human Resource Director of a company which sits on a stretch of land overlooking the sea front in Penang Island (Maznah et al., 2001: 66).

15 See Lochead (1988) for a detailed account of the Mostek struggle. Since then there has not been a strike of such immense dimension in Malaysia.

16 This account of an early attempt to mobilize young women industrial workers is provided by Chan Lean Heng who was one of the early coordinators of the Young Workers Project and currently an academic (Interview, 6 May 2003).

17 In its evolution from one organizational structure to another, the YWCEP changed its name to Young Workers Educational Project and finally to the Workers Educational Project.

18 1987 was also the year of the mass arrest of social activists under the police sweep code-named *Operasi Lalang*. See Chapter 3 for additional details of the detentions.

19 Sahabat Wanita was formed in the late 1970s by a group of women committed to support women workers in their struggles to improve their lives, communities and workplace. Their programmes include case solutions, education and training, community organizing and pre-school projects. The organization is also concerned with the larger issues of democracy, justice and equality in Malaysian society.

20 Interview with Manohara (7 June 2003).

21 See Chapter 2 for a description of the National Women's Coalition.

22 See Appendix A for details of this organization.

23 For a long time women were not allowed to venture outside weeding tasks on the grounds that they were 'naturally' unsuited to perform rubber-tapping. A more likely explanation for the division in labour at the time can be attributed to the differential wage rates between male tappers and female weeders, with the latter on the losing end of the scale. Only later when there was a shortage of rubber-tappers were women encouraged to take over this function in the rubber plantation. See Tan (1991).

24 Bank Negara statistics quoted in Healy (2000).

25 While official statistics on undocumented migrant workers – more derogatorily known as 'illegal' workers – are not available, it is widely assumed that there is at least one undocumented migrant worker for every documented one (Government of Malaysia, n.d).

26 Indonesian domestic workers who are successful abroad can sometimes save enough to build houses and start small businesses once they are back home, much to the envy of their neighbours (Ford, 2003:102).

27 For further insight into the different forms of abuse faced by female domestic workers in Malaysia, see Samanther (2002).

28 In a highly publicized case, a male police officer was arrested for raping two migrant women, one a Filipina and the other an Indonesian, who were in police custody. He was initially discharged when the judge ruled in his favour, saying that 'the sexual intercourse [between the accused and the women] seemed voluntary, just like between husband and wife' (Zarizana, 2003: 99). Later, however, the same judge came up with a completely different verdict when the case was tried again upon appeal. How this was possible is anyone's guess but, at the very least, this episode shows the vulnerability of migrant women who land in police custody.

29 Under the Memorandum of Understanding between the Philippine and Malaysian governments, employers of Filipina domestic workers are obliged to give them Sundays off; and because they are perceived as being better educated, they are also able to command a higher salary than Indonesian domestic workers. See *The Star* (17 December 2003).

30 For example, the National Office for Human Development (NOHD), the social and welfare arm of the Catholic Church had established a Migrant Desk as early as the early 1990s and has been active in providing support services to migrant

workers and refugees. The migrant workers have exercised their agency in spite of their difficult working conditions. For example they have formed migrant councils, organized activities and opened a restaurant at the Bukit Nanas Community Centre set up by NOHD in Kuala Lumpur.

31 Lasting over seven years, the trial was widely seen by many commentators and social activists, both within and outside the country, as an act of 'political persecution to silence dissenting voices' against the government. See *Malaysiakini* (9 November 2003). The case is currently under appeal.

32 See WAO paper (Samanther, 2001).

33 Even within WAO, the decision to expand its advocacy work to cover the rights of migrant women workers was initially met with resistance from within, as it was viewed as a waste of resources (Samanther, 2001).

34 See reports in *New Straits Times* (2 March 2004; 25 June 2003 and 28 March 2002).

35 A news report in 2002 noted that there was an increasing problem of young women from China, ranging from 20 to 30 years of age, being coerced into prostitution. They had come to Malaysia expecting to earn high salaries but upon arrival were forced into the flesh trade. Many of them had paid as much as RM12,000 to RM15,000 for this 'opportunity'. See *The Star* (15 May 2002).

36 For example, the Selangor government announced that it would organize courses for married women, on how to rein in philandering husbands. See *The Sun* (13 December 2003); also 'Women are not sex objects, say NGOs', *Malay Mail* (15 February 2003).

37 This alone, however, does not adequately explain the prevalence of the sex industry across the globe. For a more in-depth account that takes into consideration economic and political reasons, see Lim (1998).

38 It is estimated that in the early 1990s, the sex sector in Malaysia, Indonesia, the Philippines and Thailand accounted for between 2 per cent and 14 per cent of the gross domestic product in these countries (Lim, 1998: 7).

39 Up till the early 1930s, sex workers were allowed to ply their trade openly in what was referred to as 'known' brothels. Although the purpose for having 'known' brothels has been critiqued elsewhere (see Tan, 2003), at least these women were able to receive medical treatment and to an extent had greater ability to escape bad working conditions. Also see Chapter 7 for an elaboration.

40 Figures in 1993/1994 indicate that there were possibly close to 142,000 women in this industry. Given that trafficking in women continues unabated, and if the frequency of news reports about this phenomenon is any reflection, it is likely that the number has increased manifold.

41 For example, in some countries like Thailand and Taiwan, there are moves by women's groups to lobby the state to decriminalize sex work.

Chapter 7

1 The term sexuality includes sexual behaviour, sexual preferences, sexual orientation, sexual relations and sexual practices. It is linked to feelings we experience in relation to our bodies and ourselves.

2 Prior to Kuala Lumpur, the play had shown to packed houses in other parts of Asia, namely the Philippines, Hong Kong and Singapore.

3 The organization later held the play at a private venue.

4 Sincere thanks to Alina Rastam of the Sexuality Rights Project for her contributions to various parts of this chapter.

5 The target audience of *3R*, which stands for Respect, Relax and Respond, are those in the 15–29 age group.

6 See, 'An episode of TV series 3R banned', *The Star* (7 August 2003).

7 HIV/AIDS activists are hampered by societal inability to openly discuss matters related to sex and sexuality, and in particular they have been unable to promote the use of condoms for safe sex, just as they have not been able to effectively introduce the concept of a needle-exchange programme for intravenous drug users.

8 Inadequate sex education in schools has resulted in the majority of Malaysians having a poor understanding of matters pertaining to sexuality. Although some NGOs like the Federation of Family Planning Associations in Malaysia have attempted to address this by running sex-education workshops for youth, this is no replacement for a systematic and widespread programme that can be offered via schools. In 2005, however, after much foot-dragging, the government announced that its guidelines for sex education in schools were being finalized.

9 Even the act of celibacy is not promoted as something desirable for a 'regular' lifestyle as the only acceptable reason for this is on religious grounds.

10 In 2003, horrified at how a widely circulated Malay daily, *Utusan Malaysia*, was allowing readers to vilify and condemn lesbians and gay men in its 'Letters to the Editor' forum, a group of concerned citizens sent a letter of protest. Not surprisingly the newspaper failed to respond, much less publish this letter.

11 The shows were screened by the private television station NTV7, as part of its highly popular but highly sensationalist series *Edisi Siasat*.

12 He was also capitalizing on the 'Asian values' rhetoric prevalent at the time (see next section for details). The message was clear: 'We do not want to encourage any form of homosexuality in our society.' Posted on www.ilga.info/ Information/Legal _ survey/Asia _ Pacific/malaysia.htm.

13 See *Berita Harian* (28 August 2003).

14 Current levels of moral policing have made it easier for unscrupulous officials to extort money from unsuspecting members of public, particularly youth. In one case, two officers from DBKL were hauled up for trying to coerce a young (but unmarried) couple into giving them a sum of money to avoid being fined for 'indecent behaviour' in a public park. When the couple refused to give in to these demands on the grounds that they had done nothing wrong, the officers proceeded to issue them with a summons even though their actions were contrary to City Hall policy. See 'Couple summoned for merely holding hands', *New Sunday Times*, (10 August 2003). They have since been charged in court, but have claimed trial.

15 The three had taken part in the Miss Malaysia Petite competition but were unaware that the state of Selangor, where the contest took place, had passed a new law banning Muslim women from such events. See 'In Malaysia, pressure builds over enforcement of Islamic laws', *International Herald Tribune* (18 August 1997).

16 One woman was wearing a body-hugging shirt and the other, tight-fitting pants. The Road Transport Department head justified the ban claiming that the women had contravened the official dress code. He added that such action would prevent the recurrence of an incident where one of his officers had groped a woman's breast during a driving test. See 'Tight fitting clothes rule out women's driving test chances'. Posted in Ananova at http://www.ananova.com/news/story/sm_ 293300.html?menu = (15 May 2001).

17 The performer was heavily censured in the Malay media, and asked to shun bad Western influences and publicly apologize for her actions. See 'Fantasi seks Ning jatuhkan maruah sendiri (Ning's sexual fantasies will bring down own honour)', *Berita Harian* (26 July 2000); 'In hot soup', *The Star* (28 July 2000).

18 See *Asiaweek* (2 March 2001).

19 The information in this section is drawn from a previous work by Tan (2003).

20 To be precise, this law was introduced in the Straits Settlements – Singapore, Penang and Malacca – where the British first imposed colonial rule.

21 The CDO was introduced in 1870 before the Women and Girls Protection Ordinance replaced it in 1887.

22 See 'Insufficient evidence to prosecute Rahim', *New Straits Times* (22 October 1994); 'Father: Why make my girl's sex life public?', *New Straits Times* (23 October 1994); and 'Girl in Rahim controversy with welfare authorities', *New Straits Times* (25 October 1994) and in thenewsletter of AWAM, *WAVES*, 1995, p. 3.

23 The information in this section is drawn from a previous work by Tan (1999a).

24 Although this discourse appears to have peaked in the mid-1990s, its remnants occasionally surface when political or religious leaders feel that there is a need to assert one's Asian identity.

25 See *Asiaweek* (8 September 1995).

26 In fact, both Malaysia and Singapore are classic examples of Asian countries which have adopted a capitalist economic development framework as touted by Western nations like the US, Australia and those of Western Europe.

27 Quite apart from these older male 'clients', the *boh sia* also had male counterparts, younger men known as *boh jan*. Although *boh jan* too came under fire during this time, the level of attack against *boh sia* was much higher as was apparent from the public censure in media reports.

28 The only category of single mothers that appear rejected by society are those who have children out of wedlock. Even within this, however, there are different degrees of rejection depending on one's economic standing. While still questioned, middle-class single women who choose to adopt children, for example, are not seen in such negative light.

29 In fact, as late as the 1960s it was observed that generally in Southeast Asia, '[h]omosexuals and transvestites [were] treated with kindness and an amused tolerance; ... seldom considered a menace to society, blamed for being what they are, or made to feel that they must be kept in separate places from other people, ostracized or confined to institutions.' (Jaspan, 1969: 22–3 cited in Peletz, 1996: 123).

30 In September 1998, Anwar Ibrahim, long hailed as premier-in-waiting, was dismissed (See Chapter 1 for details). The shock was worsened by news that he was unfit for his job because of 'abnormal' sexual proclivities including sodomy. Although his first trial was for corruption, attempts to further discredit and alienate him from his supporters were undertaken by exploiting homophobic sentiments among the Malaysian public (Tan, 2000: 20). It is worth noting that such a strategy appears to be employed selectively. For example, in spite of several attempts by adversaries to brand her a lesbian, Puteri Umno chief and now Minister of Youth and Sports, Azalina Othman Said, was spared Anwar's fate. The claims against her have never been proven. (See also Chapter 8.)

31 This outfit can best be understood as an opportunistic initiative by two UMNO leaders who, it appeared, were trying to endear themselves with Mahathir. When the desired recognition was not forthcoming, one of them publicly disassociated himself and this effectively marked the group's demise.

32 Various news reports on this incident, as well as a similar episode involving two men, Fauzi and Zakaria (discussed later in this chapter), appeared in *The Star* from 2 December 1996 to 6 March 1997.

33 Up till today the Malaysian Penal Code only criminalizes male-to-male sexual acts (i.e. sodomy), and by implication enables the persecution of male homosexuals. It is silent on sexual acts between women. Nevertheless, around the mid-1990s amendments to the *Syariah* law in some states (Johor, Kelantan, Terengganu) and the Federal Territories mean that there are now also provisions

to criminalize Muslim women who engage in sexual relations with one another. See below for details.

34 Aside from police harassment faced by transvestite sex workers, another common form of harassment of transvestites occurs when the authorities swoop on their beauty pageants and detain them for 'wearing female clothes and acting like a woman in a public place', considered an offence under the *Syariah* laws. For a typical account of this kind of persecution, see 'Religious authorities bust transvestite beauty pageant' in *Malaysiakini* (30 October 2002).

35 The Federal Territories *Syariah* Laws: *Syariah* Criminal Offences (Federal Territories) Act 1997 defines *musahaqah* loosely as 'sexual relations between female persons'. This is in contrast to the Kelantan *Hudud* Bill that was proposed some years earlier, which deemed this to be the 'act of sexual gratification between females by rubbing the vagina of one against that of the other.' See Rose Ismail (1995: 116–17).

36 While this law has been enacted in Kelantan, and subsequently in Terengganu, the Federal Government has refused to approve the use of state instruments that fall under its jurisdiction – e.g. the police and prison system – for *Hudud*-related crimes. Despite protestations by PAS that it will go ahead and implement the law, it is unclear if this will ever happen. However, it must be made clear that this opposition against the Hudud by the more secular Federal government does not mean that is was doing so in protest against the *musahaqah* provision.

37 See Chapter 4 for details of the process and document.

38 These issues cut across the socio-economic, ethnic and geographical spectrum of Malaysian lesbians. Nevertheless, a Malaysian lesbian's experience with any of these forms of discrimination will be determined by the specificities of her location. For example, a middle-class, affluent and feminine-looking lesbian would be less vulnerable to persecution compared to a working-class, masculine-looking lesbian.

39 Personal communication between the writer and the WAC Organizing Committee, 24 March 1999.

40 Zainah Anwar, Sisters in Islam, Personal communication to the WAC Organising Committee, 22 March 1999.

41 The contradictions of trying to juggle words around, however, was picked up by one observer. After attending the launch of the WAC, she wrote to the Organizing Committee, expressing her concern over the way the phrase 'Someone's sexual orientation, and sexual practices *which do not involve harm to anyone*, should not be grounds for discrimination' (italics in original letter) had been worded. She noted that even though the Committee's intention may have been to rule out support for practices like paedophilia, the statement could be used to justify the very kind of discrimination that it sought to avoid. Trying to couch the sexuality dimension of the chapter in terms of health also caused another two observers to comment that health issues were not covered adequately by a chapter that was named 'Women, Health and Sexuality'. (Personal communication between the writers and the WAC Organizing Committee, 3 June 1999 and 24 March 1999 respectively.)

42 See Chapter 6 for an elaboration.

43 Support for the ruling coalition was firmly in place in the early 1990s but this changed by the 1999 elections when the Anwar crisis caused a split among Malay voters. See Chapter 2 for an elaboration.

44 This term is usually used to describe effeminate or gay men but carries with it very negative connotations.

45 During a wedding ceremony, a *mak andam* takes charge of preparations involved in beautifying the bride.

46 The movement to defend sexuality rights is in its very early days in Malaysia but, since the early 1990s, those involved have started to make a difference by adding

their voices to public discourse to protest against discrimination on the basis of sexuality.

47 She claimed that this new law would violate women's rights. In all likelihood, her attack was more politically motivated to discredit the Islamic political party PAS, the main rivals of UMNO, 'Warning on sodomy law', *The Star* (30 August 2003).

48 Instead of dealing with the *mak nyah* community's request to be officially recognized as women, and thus be granted the same rights, the minister suggested that they first change their name to something that was 'more feminine' and 'dignified'.

49 See 'Suhakam ticks off media on "effeminate" men and "masculine" women', *Malaysiakini* (28 August 2003).

Chapter 8

1 This area of study is the unique contribution of Antonio Gramsci, who wrote many of his works while being imprisoned by the Italian Fascist government from 1926 to his death in 1937.

2 See 'Violence prevention campaign to involve ministries, agencies', *New Straits Times* (15 August 2003).

3 The 2003 budget was seen as the then Prime Minister Mahathir Mohamad's 'parting gift' to the nation before he stepped down in October. It was also looked upon as an 'election' budget, as the 11th general election was expected any time then. The category of single mothers and women in small businesses were made a target beneficiary, as the allocation would allow this group to have wider access to loan and credit facilities.

4 For example, several PAS women candidates contested in the 2004 general election, a turnaround from the 1999 election when the party's women members were not allowed to contest.

5 Among Mahathir's other infamous sayings is the following: 'Many say two men living together is a family, two women living together is a family, an unmarried woman and her child are a family. To Asians those are not families. A family exists when a man and a woman are joined in marriage and have children. The Western redefinition of the family is totally unacceptable' (1995: 86).

6 The experience of women's NGOs in Malaysia with funding has been varied. The following discussion pertains to groups which are autonomous or semi-autonomous in nature, rather than those which support the establishment or *status quo*.

7 Donors cited the need to switch funding priorities into geographical regions such as the Mekong region, Eastern Europe and Central Asia as reasons for this pull-out. They turned a deaf ear to counter-arguments by local women's groups that economic development should not be used as a yardstick in countries where the state has blocked access to women's and human rights.

8 It was only at the end of 2004, after much lobbying by women's groups, that the government announced that it would be setting up women's shelters. See below for details.

9 The discussions and debates raised around and at the World Conference on Human Rights in Vienna, Austria, in 1993, were a key to raising this approach into prominence.

10 The United Nations treaty body system is best understood as a set of international laws and mechanisms which provide for certain standards that should be upheld by all countries that have agreed to be bound by these (a country is bound when its government ratifies a treaty). Apart from CEDAW and the Convention on the Rights of the Child, these include: the International Covenant on

Economic, Social and Cultural Rights, the International Covenant on Civil and Political Rights, the Convention Against Torture, the Convention on the Elimination of All Forms of Racial Discrimination, and the Convention on the Protection of the Rights of All Migrant Workers and Members of Their Families.

11 See *Media and Gender Monitor*, September 2003, p. 4.

12 See 'Report: Women will head more households', *The Star* (13 April 2005).

13 Unlike in the past when women's NGOs were the main bodies interested in organizing and mobilizing to commemorate International Women's Day, Red Communications – the company behind the highly successful television series for young women *3R* – appears to have taken over this role in recent years.

14 Founded by Chong Sheau Ching, a single mother who was a journalist with a young daughter, the group was started for women in her situation. While the group began with middle-class women, it has recently started working with urban-based low income and unemployed home-makers, particularly single mothers, care-givers and the disabled.

15 One of the winners was quoted as saying that 'playing jigsaw puzzles with my daughter and making roast chicken and home-baked buns are the "luxuries" of working from home'. See 'Fight sex crimes: Abdullah wants tougher laws', *The Star* (12 May 2004).

16 See Anthea De Lima, 'Radio just for women', *New Straits Times* (12 February 2005).

17 Items for consumption that do not contain anything that is forbidden by Islam, such as alcohol, pork and other specific animals.

18 See Rose Ismail, 'Exploiting *halal* potential', *New Straits Times* (18 August 2004).

19 We would like to thank Judith Loh, a key mover of MAN.V for the above information.

20 The White Ribbon Campaign (WRC) was started in Canada in 1991 by a handful of men who felt that they had a responsibility to urge men to speak out against violence against women. Spearheaded by Michael Kaufman, who was invited by AWAM to lead a workshop in Malaysia, WRC has held similar campaigns in about 30 countries – the largest effort to end men's violence against women.

21 In this regard, it also shares similarities with women's organizations worldwide.

22 Take the issue of sexuality, for example. In a revealing discussion among younger urban women, held to elicit feedback on their main concerns, there was overwhelming agreement that sexuality was an area which needed more attention, going beyond the realm of violence into a sphere where informed sexual choices could be made. This was expressed during the 'Dialogue among younger women', a meeting organized by WDC on 6 September 2003.

23 There is, for instance, a listserv dubbed 'Writers for Rights' that was started in 2004 by a 19-year-old woman. She wanted it as a space where younger women could freely discuss and exchange views on topical issues, and when necessary, to express these via the media so that the voices of younger women will count.

24 His desire to establish a government that is transparent, accountable and void of corruption was almost deliberately well publicized by the media, where his appointees or lobbyists are now in charge.

25 This is not to say that Pak Lah is without critics. Several commentators have noted how his efforts to stamp out corruption have not addressed some of the 'big fish' allegedly including certain members of his cabinet. Human rights advocates have taken him to task for his refusal to abolish the Internal Security Act, a stance he has upheld since his days as Deputy Prime Minister and Home Minister.

26 Only 99 women candidates stood for election compared to the 1,564 hopefuls who offered themselves for both state and parliamentary seats. See *New Straits Times* (25 March 2004).
27 This solved the problem of overlapping roles between the two ministries, especially in relation to the issue of domestic violence. Domestic violence, for example, requires referrals of social welfare officers who worked under the other ministry; as a result, the Ministry of Women and Family Development often found it difficult to promote a holistic campaign against VAW. See Chapter 4.
28 See *The Star* (12 May 2004).
29 See 'Women shelters to be gazetted', *The Star* (7 December 2004).
30 In fact, these 'gender focal points' were already set-up by the early 1990s. However, they failed to function effectively and hence needed to be revived.
31 Polygamy, for example, is defended by some Muslim feminists because a strident campaign that promotes monogamy is perceived as undermining the greater purpose and identity of the Islamic religious community. In fact, some Muslim women's groups emphasize that polygamy is a 'small matter' compared with the issue of oppression against the Islamic community and widespread but unchecked moral ills such as free sex among youths. See 'Sisters in Islam.perlu anjurkan kempen cegah maksiat (Sisters in Islam should campaign against moral decay)': http://harakahdaily.net (2 June 2003).
32 A female MP from the Malaysian Indian Congress, the Indian-based component of the BN, even went so far as to refute claims by women's groups that a critical number of women politicians was necessary before women could be effective in their decision-making roles in government. She was also quoted as saying that, despite their small numbers, all elected women representatives had always championed women's rights. See *The Malay Mail* (20 March 2004).

Appendix A

1 In 2005, the Joint Action Group against Violence Against Women (JAG-VAW) was renamed the Joint Action Group for Gender Equality (JAG).

Appendix B

1 This is the Introduction to the Women's Agenda for Change document, launched in 1999.
2 The ten issues were: development; participatory democracy; culture and religion; violence against women; land; health services; law; work; HIV/AIDS; and environment.

Bibliography

Alvarez, Sonia (1990) *Engendering Democracy in Brazil: Women's Movement in Transition Politics*. Princeton, NJ: Princeton University Press.

——(1991) 'Women's Movement and Gender Politics in the Brazilian Transition'. In Jane Jaquette (ed.) *The Women's Movement in Latin America*, Boulder, CO: Westview.

——(1999) 'Advocating Feminism: The Latin American Feminist NGO 'Boom''. *International Feminist Journal of Politics*. Vol.1, No. 2: pp. 181–209.

Alina, Rastam (ed.) (2002) *The Rape Report: An Overview of Rape in Malaysia*. Petaling Jaya: All Women's Action Society (AWAM) and Strategic Info Research Development (SIRD).

Aliza, Jaafar (1994) 'Jadilah Mujadidah Sejati (Be a Genuine Women's Advocate)'. In *Perjuangan Wanita Kini: Halatuju dan Peranan Wanita Islam* (The Struggle of Women Today: Direction and Role of Islamic Women). Kuala Lumpur: Pertubuhan Jamaah Islah Malaysia. pp. 99–103.

All Women's Action Society (AWAM) (1989) *Women Alert*. Issue Number One. May/June.

——(1993) *Waves. Newsletter of the All Women's Action Society*. Issues Nos. 12 and 13. Bumper Edition. March–August.

——(1995) *Waves. Newsletter of the All Women's Action Society*. Issue No. 17. June–August.

——(2000) 'A Preliminary Proposal on Anti-Rape Reforms'. Memorandum presented to the Attorney General of Malaysia. 24 April.

——(2001) 'A Preliminary Proposal: Amendments to Laws Relating to Rape in Malaysia'. Presented to the Attorney General of Malaysia. 18 September.

——(2002) 'Memorandum on Laws Related to Rape: Review and Proposals for Amendments'.

Aminah, Ahmad (1999) 'Participation of Malaysian Women in Employment: A Gender Stratification Analysis'. In Maimunah Ismail and Aminah Ahmad (eds) *Women and Work: Challenges in Industrializing Nations*. London: ASEAN Academic Press.

Anantaraman, V. (1997) *Malaysian Industrial Relations: Law and Practice*. Serdang: Universiti Putra Malaysia Press.

Arat, Yesim (1998) 'Feminists, Islamists, and Political Change in Turkey'. *Political Psychology*. Vol. 19, No. 1, pp. 117–31.

Arudsothy, Ponniah (1994) 'New Strategies of Labour Control: The State, Transnationals and Trade Unionism in Malaysia'. In Sukhan, Jackson, *Contemporary*

Developments in Asian Industrial Relations. University of New South Wales Studies in Human Resource Management and Industrial Relations in Asia. Number 3.

Batliwala, Srilatha (2003) *Resource Net.* 25 April. Toronto: Association of Women's Rights in Development, interview.

bh. (2000) 'Brothel's Keeper'. Vox. *The Sun.* 17 December.

Bhopal, Mhinder and Rowley, Chris. n.d. 'Ethnicity as a Management Issue and Resource: Examples from Malaysia'. Unpublished manuscript.

Blondet, Cecilia. (2002) 'The Devil's Deal: Women's Political Participation and Authoritarianism in Peru'. In Maxine Molyneux and Shahra Razavi (eds) *Gender Justice, Development and Rights.* Oxford: Oxford University Press. pp. 277–305.

Boreham, Paul, Clegg, Stewart and Dow, Geoff (1989) 'Political Organisation and Economic Policy'. In Graeme Duncan (ed.) *Democracy and the Capitalist State.* Cambridge: Cambridge University Press. pp. 253–76.

Boserup, Ester (1970) *Women's Role in Economic Development.* London: Allen and Unwin.

Brown, Carl L. (2000) *Religion and State: The Muslim Approach to Politics.* New York: Columbia University Press.

Burawoy, M. (1983) 'Between Labour Process and the State: The Changing Face of Factory Regimes Under Advanced Capitalism'. *American Sociological Review.* 18 October. pp. 587–605.

Cabrera-Balleza, Mavic (1999) 'Fighting an Uphill Battle'. *Women in Action,* No. 2, pp. 26–9.

Cardosa, Mary and Wan Fauziah (1994) 'Health Consequences of VDT Work in Malaysia: Some Preliminary Findings'. In Cecilia Ng and Anne Munro-Kua (eds) *Keying Into the Future: The Impact of Computerization on Office Workers.* Kajang and Serdang: Women's Development Collective and Women's Studies Unit. Universiti Pertanian Malaysia.

Carroll, Barbara Wake and Carroll, Terrance (2000) 'Accommodating Ethnic Diversity in a Modernizing Democratic State: Theory and Practice in the Case of Mauritius'. *Ethnic and Racial Studies.* Vol. 23, No. 1, January. pp. 120–42.

Cawson, Alan (1989) 'Is There a Corporatist Theory of the State?'. In Graeme Duncan (ed.) *Democracy and the Capitalist State.* Cambridge: Cambridge University Press. pp. 233–52.

Chan, Lean Heng (1991) 'Reflection of an Organiser'. In Loh Cheng Kooi and Cheung Choi Wan (eds) *Many Paths One Goal: Organising Women Workers in Asia.* Hong Kong: Committee for Asian Women (CAW).

Chee, Heng Leng and Subramaniam, Mano (1994) 'Speaking Out: Women Workers Talk About Safety and Health in Electronics'. In Chee Heng Leng (ed.) *Behind the Chip* Petaling Jaya: Women's Development Collective and Persatuan Sahabat Wanita.

Chen, May Yee (1999) 'Malaysia's Political Parties Shift to Courting Women'. *Asian Wall Street Journal.* 28 July.

Chhachhi, Amrita and Pittin, Renee (1996) 'Multiple Identities, Multiple Strategies'. In Amrita Chhachhi and Renee Pittin (eds) *Confronting State, Capital and Patriarchy: Women Organising in the Process of Industrialisation.* Basingstoke and London: Macmillan Press.

Chhachhi, Amrita (1998) '*Gender, Flexibility, Skill and Industrial Restructuring in the Electronics Industry in India*'. Paper presented at the Regional Conference and Technology in Asia. Bangkok: Asian Institute of Technology. 4–7 August.

Connell, R. W. (1994) 'The State, Gender and Sexual Politics: Theory and Appraisal'. In H. Lorraine Radtke and Henderikus J. Stam (eds) *Power/Gender: Social Relations in Theory and Practice*. London: Sage Publications.

Crouch, Harold (1992) 'Authoritarian Trends, the UMNO Split and the Limits to State Power'. In Joel Kahn and Francis Loh (eds) *Fragmented Vision: Culture and Politics in Contemporary Malaysia*. Sydney: Asian Studies Association of Australia in association with Allen and Unwin.

D'Cunha, Jean (2003) '*Protecting Women Migrants in Asia: Gender and Rights-based Analysis and Action*'. Paper presented at the Regional Workshop on Protecting Women Migrant Workers in Asia: Meeting the Challenges. 9–11 December. Jakarta, Indonesia.

Dancz, Virginia H. (1987) *Women and Party Politics in Peninsular Malaysia*. Singapore: Oxford University Press.

Deveaux, Monique (2000) 'Conflicting Equalities? Cultural Group Rights and Sex Equality'. *Political Studies*. Vol. 48.

Dewan Muslimat PAS. (2001) *Halwa Perjuangan*, Lajnah Penerangan dan Hal Ehwal Luar (*Mission Directions*, Information and External Relations Bureau). Kuala Lumpur: PAS Publication.

Deyo, Frederick (1997) 'Labour and Industrial Restructuring in South-East Asia'. In Garry Rodan, Kevin Hewison and Richard Robison (eds) *The Political Economy of South-East Asia*. Melbourne: Oxford University Press.

Dunleavy, Patrick and O'Leary, Brendan (1987) *Theories of the State: The Politics of Liberal Democracy*. London: Macmillan Education.

Elson, Diane and Pearson, Ruth (1981) 'The Subordination of Women and the Internationalisation of Factory Production'. In Kate Young *et al.*, *Of Marriage and the Market*. London: CSE Books.

Entwistle, Harold (1979) *Antonio Gramsci: Conservative Schooling for Radical Politics*. London: Routledge and Kegan Paul.

Esposito, John and J. O. Voll (1996) *Islam and Democracy*. New York: Oxford University Press.

Fernandez, Irene (1992) 'Mobilising on All Fronts: A Comprehensive Strategy to End Violence Against Women in Malaysia'. In Margaret Schuler (ed.) *Freedom from Violence: Women's Strategies From Around the World*. New York: UNIFEM. pp. 101–20.

Ford, Michele. (2002) 'Public Accounts of Indonesian Women Workers' Experiences Overseas'. Research Note. *Asian Journal of Women's Studies*. Vol. 8, No. 4. Seoul: Ewha Women's University Press. pp. 101–15.

Franceschet, Susan (2003) 'State Feminism and the Women's Movements: The Impact of Chile's Servicio Nacional de la Mujer on Women's Activism'. *Latin American Research Review*, Vol. 38, No. 1, pp. 9–40

Gellner, Ernest (1994) *Conditions of Liberty: Civil Society and Its Rivals*. London: Penguin.

Ghosh, Jayati (1997) *Impact of Globalisation on Women: Women And Economic Liberalisation In The Asian And Pacific Region*. Paper prepared for ESCAP.

Gilpin, Robert (2001) *Global Political Economy: Understanding the International Economic Order*. Princeton, NJ: Princeton University Press and Oxford University Press.

Gole, Nilufer (1996) *The Forbidden Modern: Civilization and Veiling*. Ann Arbor, MI: University of Michigan Press.

Government of Malaysia (1991) *Sixth Malaysia Plan 1991–1995*. Kuala Lumpur: National Government Printers.

——(2001) *Eighth Malaysia Plan 2001–2005*. Kuala Lumpur: National Government Printers.

——(2001) *The Third Outline Perspective Plan 2001–2010*. Kuala Lumpur: National Government Printers.

Grace, Elizabeth (1990) *Shortcircuiting Labour: Unionising Electronic Workers in Malaysia*. Kuala Lumpur: INSAN.

Griffen, Vanessa (2002) *Globalisation and Re-inventing the Politics of a Women's Movement*. Occasional Paper No. 6. Toronto: Association for Women's Rights in Development.

Grossman, Rachel (1979) 'Changing Role of Southeast Asian Women: The Global Assembly Line and Social Manipulation of Women'. *Joint Issue of Southeast Asia Chronicle/Pacific Research*. SEAC 66/PSC, 9/5.

——(1979) 'Women's Place in the Integrated Circuit'. *Joint Issue of Southeast Asia Chronicle/Pacific Research*. SEAC 66/PSC, 9/5.

Habermas, J. (1973) *Legitimation Crisis*. London: Heinemann.

Haji Muhammad Nur Lubis (2000) '*Hukum dan Persoalan: Wanita Dilantik Sebagai Ketua Negara, Hakim atau Menteri* (Rules and Question: Women Appointed as Head of States, Judges or Ministers)'. Kuala Lumpur: Al-Hidayah Publishers.

Harlina, Halizah Siraj (2000) 'Pengukuhan Kepemimpinan Wanita JIM: Mengorak Langkah ke Arah Menerajui Dakwah dan Ummah (The Strengthening of JIM's Women's Leadership: Steps in Achieving Mission Work and Ummah)'. In Mohamed Hatta, Shaharom, Ahmad Sodikin, Kasimin and Mohd. Radzi, Shaari (eds) *Risalah Pemimpin: Penulisan Jawatankuasa Pusat JIM* (Leadership Manifesto: Writings of Central Committee Members, JIM). Kuala Lumpur: Pertubuhan Jamaah Islah Malaysia.

Healy, Lucy (2000) 'Gender, 'Aliens', and the National Imaginary in Contemporary Malaysia'. *Journal of Social Issues in Southeast Asia*. October. Vol. 15, No. 2, pp. 222.

Held, David (1987) *Models of Democracy*. Cambridge: Polity Press.

Hermida, Alfred (2001) 'Wired Mothers Do It for Themselves'. *BBC News Online*. 7 November 2001: http://news.bbc.co.uk/2/hi/science/nature/1641425.stm (date accessed: 11 March 2004).

Hooi, You Ching (2004) 'Mothers @ work'. *Star Online*: http://202.186.86.35/special/online/momsnet/default.htm (date accessed: 11 March 2004).

Jagger, Alison (1983) *Feminist Politics and Human Nature*. Sussex: Harvester Press.

Jayaseelan, Julian. n.d. 'What's AIDS Got to Do with It?' Unpublished paper.

Jayawardeena, Kumari (1986) *Feminism and Nationalism in the Third World*. London: Zed Press.

Jesudason, James. (1995) 'Statist Democracy and the Limits to Civil Society in Malaysia'. *The Journal of Commonwealth and Comparative Politics*. Vol. 33, No. 3. November. pp. 335–56.

Joint Action Group against Violence against Women (1986) '*Proceedings of a Workshop-cum-Exhibition on Violence Against Women*'. Petaling Jaya: JAG-VAW.

Jomo, K. S. and Patricia Todd. (1994) *Trade Unions and the State in Peninsular Malaysia*. Kuala Lumpur: Oxford University Press.

Jomo, Kwame Sundaram (1988) *Race, Religion and Repression: National Security and the Insecurity of the Regime,* London: CARPA.

Josiah, Ivy Nallammah, Lee Shook Fong and Naidu, Wathshlah G. (2001) *'Malaysia's Experience with the Domestic Violence Act 1994 (Act 521) Malaysia'*. Paper written for the United Nations Special Rapporteur for Violence against Women Consultation. Organized by APWLD. Colombo, Sri Lanka. 12–13 August.

Kamilia, Ibrahim (1998) 'Women's Involvement in Politics and the Need for a Paradigm Shift'. In Sharifah Zaleha Syed Hassan (ed.) *Malaysian Women in the Wake of Change*. Kuala Lumpur: University of Malaya, Gender Studies Programme.

Kandiyoti, Deniz (1989) 'Women and the Turkish State: Political Actors or Symbolic Pawns?' In Floya Anthias and Nira Yuval-Davis (eds) *Women-Nation-State*. Houndmill: Macmillan.

Kazemi, Farhad (2000) 'Gender, Islam and Politics'. *Social Research*. Vol. 67, No. 2.

Kessler, Clive (1992) 'Arcahism and Modernity: Contemporary Malay Political Culture'. In Joel Kahn and Francis Loh (eds) *Fragmented Vision: Culture and Politics in Contemporary Malaysia*. Sydney: Allen and Unwin.

Khalijah, Mohd. Salleh (1996) 'Wanita Sebagai Pendakwah dan Pembangun Ummah (Women as Missionary and Builder of Ummah)'. In Md Sidin Ahmad Ishak. *Angkatan Belia Islam Malaysia, 1971–1996*. Petaling Jaya: Angkatan Belia Islam Malaysia.

Khoo, K. K. (1994) 'Malaysian Women's Participation in Politics: A Historical Perspective'. In Haas Robert and Rahmah Hashim (eds) *Malaysian Women Creating Their Political Awareness*. Kuala Lumpur: Friedrich Naumann Foundation/Asian Institute for Development Communication.

Khoo, Philip (1999) 'Thinking the Unthinkable: A Malaysia not Governed by the BN?' *Aliran Monthly*. Vol. 19, No. 5, pp. 2–8.

——(2002) 'Beyond UMNO and PAS: Elections as Opportunity'. *Aliran Monthly*, Vol. 22, No. 10.

Langenbach, Ray (1994) 'Epistememission: (s)eX in the (t)eX(t)'. In Maznah Mohamad and Wong Soak Koon (eds) *Feminism: Malaysian Critique and Experience*. Special Issue of *Kajian Malaysia*. Vol 12, Nos. 1 and 2 (June/December), pp. 226–52.

Lai, Suat Yan (1996) *'Competing Discourses on Sexuality Between the Women's Movement and the State in Malaysia: The Domestic Violence Act'*. Unpublished MA Paper. The Hague: Institute of Social Studies.

Lawrence, Philip K. (1989) 'The State and Legitimation: The Work of Jurgen Habermas'. In Graeme Duncan (ed.). *Democracy and the Capitalist State*. Cambridge: Cambridge University Press. pp. 133–58.

Lee, Rose J. and Clark, Cal (2000) *Democracy and the Status of Women in East Asia*, Boulder, CO and London: Lynne Rienner Publishers.

Lim, Lin Lean (ed.) (1998) *The Sex Sector: Economic and Social Bases of Prostitution in Southeast Asia*. Geneva: International Labour Office.

Lim, Linda (1978) *'Women Workers in Transnational Corporations: The Case of the Electronics Industry in Malaysia and Singapore'*. Michigan Occasional Papers No. 9. Ann Arbor: University of Michigan Press.

Ling, L. H. M. (2000) 'The Limits of Democratization for Women' In Rose J. Lee and Cal Clark (eds) *Democracy and the Status of Women in East Asia*. Boulder, CO and London: Lynne Rienner.

Lipjhart, Arend. (1969) 'Consociational Democracy'. *World Politics*. Vol. 21. No. 2. pp. 207–25.

——(1977) *Democracy in Plural Societies: A Comparative Exploration*. New Haven, CT: Yale University Press.

Lochhead, J. (1986) *Retrenchment in a Malaysian Free Trade Zone*. Penang: Project *KANITA*. Universiti Sains Malaysia.

Lochhead, James (1988) 'Retrenchment in a Malaysian Free Trade Zone'. In Noeleen Heyzer (ed.) *Daughters in Industry: Work, Skills and Consciousness of Women Workers in Asia*. Kuala Lumpur: Asian and Pacific Development Centre.

Loh, Francis K. W. (2000) 'State–Societal Relations in a Rapidly Growing Economy: The case of Malaysia, 1970–97'. In R. B. Kleinberg and J. Clark (eds) *Economic Liberalisation, Democratisation and Civil Society in the Developing World*. New York: St. Martin's Press.

——(2002) 'Developmentalism and the Limits of Democratic Discourse'. In Francis Loh and Khoo Boo Teik (eds) *Democracy in Malaysia: Discourse and Practice*. Richmond, Surrey: Curzon Press.

Loh, Francis and Khoo, Boo Teik (eds) (2002) *Democracy in Malaysia: Discourse and Practice*. Richmond, Surrey: Curzon Press.

Loh, Francis and Saravanamuttu, Johan (eds) (2003) *New Politics in Malaysia*. Singapore: Institute of Southeast Asian Studies (ISEAS).

Loh, Lee Lee (2001) *Chinese Women in Industrial Home-Based Subcontracting in the Garment Industry in Kuala Lumpur, Malaysia: Neither Valued nor Costed*. PhD thesis. Kuala Lumpur: University of Malaya.

MacKinnon, Catherine (1979) *Sexual Harassment of Working Women: A Case of Sex Discrimination*. New Haven, CT: Yale University Press.

Macpherson. C. B. (1989) 'Do We Need a Theory of The State?'. In Graeme Duncan (ed.) *Democracy and the Capitalist State*. Cambridge: Cambridge University Press. pp. 13–14.

Mahathir Mohamad (1970) *The Malay Dilemma*. Singapore: Donald Moore Press.

Mahathir Mohamad and Shintaro Ishihara (1995) *The Voice of Asia: Two Leaders Discuss the Coming Century*. Tokyo: Kodansha International Ltd.

Mandaville, Peter (2001) *Transnational Muslim Politics: Reimagining the Umma*. London and New York: Routledge.

Manderson, Lenore (1980) *Women, Politics and Change: The Kaum Ibu UMNO Malaysia, 1945–1972*. Kuala Lumpur: Oxford University Press. pp. 113–14.

Mann, Susan Archer (2005) 'The Decentering of Second Wave Feminism and the Rise of the Third Wave', *Science and Society*, Vol. 69, No. 1, January, pp. 56–91: http://proquest.umi.com/pdqweb?index=12&sid=9&srchmode=1&vinst=PROD& fmt = 3 (date accessed: 21 March 2005)

Marcuse, Herbert (1964) *One-Dimension Man: Studies in the Ideology of Advanced Societies*. Boston: Beacon.

Marina, Mahathir (2004) 'HIV/AIDS in Malaysia: Moving Forward Slowly'. In Bridget Welsh (ed.) *Reflections: The Mahathir Years*. Southeast Asia Studies Program. The Paul H. Nitze School of Advanced International Studies (SAIS). Washington, DC: Johns Hopkins University. pp 461–72.

Maznah, Mohamad (ed.) (2000) *Muslim Women and Access to Justice: Historical, Legal and Social Experience of Women in Malaysia*. Penang: Women's Crisis Centre.

——(2001) 'At the Centre and Periphery: The contributions of women's movement to democratisation'. In Loh Kok Wah and Khoo Boo Teik (eds) *Democracy in Malaysia: Discourse and Practice*. London: NIAS/Curzon Press.

——(2001 a) 'The Unravelling of the "Malay Consensus"'. *Southeast Asian Affairs 2001*. Singapore: Institute of Southeast Asian Studies.

——(2002) 'Malaysian Women's Movement at the Centre and Periphery: Contributions in the Democratisation of Politics'. In Loh Kok Wah and Khoo Boo Teik (eds) *Democracy in Malaysia: Discourse and Practice*. Richmond, Surrey: Curzon Press. pp. 216–40.

——(2003) 'The Contest for Malay Votes in 1999: UMNO's most Historic Challenge?' In Francis Loh Kok Wah and Johan Saravanamuttu (eds) *New Politics in Malaysia*. Singapore: ISEAS. pp. 66–86.

——(2004) 'Women's Engagement with Political Islam in Malaysia'. *Global Change, Peace and Security*. Vol. 16, No. 2, June.

Maznah, Mohamad and Ng, Cecilia. (1988) 'The Reconstitution of Rural Women's Labour: The Malaysian case'. In Bina Agarwal (ed.) *Structures of Patriarchy: State, Community and the Household in Modernising Asia*. London: Zed Books. pp. 52–82.

Maznah Mohamad, Ng, Cecilia and Tan, beng hui. (2001) 'Globalization, Industrialization and Crisis: The Coming of Age of Malaysian Women Workers?' In Sandra J. Maclean, Fahimul Quadir, and Timothy Shaw (eds) *Crises of Governance in Asia and Africa*. Hants: Ashgate.

Md Sidin, Ahmad Ishak (ed.) (1996) *Angkatan Belia Islam Malaysia, 1971–1996*. Petaling Jaya: Angkatan Belia Islam Malaysia.

Mies, Maria and Jayawardena, Kumari (1981) *Feminism in Europe: Liberal and Socialist Strategies 1789 – 1919*.The Hague: Institute of Social Studies.

Milne, R. S. and Mauzy, Diane K. (1978) *Politics and Government in Malaysia*. Vancouver: University of British Columbia Press.

Mohamed Hatta, Shaharom, Ahmad Sodikin, Kasimin and Mohd. Radzi, Shaari (eds) (2000) *Risalah Pemimpin: Penulisan Jawatankuasa Pusat JIM* (Leadership Manifesto: Writings of Central Committee Members, JIM). Kuala Lumpur: Pertubuhan Jamaah Islah Malaysia.

Molyneux, Maxine (1995) 'Mobilisation Without Emancipation? Women's Interests, the State and Revolution in Nicaragua'. *Feminist Studies*, Vol. 11, pp 227–54.

——(1998) 'Analysing Women's Movements'. In Cecile Jackson and Ruth Pearson (eds) *Feminist Visions of Development: Gender Analysis and Policy*. London and New York: Routledge.

Molyneux, Maxine and Shahra Razavi. (2002) *Gender Justice, Development, and Right*. Oxford: Oxford University Press.

Mostov, Julie (2000) 'Sexing the Nation/Desexing the Body: Politics of National Identity in the Former Yugoslavia'. In Tamar Mayer (ed.) *Gender Ironies of Nationalism: Sexing the Nation*. London and New York: Routledge.

Murshidah, Mustaffa n.d. Perancangan Yahudi di Sebalik Penolakan Poligami (Jewish Plot Behind Rejection of Polygamy) in magazine-formatted publication, *Rahsia Pembentukan Keluarga Supe*.

Nagaraj, Shyamala and Siti Rohani Yahya (1998) 'Prostitution in Malaysia'. In Lim Lean Lin (ed.) *The Sex Sector: Economic and Social Bases of Prostitution in Southeast Asia*. Geneva: International Labour Office. pp. 67–99.

National Office for Human Development (2003) 'Guide for Ministry with Migrants and Refugees. 2002–3'. Kuala Lumpur: Migrants Services Secretariat NOHD.

Ng, Cecilia (ed.) (2001) *Teleworking and Development in Malaysia*. Penang: Southbound.

——(1994) 'The Woman Question: Problems in Feminist Analysis'. *Kajian Malaysia*. Vol. 12, Nos. 1 & 2, June/December.

——(1999) '*Social Movements, Women's Movements and the State in Malaysia: The Politics of Engagement*'. Paper presented at the DAWN Asia-Pacific Workshop on Political Restructuring and Social Transformation. 8–11 October. Chiang Mai, Thailand.

——(1999) *Positioning Women in Malaysia: Class and Gender in an Industrializing State*. Houndmills: Macmillan Press.

Ng, Cecilia and Carol Yong (1990) *Malaysian Women at the Crossroads*. CHANGE International Report No. 17. London: Calverts Press.

Ng, Cecilia and Maznah Mohamad (1997) 'The Management of Technology and Women in Two Electronics Firms in Malaysia'. *Gender, Technology and Development*. Vol. 1, no. 2, pp. 178–203.

Ng, Cecilia, Siti Nor Hamid and Syed Husin Ali (1987) 'Rural Development Programmes, Women's Participation and Organisations in Malaysia'. In Noeleen Heyzer (ed.) *Women Farmers and Rural Change in Asia: Towards Equal Access and Participation*. Kuala Lumpur: Asia and Pacific Development Centre.

Ng, Cecilia, Zanariah Mohd Noor and Maria Chin Abdullah (2003) *A Pioneering Step: Sexual harassment and the Code of Practice in Malaysia*. Petaling Jaya: All Women's Action Society and Women's Development Collective.

Nicholson, Linda (ed.) (1990) *Feminism/Postmodernism*. New York and London: Routledge.

Ong, Aihwa (1995) 'State Versus Islam: Malay Families, Women's Bodies, and the Body Politic in Malaysia'. In Aihwa Ong and Michael Peletz (eds) *Bewitching Women, Pious Men: Gender and Body Politics in Southeast Asia*. Berkeley, CA: University of California Press.

——(1987) *Spirits of Resistance and Capitalist Discipline: Factory Women in Malaysia*. Albany, NY: State University of New York Press.

Paidar, Parvin (2001) 'Encounters Between Feminism, Democracy and Reformism in Contemporary Iran'. In Maxine Molyneux and Shahra Razavi (eds) *Gender Justice, Development and Rights*. Oxford: Oxford University Press. pp. 239–76.

Peletz, Michael. (1996) *Reason and Passion: Representations of Gender in a Malay Society*. Berkeley, CA: University of California Press.

Phillips, Anne (2002) 'Multiculturalism, Universalism, and the Claims of Democracy'. In Maxine Molyneux and Shahra Razavi (eds) *Gender Justice, Development and Rights*. Oxford: Oxford University Press. pp. 115–40.

Pringle, Rosemary and Watson, Sophie (1992) 'Women's Interests and the Post-Structural State'. In Michele Barrett and Ann Phillips (eds) *Destabilising Theory: Contemporary Feminist Debates*. Cambridge: Polity Press.

Purvis, Jennifer. (2004) 'Girls and Women Together in the Third Wave: Embracing the Challenges of Intergenerational Feminism(s)'. *NWSA Journal*, Vol. 16, No. 3, October, pp. 93–123

Rai, Shirin (1996) 'Women and the State: Some Issues for Debate'. In Shirin Rai and Geraldine Lievsley (eds) *Women and the State: International Perspectives*. London: Routledge.

——(ed.) (2000) *International Perspectives on Gender and Democratisation*. Women's Studies at York. London: Macmillan Press.

Rai, Shirin and Lievesley, Geraldine (1996) (eds) *Women and the State: International Perspectives*. London: Routledge.

Rashila, Ramli (1998) 'Democratisation in Malaysia: Toward Gender Parity in Polit-ical Participation'. *Akademika*. July. pp. 72–75.

Rasiah, Rajah (1996) 'The Changing Organisation of Work in Malaysia's Electronics Industry'. *Asia-Pacific Viewpoint*. Vol. 37, No. 1, pp. 21–37.

Ray, R. and Korteweg, A. C. (1999) 'Women's Movements in the Third World: Iden-tity, Mobilization, and Autonomy'. *Annual Review of Sociology*. Vol. 27, pp. 47–71.

Roff, William (1967) *The Origins of Malay Nationalism*. New Haven, CT: Yale University Press.

Rohana, Ariffin (1988) 'Malaysian Women's Participation in Trade Unions'. In Noeleen Heyzer (ed.) *Daughters in Industry: Work, Skills and Consciousness of Women Workers in Asia*. Kuala Lumpur: Asian and Pacific Development Centre.

——(1994) 'Patriarchy in Labour Unions'. In Maznah Mohamad and Wong Soak Koon (eds) *Feminism: Malaysian Critique and Experience*. (Special Issue of *Kajian Malaysia*). Vol. 12, No. 1 and 2 (June/December).

Rose Ismail. (ed.) (1995) *Hudud in Malaysia: The Issues at Stake*. Kuala Lumpur: SIS Forum (Malaysia) Berhad..pp. 116–17

Roy, Olivier. (1999) *The Failure of Political Islam*. London and New York: I. B Tauris Publishers.

Samanther, Meera (2001) *'Women's Aid Organisation's (WAO) Advocacy on the Issue of Foreign Domestic Workers in Malaysia'*. Paper presented at the NGO Forum on the World Conference Against Racism. Durban, South Africa. 31 August.

——(2002) *'Is the Domestic Worker Safe at Home?'*. Unpublished paper prepared presented by Meera Samanther of Women's Aid Organisation at the National Consultation on Foreign Domestic Workers, 31 July.

Saravanamuttu, Johan (1991) *'Industrialization and the Institutionalization of Authori-tarian Political Regimes'*. Occasional Paper Series Number 8. Yokohama: International Peace Research Institute Meigaku (PRIME), Meiji Gakuin University.

——(2001) 'The Roots and Future of the Reformasi Movement'. *Communique*. No. 58. March–August. An occasional publication of the Asian Regional Exchange for New Alternatives (ARENA).

——(2002) *'Politics and Religion: State, Church, Mosque and Civil Society'*. Talk presented at Seminar on Religion and Politics, Petaling Jaya.

——(2002) 'Multiculturalisms in Crisis: Reflections from Southeast Asia'. *Macalester International*. Special issue on Malaysia: Crossroads of Diversity in Southeast Asia. Vol. 12, Autumn. pp. 3–36.

Sattherthwaite, Meg (2003) *'Human Rights Protections Applicable to Women Migrant Workers. A Unifem Legal Analysis'*. Unpublished paper.

Schild, Veronica (2001) 'Engendering the New Social Citizenship in Chile: NGOs and Social Provisioning under Neo-liberalism'. In Maxine Molyneux and Shahra Razavi (eds) *Gender Justice, Development and Rights*. Oxford: Oxford University Press. pp. 170–203.

Schuler, Margaret (ed.) (1992) *Freedom from Violence: Women's Struggles From Around the World*. New York: UNIFEM.

Shaheed, Farida (1994) 'Controlled Or Autonomous: Identity and the Experience of the Network, Women Living Under Muslim Laws'. *Signs*. Vol. 19, No. 4, Summer. pp. 997–1020.

Shamsul, Amri Baharuddin (1986) *From British to Bumiputera Rule: Local Politics and Rural Development in Peninsular Malaysia*. Singapore: Institute of Southeast Asian Studies.

Sharifah Zaleha, Syed Hassan (2002) *'Domesticated but Empowered: Islamic Resurgence and Muslim Women in Malaysia'*. Paper presented at the 4th SAMA Annual Conference on Gender Studies. Bangi, Malaysia.

Suaram (1998) *Malaysian Human Rights Report*. Petaling Jaya: Suaram Komunikasi.

Suriani Abdullah (1999) *Rejimen Ke-10 dan Kemerdekaan*. Hong Kong: Nan Dao Publisher.

Tan, beng hui (1991) 'Indian Rubber Estate Workers in Malaya/West Malaysia: c.1880 – c.1980 (with Special Emphasis on Indian Women)'. Unpublished Honours Thesis. University of Sydney.

——(1999a) 'Women's Sexuality and Asian Values'. In Evelyn Blackwood and Saskia E. Wieringa (eds) *Female Desires: Same-Sex Relations and Transgender Practices Across Cultures*. New York: Columbia University Press.

——(1999b) 'Women Organising for Change: Costing the Domestic Violence Act Campaign in Malaysia (c.1985–96)'. *Kajian Malaysia*. Vol. XVII, No. 1, June. pp. 48–69.

——(2000) 'Time's Up! Moving Sexuality Rights in Malaysia into the New Millennium'. *Women in Action*. pp. 20–23.

——(2003) "Protecting' Women: Legislation and Regulation of Women's Sexuality in Colonial Malaya'. *Gender, Technology and Development*. Vol. 7, No. 1. New Delhi: Sage Publications. pp. 1–30.

Tan, beng hui and Ng Cecilia. (2003) 'Embracing the Challenge of Representation: The Women's Movement and Electoral Politics in Malaysia' In Loh, Francis and Johan Saravanamuttu (eds) *New Politics in Malaysia*, Singapore: Institute of Southeast Asian Studies.

Tan, Boon Kean and Bishan Singh (1990) 'Uneasy Alliance: The State and NGOs in Malaysia'. Unpublished manuscript.

Taylor, Viviene (2003) 'Political Restructuring and Social Transformation'. Paper presented at DAWN Training Institute. Bangalore 14 September–3 October.

Tinker, Irene (1990) *Persistent Inequalities*. New York: Oxford University Press.

Tong, Rosemary (1992) *Feminist Thought: A Comprehensive Introduction*. London: Routledge.

Turner, Donna (2002) 'The K-Economy Transition and the Politics of Labour Reform: Some Socio-Political Implications for Labour'. Working Paper Series. Bangi: Institute of Malaysian and International Studies. Universiti Kebangsaan Malaysia,

UNDP, (2001) *Human Development Report: Making New Technologies Work for Human Development*. New York: Oxford University Press.

Valte, Maricris (forthcoming) *'Building Civil Society: Old Themes, New Challenges in the Age of Globalisation'*. Bangi: IKMAS.

Wad, Peter and Jomo. K. S. (1994) 'In-House Unions: "Looking East" for Industrial Relations'. In K. S. Jomo *Japan and Malaysian Development: In the Shadow of the Rising Sun*. London and New York: Routledge.

Walby, Sylvia (2001) 'Globalisation and Regulation: The New Economy and Gender in the UK'. Occasional Paper Series. No. 7. College of Urban. Labor and Metropolitan Affairs. Wayne State University.

Wanita UMNO (1989) 'Usul-Usul Wanita UMNO Memperjuangkan Hak-Hak Kaumnya (Resolutions of Wanita UMNO in Advocating for Women's Rights)'. In *Pergerakan Wanita UMNO, 40 Tahun Ulangtahun, Buku Cenderamata* (Wanita UMNO's 40th Anniversary Souvenir Book).

WAO (2004) 'Abolishing the Marital Rape Exception: Evidence from Around the World'. Unpublished paper.

Waylen, Georgia (1996) 'Women's Movements, the State and Democratization in Chile: The Establishment of SERNAM'. In Anne Marie Goetz (ed.) *Getting Institutions Right for Women in Development*. London: Zed Books. pp. 90–103.

Wieringa, Saskia (1994) 'Women's Interests and Empowerment: Gender Planning Reconsidered'. *Development and Change*. Vol. 24, No. 4, pp. 829–48.

——(ed.) (1995) *Subversive Women: Women's Movements in Africa, Asia, Latin America and the Caribbean*. London: Zed.

Women's Agenda for Change (1999) *Women's Agenda for Change*. Kuala Lumpur: Women's Agenda for Change.

Women's Aid Organisation (2000) 'Malaysia's Campaign for the Domestic Violence Act'. Online at: http://www.wao.org.my/news/20001130Day06.htm.

Women's Crisis Centre. (1999) 'Memorandum on the Domestic Violence Act 1994: Review and proposals for amendments'. Unpublished paper

Zainah, Anwar (2001) 'What Islam, Whose Islam? Sisters in Islam and the Struggle for Women's Rights'. In Robert W. Hefner (ed.) *The Politics of Multiculturalism: Pluralism and Citizenship in Malaysia, Singapore and Indonesia*. Honolulu: University of Hawaii Press.

Zarizana, Abdul Aziz (2003) 'Women and Justice: Rights and Detention in Malaysia'. Report of the 3rd Expert Meeting on Women and Justice in Penang, Malaysia 12–14 January. Organized by the Asian Women's Fund in Penang, Malaysia. 12–14 January. pp. 99–107.

Zarizana, Abdul Aziz and Marrison, Anna (2001) 'The Status of Women Under Malaysian Laws'. Women's Crisis Centre. July: http://www.wccpenang.org/women-status.htm

Index

LIVERPOOL JOHN MOORES UNIVERSITY
Aldham Roberts . R.C.
TEL. 0151 231 3701/3634

WCC 24, 28, 46, 56, 58–9, 162, 164, 171
WCI 31, 75
WDC 24–5, 28, 44–5, 58, 60, 71, 80–1,
103, 112, 126, 172, 185n10
WGPA 136–7, 139–41
WGPO 136–9, 196n21
White Ribbon Campaign 163, 199n20
WID 65–6, 67–9, 73
Wieringa, Saskia 3, 6
woman question 35, 68, 100, 159
WoMEC 81, 172
Women and Girls Protection Act
(WGPA); *see* WGPA
Women and Girls Protection Ordinance
(WGPO); *see* WGPO
Women in Development (WID); *see* WID
Women Monitoring Election Candidates
(WoMEC); *see* WoMEC
Women Teachers Union 19
women workers; *see* labour, women
working class
women: differences 2, 12, 167; divided 2,
6, 13, 23, 83, 165, 168; leaders 17, 20,
28, 48, 96–7, 103, 113; middle-class 10,
13, 20, 24, 28–9, 38, 42–3, 83,101, 125,
128, 130, 168, 196n28; rural 26–27, 67,
124; working-class 5, 10, 13, 26, 82
Women's Agenda for Change (WAC);
see WAC
Women's Aid Organisation (WAO); *see*
WAO

Women's Candidacy Initiative (WCI);
see WCI
Women's Centre for Change, previously
Women's Crisis Centre (WCC); *see*
WCC
Women's Charter 19
Women's Development Collective
(WDC); *see* WDC
women's empowerment 21, 32, 38, 42,
95, 100, 120–1, 130, 148–9, 155, 160,
171; *see also* economic empowerment
Women's Manifesto 70–2, 74, 147, 173,
175–81
women's movement: associational 6;
autonomous 15, 75, 82, 152; democracy 153, 166, 168, 172; directed 6–7,
10, 35–6, 105
women's rights, *see* rights
workers; *see* labour; women
World Conference on Women, UN 25,
63, 72–3, 173; *see also* Beijing

Young Women's Christian Association
(YWCA), *see* YWCA
younger women 146, 156, 164–5; *see also*
feminism
YWCA 19, 183n2

Zainah Anwar 98–9
Zaleha Ismail 55

eBooks – at www.eBookstore.tandf.co.uk

A library at your fingertips!

eBooks are electronic versions of printed books. You can
store them on your PC/laptop or browse them online.

They have advantages for anyone needing rapid access
to a wide variety of published, copyright information.

eBooks can help your research by enabling you to
bookmark chapters, annotate text and use instant searches
to find specific words or phrases. Several eBook files would
fit on even a small laptop or PDA.

NEW: Save money by eSubscribing: cheap, online access
to any eBook for as long as you need it.

Annual subscription packages

We now offer special low-cost bulk subscriptions to
packages of eBooks in certain subject areas. These are
available to libraries or to individuals.

For more information please contact
webmaster.ebooks@tandf.co.uk

We're continually developing the eBook concept, so
keep up to date by visiting the website.

www.eBookstore.tandf.co.uk